A Treasury of

READER'S DIGEST
Wit and Humor

SELECTED BY THE EDITORS OF THE READER'S DIGEST
IN COLLABORATION WITH BOB HOPE, BENNETT CERF, GROUCHO MARX,
DON HEROLD, OGDEN NASH AND J. P. McEVOY

With Illustrations by Robert Day

THE READER'S DIGEST ASSOCIATION, INC.
Pleasantville, N. Y.

PRINTED IN THE UNITED STATES OF AMERICA

What's Funny?

By J. P. McEvoy

HAT'S FUNNY? You might think the answer is simply "anything that amuses me." But what amuses you? That is a mighty serious question if you are in the grim business of making people laugh. Professional comedians are notoriously unhappy; radio gagwriters and movie "comedy constructionists" are constantly taking time out to have their ulcers retreaded; the children of humorists grow up humpbacked from hiding under the bed when Father staggers home after a hard day of cracking jokes, while the editors who select material for books like this cry themselves to sleep nights worrying over what's funny — to you.

For many years I wrote daily humorous columns for newspapers and later comedies and revues for Broadway, including three editions of the *Ziegfeld Follies*. I have asked every important comedian of our time the question, "What's funny?"

I like Ed Wynn's answer the best. "What was your funniest sketch — and why was it funny?" Wynn replied, "That's what the sketch was about: My straight man comes out to the middle of the stage while I lean against the proscenium arch and he proceeds to tell three of my best stories, one after the other. The audience laughs politely. He turns to me and says indignantly, 'What's wrong? When *you* tell these same stories they get big laughs.' And I say, 'Well, maybe the audience doesn't think they're funny.'

"Then he says, 'Well what *is* funny?' and I say, 'Darned if I know,' and I walk over to him and take his new straw hat off his head and admire it. I ask him if he likes his new hat very much and he says, 'Certainly,' and I say, 'Cost a lot of money?' and he says, 'Very expensive.' And while I'm talking to him I take one of those big Boy Scout knives out of my pocket, snap it open and then slowly proceed to cut huge slices off the hat until there is nothing left but the crown, which I gravely put back on his head.

"Then I ask him, 'Do you think that's funny?' and he shouts indignantly, 'No!' I point to the audience which greeted each slice with a great roar of happy laughter and say, 'Look! they think it's funny.' And then I take his necktie and while he's protesting I cut it off — right at the knot — and drop it on the stage. And then deliberately I cut off all his coat buttons, and while he's grabbing for his coat I cut off his suspender buttons, and while he's trying to hold his clothes on and the audience is falling out of their seats laughing I say, 'Do you think that's funny?' He screams, 'No, No!' Then I point to the audience as I walk off and say, 'Look — they do.' "

Now, as I rove the world for The Reader's Digest, I am invariably asked two questions: "Do you write those funny things at the bottom of the page which I always read first?" To which I reply unhappily that my job, alas, is writing those long pieces so that the little ones can be separated. The other question is: "Could you fix it so I could get my copy of the Digest a few days ahead of anybody else in town?" Then I hear that familiar heartbreaking tale: How that funny story they had just read in the new Digest was greeted with deafening silence when they told it at the Rotary lunch or the dinner table, because everyone present had already read it in *his* copy.

I have always assured these frustrated Fred Allens that if only they would wait a few months the same quips would be fresh and unfamiliar again. And now this stunning collection comes along to prove it. Here is a mad, glad harvest of sock jokes and pithy sayings, old saws with new teeth and naughty favorites restyled in Shocking Pink. Here you will find the now immortal story of the distracted lady who said, "I'm sure I had two when I came here"; and my favorite, about the man who played one note continuously on his one-stringed fiddle and, when his wife complained that other players had four strings and moved their fingers up and down, replied, "They're looking for the place, but I've found it."

If this book isn't funny, what's funny?

Rising to the Occasion

The toastmaster introduced the speaker with great fervor, stressing her years of faithful service to the club and eulogizing her ability and charm. Somewhat overwhelmed, the speaker faced the audience. "After such an introduction," she said disarmingly, "I can hardly wait to hear what I'm going to say." — Adnelle H. Heskett

At a dinner concluding a long and boring convention, a parade of reluctant speakers had been pried from their chairs to "say a few words." As the 16th orator took his seat, a sigh of expectation filled the room. Deliverance was in sight. But no! The chairman was on his feet again. "I'm sure this meeting does not want to break up without hearing from our good friend, Ken Roe."

Mr. Roe stood up. "Gentlemen," he said, "I am reminded of the story of the two skeletons. For days they had been imprisoned in the mustiest closet imaginable. Finally, one skeleton said to the other, 'What are we doing here, anyhow?' Whereupon, the other skeleton replied, 'I'll be darned if I know. But if we had any guts, we'd get the hell out of here.'" — Matt Roberts in *The Saturday Evening Post*

One of the major embarrassments to which lecturers are submitted is the audience's looking at their watches. I once asked John Erskine if he found the ordeal particularly trying.

"No," he replied, "not until they start shaking them!" — Frank Crowninshield in *Vogue*

Speeches are like steer horns — a point here, a point there and a lot of bull in between.
— *Liberty*

One evening Chauncey Depew, then over 90, occupied a box in a New York theater where Will Rogers was whirling his rope and wise-cracking his way to fame. At the end of the act, when Will introduced Mr. Depew, the audience applauded vigorously. The famous wit rose to acknowledge the tribute and, in a voice a little quavery with age, said: "I've been making speeches for over 50 years, but I've never found it necessary to use a rope to hold an audience."
The crowd roared, and Will Rogers laughed hardest of all.
— Josh Lee, *How to Hold an Audience Without a Rope* (Ziff-Davis)

After-dinner speaker's remark: "Now before I start I want to say something."

A toastmaster is a man who eats a meal he doesn't want so he can get up and tell a lot of stories he doesn't remember to people who've already heard them.
— George Jessel

Wilton Lackaye was on the program for a speech at a gathering in Chicago. It was late in the evening, and everyone had been bored by the other speakers. When the toastmaster announced, "Wilton Lackaye, the famous actor, will now give you his address," Mr. Lackaye arose and said, "Toastmaster and Gentlemen, my address is the Lambs Club, New York." He sat down to tremendous applause.

On a lecture tour, Louis Untermeyer told a Texas audience all his best stories. After the lecture he was presented with his check, which he realized had been rather a burden on the committee. With a wave of his hand, he offered it back to be put to some good use. The committee faltered. They retired to a back room to decide what to do. The problem settled, they returned, accepted the check, and said that it would be the beginning of a special fund. "And the purpose of this fund?" asked Mr. Untermeyer. Their eyes fluttered unhappily. "It's a fund to get better lecturers next year," they said.
— *The Stage*

Pardon, Your Slip Is Showing

The following correction appeared in a small town paper: "Our paper carried the notice last week that Mr. John Jones is a defective in the police force. This was a typographical error. Mr. Jones is really a detective in the police farce."

— Quoted in *The Link*

An advertisement in the Seattle *Post-Intelligencer:* "Large wicked davenport — Was $24.50. Now $19.50."

From the society column of the Boulder, Colo., *Daily Camera:* "Members of Thursday Club met yesterday at the home of Mrs. Frank Spencer for luncheon and contract. Guests were Mrs. I. D. Linder, Mrs. A. A. Parkhurst and Mrs. Neil Wilkinson. Mrs. Wilkinson was high."

In the Monterey, Calif., *Peninsula Herald:* "The area in which Miss Garson was injured is spectacularly scenic."

From the Barnesboro, Pa., *Star:* "Both high school bands will be present to dispense with fine music."

Church notice from the Parkersburg, W. Va., *News:* " 'Change Your Wife Through Prayer' will be the sermon subject Sunday."

Classified ad in a Washington paper: "Secretary about to be married urgently, needs a 2 rm. apt."

From the Rice Lake, Wis., *Chronotype:* "Watch out for the pancake supper sponsored by the Mikana Ladies' Aid."

— Quoted in *Successful Farming*

From the trade journal *Tobacco:* "It has been 15 years since Tipton, Calif., has had a mayor who smoked. Mayor North never smoked, ex-Mayor Calman doesn't smoke, and Mayor Chapman never smoked when living."

From a department-store advertisement in the Elmira, N. Y., *Star-Gazette:* "Whatever type your father is, we know we can help you choose a gift to make him grim all over."

Item in *House & Garden:* "Nothing gives a greater variety to the appearance of a house then a few undraped widows."

From the Angola, Ind., *Steuben Republican:* "Mrs. Glen Golden is general chairman of the affair. Mrs. LeLand Ax and Mrs. Ben Gordon have charge of invitations. Mrs. John Estrick, Mrs. E. J. Ries and Mrs. Harold Stevens have charge of Harold Stevens."

Item from the Cincinnati *Post:* "Representatives of teachers' organizations appeared before the board to ask for a further cost-of-loving adjustment in wages."

Brief Encounters

A man was carrying a grandfather's clock down a crowded main street to a repair shop. As the clock limited his vision, he unintentionally collided with a woman, knocking her down. After collecting her composure and packages, the  woman struggled to her feet and scathingly inquired: "Why don't you carry a wrist watch like everybody else?" — Robert W. Ensley

In a night club one evening a very pretty girl was wearing, around her neck, a thin chain from which hung a tiny golden airplane. One of the young men in the party stared at it so that the girl finally asked him: "Do you like my little airplane?"

"As a matter of fact," he replied, "I wasn't looking at it. I was really admiring the landing field." —Athos Cadilhe Abilhoâ

Late for an appointment, a friend of mine dashed into the entrance of a New York cocktail lounge and collided with a lady just emerging. Hurried "beg pardons" ensued. Then began one of those ludicrous dances with each party jumping from side to side in unison, blocking instead of side-stepping the other.

Finally, flushed and embarrassed, my friend exclaimed, "Well — we seem to be at an impasse! I wonder what Emily Post would do in a case like this?"

Said the other lady, "She'd feel just as awkward as you. I know, because it happens that I am Emily Post." — Olga Swanson

In a New York restaurant artist James Montgomery Flagg saw Beatrice Lillie sitting at a nearby table. With her was a most attractive young woman, so attractive in fact that Flagg decided he could use her as a model. When the beauty left the table for a few minutes, Flagg scribbled a note to Miss Lillie: "Who *is* that marvelous, gorgeous creature?" he pleaded. The waiter immediately brought back Beatrice's brief reply: "Me!"   — Don Fairbairn in Philadelphia *Bulletin*

A young lady, calling on Agnes Repplier, got ready to go, put on her hat and coat, put her hands in her muff, took them out, picked up a parcel, laid it down, shifted from one foot to another and then said, "There was something I meant to say but I've forgotten." "Perhaps, my dear," Miss Repplier replied, "it was *good-bye*."
— Loren Carroll, *Conversation, Please* (Bobbs-Merrill)

A man who had learned to share taxis in Washington jumped in with another passenger at Boston's South Station, having overheard the first fare give a destination close to his. He sat back with a cheery smile and, turning to the other passenger, said pleasantly, "My name's Jennings."

"Mine," said the Bostonian, "is not."   — Boston *Globe*

Ladies' Daze

Some weeks after receiving £400 compensation for the loss of her jewelry an elderly woman informed an Auckland insurance company that she had found the missing property in a cupboard. "I didn't think it would be fair to keep both the jewels and the money, so I thought you would be pleased to know that I have sent the £400 to the Red Cross," she wrote.   — Christchurch, New Zealand, *Star-Sun*

The two chorus girls were great friends, although one was a live wire, the other quiet and reserved. One day the vivacious Phyllis said, "Look, Ruth, I don't mind digging up dates for us, but you just sit around like a zombie and never open your mouth. Why don't you read up and get something to talk about?"

Ruth promised to try.

Next town they hit, Phyllis had two local Lotharios waiting for them at the stage door. Later in the evening, one of those painful silences enveloped the party. Ruth fidgeted, gulped once or twice, and then let them have it.

"Isn't it too bad," she inquired, "what happened to Marie Antoinette?"

— Kay Painton

A Minneapolis teacher gave $500 to a charming gyp for a half interest in a mythical training school — and then the man skipped out and couldn't be found.

When she came to the Better Business Bureau with her tale of woe, the Bureau man asked: "Why didn't you investigate first? Didn't you know about our service?"

"Oh, yes, I've known about the Bureau for years," she answered. "But I was afraid you'd tell me not to do it!"

— Frank W. Brock in *Coronet*

A pretty girl taking public-service examinations had this problem put to her: If a man buys an article for $12.25 and sells it for $9.75, does he gain or lose by the transaction?

The young thing pondered deeply, then answered: "He gains on the cents but loses on the dollars."

— *The Vagabond*

A young lady, with a touch of hay fever, took with her to a dinner party two handkerchiefs, one of which she stuck in her bosom. At dinner she began rummaging to right and left in her bosom for the fresh handkerchief. Engrossed in her search, she suddenly realized that conversation had ceased and people were watching her, fascinated.

In confusion she murmured, "I *know* I had two when I came."

— John Erskine

The Answer Men

A midwestern university held entrance exams for a group of ex-GIs. One of the questions was, "Name two ancient sports."

An ex-sergeant racked his brain, finally came up with an answer that passed him. He wrote, "Antony and Cleopatra."

— Stanley J. Meyer in *The American Legion Magazine*

A recent newspaper ad of the Oklahoma School of Accountancy was headed: "Short Course in Accounting for Women."

Not long after the ad appeared, a note reached the school's president. It said: "There is NO accounting for women." — Tulsa *Tribune*

An employer had spent a great deal of money to ensure that his men should work under the best conditions. "Now, whenever I enter the workshop," he said, "I want to see every man cheerfully performing his task, and therefore I invite you to place in this box any further suggestions as to how that can be brought about."

A week later the box was opened; it contained only one slip of paper, on which was written: "Don't wear rubber heels."
— *The Hartford Agent Magazine*

A Topeka, Kans., assessor recently ran across the best answer yet to the question on the tax assessment blank: "Nature of taxpayer." The answer: "Very mean." — *Liberty*

A man who took great pride in his lawn had a heavy crop of dandelions. After trying every known device to get rid of them, he wrote the Department of Agriculture enumerating all the things he had tried, and ending, "What shall I do now?"

In due course came a reply, "We suggest you learn to love them."
— *Family Herald and Weekly Star*

Letter to the editor of a correspondence column: "I am only 19 and I stayed out till two the other night. My mother objects. Did I do wrong?"

The answer: "Try to remember." — Cecil Hunt, *Laughing Gas* (Methuen)

Gallic Gallantry

The mayor of a French city visited New York and was taken on a tour of the city. He went to the top of the Empire State Building to see the view, began to blow kisses ecstatically, and said: "Ah, it reminds me of a woman's curves."

"But why should it?" asked his puzzled host.

"M'sieur," explained the French mayor, "*everything* reminds me of a woman's curves."
— Leonard Lyons

An American professor met three staid members of the *Académie Française* in Paris and asked for their definition of *savoir-faire* to include in his modern dictionary. "Eet is not deefeecult," one said. "Eef I go home and find my wife kissing another man and I teep my hat to them and say: 'Excuse me,' that is *savoir-faire*."

"Not quite," said the second. "Eef I go home and find my wife kissing another man and I teep my hat and say: 'Excuse me. Continue,' that is *savoir-faire*."

"No — not quite," rumbled the third, fingering his beard. "Eef I go home and find my wife kissing another man and teep my hat and say: 'Excuse me. Continue,' and he *can* continue — *he* has *savoir-faire*."
— Irving Hoffman in *The Hollywood Reporter*

In the French Parliament, one of the Deputies, making a speech urging the improvement of the legal status of women, cried: "After all, there is very little difference between men and women!"

The entire Chamber of Deputies rose and shouted as one man: "*Vive la différence!*"
— Milton Wright, *The Art of Conversation* (Whittlesey)

M. le Vicomte Sorigny, a distinguished member of the French Embassy, was present at the silver-wedding anniversary celebration of a bishop. Leaning over to his neighbor, the bishop's nephew, the vicomte asked, *sotto voce:* "Tell me, what is this silver wedding which we celebrate? I do not quite understand."

"Oh," replied the bishop's nephew, "don't you know? Why, my uncle and aunt have lived together for 25 years without ever having been separated."

"Ah," exclaimed the diplomat heartily, "and now he marry her? Br-ravo!"
— Tom Masson's *Annual* (Doubleday)

An American woman, driving her car very fast down a Paris boulevard, was stopped by a gendarme. "*Alors, alors, alors!*" he cried, and sharply demanded what she meant by driving at such a rate. Thinking fast, the lady explained that she was pursuing her husband and another woman, who were in a car ahead.

The gendarme stepped aside. "After them, *Madame*, after them!" he said, gallantly waving her on.

Enough to Drive You Crazy

Stop Signs: On rear of car, "BEWARE OF SUDDEN STOPS — TEACHING WIFE TO DRIVE." On back of Austin, "HIT SOMEONE YOUR OWN SIZE."

A young Cleveland matron stalled her car at a traffic light one winter day. She stamped on the starter, tried again, choked her engine, while behind her an impatient citizen honked his horn steadily. Finally she got out and walked back.

"I'm awfully sorry, but I don't seem to be able to start my car," she told the driver of the other car. "If you'll go up there and start it for me, I'll stay here and lean on your horn."   — Harriet L. Clark

A Hollywood writer had a motorcar with a short bar through the steering column which allowed him to guide the car with his knees; the steering wheel was removable. Spinning along through traffic, he'd complain to an uninitiated passenger of a sudden illness. After a couple of close shaves, with the driver plainly getting dizzier, the passenger would beg him to stop.

"No, I'll be okay in a minute," the writer would gasp. "Here, you take the wheel —" and he'd snatch off the wheel and thrust it into the hands of his gibbering companion.

— Paul Harrison in New York *World-Telegram*

Two thoroughly inebriated men were driving like mad in an automobile. "Shay," one fumbled his words, "be sure to turn out for that bridge that's comin' down the road toward us."

"What do you mean, me turn out?" the other retorted. "I thought you were drivin'."

— Donald MacGregor

A woman trying to maneuver her sedan out of a parking space banged into the car ahead, then into the car behind and finally, pulling into the street, struck a passing delivery truck. A policeman who had been watching approached her. "Let's see your license," he demanded.

"Don't be silly, officer," she said. "Who'd give *me* a license?"

— Montreal *Star*

Motorist's definition of a split second: The interval of time between the change of a stop light to green and the fellow behind you tooting his horn.

One frosty morning I watched a county constable in the Tennessee mountains struggle in vain to get his old Model T started. Removing his topcoat, he cranked vigorously. His mutterings and curses turned the air blue, but there was no response from the engine. He tried the hot-water treatment. No luck. He pushed, cranked some more and glared. Finally, in utter disgust, he pulled his .45 from its holster, fired six rounds into the hood, and stalked away. — Ernest M. Wright

Individual Approach

A farmer hired a hand and set him to chopping wood. In the middle of the morning the farmer went down to see how the hand was coming along. To his astonishment he found the wood all chopped. Next day

the farmer told the man to stack the wood in the shed. This involved a lot of toting and the farmer figured the job would keep the man busy. But by noon he had it done.

On the third day the farmer, thinking he'd give the man a light job for a change, told him to sort out the potatoes in the bin. "Put the good ones in one pile, the doubtful in another, and throw out the rotten ones," said the farmer.

An hour or so later he went back to see how the job was coming. He found the hired man passed out cold, with virtually nothing done. After throwing water in the man's face and bringing him around, the farmer demanded an explanation.

"Hell," the man said wearily, "it's making them decisions that's killing me."

In the crowded bus a lanky Kentuckian sat opposite a young woman whose skimpy skirt kept creeping up over her knees. She fought a constant battle with it, pulling it down, but as soon as she released her hold, up it crept.

After one hard yank, she looked up and met the gaze of her traveling companion.

"Don't stretch your calico, sister," he advised her. "My weakness is liquor."   — Mabel Osborne

My escort had climbed a fence into a small field to gather me some particularly lovely wild flowers while I waited in the car. Suddenly he called excitedly to a farmer hoeing tobacco in the next field, "Hey! Is this bull over here safe?"

"Well," said the farmer composedly, "he's a dern sight safer'n you are."   — Jean Condra

A doctor in Sequatchie Valley in Tennessee was called to examine the young wife of an elderly, deaf mountaineer.

"Your wife is pregnant," he told her husband.

The mountaineer, hand behind his ear, queried, "Eh?"

The doctor shouted, "I said your wife is pregnant."

"Eh?"

Finally the doctor screamed, "Your wife is going to have a baby."

The man walked to the edge of the porch, spat out a mouthful of tobacco juice, and drawled, "I ain't a bit surprised. She's had ev'ry opportunity."   — Dolce Ogden

A Faculty for Fun

John Howard Van Amringe of Columbia University was a sworn enemy of coeducation. "It's impossible," he asserted, "to teach a boy mathematics if there's a girl in the class."

"Oh, come, professor," objected someone, "surely there might be an exception to that."

"There might be," snapped Amringe. "But he wouldn't be worth teaching!"

— The Wall Street Journal

When a girl applies for admission to Vassar, a questionnaire is sent to her parents. A father in a Boston suburb, filling out one of these blanks, came to the question, "Is she a leader?" He hesitated, then wrote, "I am not sure about this, but I know she is an excellent follower."

A few days later he received this letter from the president of the college: "As our freshman group next fall is to contain several hundred leaders, we congratulate ourselves that your daughter will also be a member of the class. We shall thus be assured of one good follower."

— The Journal of Education

Just before Christmas a college professor read the following on an examination paper: "God only knows the answer to this question. Merry Christmas." Across the paper the professor wrote: "God gets an A; you get an F. Happy New Year."

Sir James Barrie's favorite story was about the professor of biology who explained to his class the spawning of fish. "So you see," he concluded, "the female fish deposits her eggs, the male fish comes along and

fertilizes them, and later the little fish are hatched." One of the girls held up her hand. "You mean, Professor, that the father and mother fish — that they — that before that nothing happens?"

"Nothing," said the professor, "which doubtless explains the expression, 'Poor fish.'"   — Henry P. Moriarty in *Coronet*

Enjoying the Signery

Sign in a Florida cocktail lounge: "Please don't stand up while the room is in motion."

Sign outside a kennel near Poughkeepsie, N. Y.: "The only love that money can buy. Puppies for sale."

On a Negro dressmaker's shingle in New Orleans: "Skirts that Strut."

A GI returned to camp exhausted after a week-end of Wine, Women and Song. On the bunk that held his recumbent form, his buddies hung a sign: "Temporarily Out of Ardor."   — James T. Shaw

Church bulletin, Seaford, N. Y.: "Come In and Have Your Faith Lifted."   — *PM*

Traffic warning, New Rochelle, N. Y.: "Go slow. This is a one-hearse town."

Sign on a newly seeded lawn at Wellesley College: "Don't Ruin the Gay Young Blades!"   — Bruce S. Colpas

Sign in a West Coast dance hall: "The management reserves the right to exclude any lady they think proper."   — *This Week Magazine*

A St. Louis haberdasher arranged a window display of shirts and ties in bright and wildly clashing colors. In the midst of it was a large placard with the simple injunction: "Listen!" — *The Christian Science Monitor*

Sign on a road very much in need of repair near Bremerton, Wash.: "Men Should Be Working."   — Marie Reslock

Intrepid Airman, I

Condensed from London Daily Mail

Patrick Campbell

I'll take three hours in the dentist's waiting-room, with four cavities and an impacted wisdom tooth, in preference to 15 minutes at any airport, waiting for an airplane.

You may class this as hysteria, you may regard it as ungenerous criticism of a system of transportation that has established itself as the fastest, safest and most convenient in the world. But where airplanes are concerned I'm a case for quiet conditions in the padded room.

I'm all right at the terminus; indeed, when I see people queueing at counters labeled "New York," "Chungking" and "Bermuda," I feel a certain regret that I too am not bound for similar romantic destinations. But the urge for far-flung travel evaporates as soon as I get into the airport bus.

The first thing I do in the bus is to look round at the other passengers to see if they are the kind of people with whom I should be content to die. They always, for some reason, fail to measure up to my standards. By the time we arrive at the airport, I have lost about a pound in weight.

At the airport I try to fall into conversation with the pilot or some member of the crew. I have a number of questions to ask — apparently offhand, casual questions, but they go to the root of the matter.

I wish to ask the pilot:

1. Are the very best engineers even now checking every inch of our airplane?

2. Have you, or any member of your family, ever been subject to giddiness, loss of memory or nervous attacks?

3. Will you drive it very fast?

4. Will it be necessary for us to travel at much more than 50 feet above the ground?

To the radio operator:

Can you, even if they send it out very quickly, be perfectly sure of understanding the Morse code?

And, finally, to the air hostess:

If anything goes wrong, would you be so kind as to inform me personally, some time in advance of the other passengers?

Reassured about these matters — and I must admit that all air crews are immensely reassuring — I enter the plane. I cannot decide whether it is better to sit in the front and bear the full brunt of the impact, or in the back and run the risk of being carried away when the tail unit falls off. I choose a central position, where I can watch the wings and see that the propellers are going round.

Five minutes after we are airborne, I disentangle my fingernails from the upholstery of the seat and release the safety belt which I had drawn so tight that it stopped my breathing. I sit back to enjoy the cloud panorama.

The door of the pilot's cabin opens — and the pilot himself comes out! What recklessness is this? He has left some half-fledged boy at the wheel! I watch with horror as he strolls down the aisle, chatting with passengers. I know what he's doing. He's telling them both engines have fallen off but he's saying it's all right.

When my turn comes, the pilot says, "Good morning — are you having a pleasant trip?" I merely nod, speechless. All I want him to do is to get back to his work and remove that mad office boy from the controls. I relax again as he shuts the door of his cabin behind him.

An hour goes by. I had a bad moment when the hostess leaned over and said something I was unable to hear. It sounded like, "We are falling into the sea." I was halfway out of my seat when I realized she was asking me if I would like some tea.

Suddenly we are losing altitude. I look down and the earth is carpeted with railway lines, red-brick houses, factory chimneys and telegraph poles. This is it.

The percussion valve in the port cylinder has blown out. This is the emergency landing. I sink the old nails right back into the upholstery and close my eyes. There is a bump, a faint screech — we have gone through a cow? — and then all is silent. We are alive, but where?

I open my eyes. We are on the apron outside the terminal building. They are pushing up a ladder to the door. I leave the plane with a slight swagger. Openmouthed sight-seers stand behind the railings. Well may they stare. They are looking at one of the intrepid birdmen of the modern era — in Dublin, a little more than an hour ago: now, as large as life, at Northolt airport.

What I say is that airplanes provide the safest, fastest, most convenient means of travel in the world.

When Critics Crack the Quip

One of the briefest musical criticisms on record appeared in a Detroit paper: "An amateur string quartet played Brahms here last evening. Brahms lost."

I have knocked everything except the knees of the chorus girls, and God anticipated me there.   — Percy Hammond in New York *Herald Tribune*

Tallulah Bankhead barged down the Nile last night as Cleopatra — and sank.   — John Mason Brown in New York *Post*

When Mr. Wilbur calls his play Halfway to Hell, he underestimates the distance.   — Brooks Atkinson in New York *Times*

Katherine Hepburn [in *The Lake*] runs the gamut of emotions from A to B.   — Dorothy Parker

He played the King [in *King Lear*] as though someone had led the ace.   — Eugene Field in *Boston Globe*

Barbed Reviews: Monty Woolley, "For the first time in my life I envied my feet. They were asleep!" (Hedda Hopper) . . . The revue was a lot of ham and legs (Ruth Capesius) . . . The show is a riot of off-color (Time) . . . It's a run-of-the-morgue whodunit (Time)

A movie company was shooting scenes for a picture in San Francisco when two elderly women walked in the line of the camera. A movieman shouted, "Don't go through there! A movie is being shot."

"Well!" exclaimed one woman. "If it's anything like the one I sat through last night, it certainly deserves to be."   — Mrs. F. A. Gilman

Frances Perkins, former Secretary of Labor, tells about turning to a gentleman seated behind her at a movie, and saying, "If my hat prevents your seeing this picture, I'd be happy to take it off."

"Please don't," said the man. "The hat's much funnier than the movie."   — Joe Laurie, Jr., Press Features

Mad Hatters

A member of an old Boston family, now 80, still lives on Beacon Hill and carries on the family traditions. Last winter she entertained a guest from the Middle West to whom she presented her small but select circle of friends. Shortly before leaving, the guest remarked, "Emily, your friends are wonderful women, but tell me, where *do* they get their hats?"

"Oh, my dear," the Bostonian said with pained surprise, "we don't *get* our hats. We *have* our hats."   — Mrs. Paul W. Alexander

A woman walked into a millinery shop and pointed out a hat in the window. "That red one with the feathers and berries," she said. "Would you take it out of the window for me?"

"Certainly, madam," the clerk replied. "We'd be glad to."

"Thank you very much," said the woman moving toward the exit. "The horrible thing bothers me every time I pass." — *Successful Farming*

An elderly woman was shopping for a hat and the salesgirl kept showing her new types of headgear which didn't suit the old lady at all. Finally she said, "Listen, I wear a corset and I wear drawers, and I want a hat to match."
— Cedric Adams in Minneapolis *Tribune*

A woman, pricing a hat, gasped when told it was $75. "Why, there isn't anything on that hat!"

"You are paying for the restraint," the saleswoman replied quietly.
— Raymond C. Mayer, *How to Do Publicity* (Harper)

Laughing Matter

Samuel Hopkins Adams, who was always willing to try anything once, had accepted an invitation to a nudist party. Describing his experience to some friends the next day, he said, "They didn't do things by halves. Even the butler who opened the door for me was completely nude."

"If he wasn't uniformed, how did you know it was the butler," asked Mr. Adams' literal-minded publisher.

"Well," said Mr. Adams, "it certainly wasn't the maid."
— Bennett Cerf in *The Saturday Review of Literature*

"How's your insomnia?"

"Worse. Can't even sleep when it's time to get up." — *Partner*

Journalist Heywood Broun was standing next to a prim old lady at a wedding. "Can you imagine," she whispered as the couple met at the altar, "they've known each other scarcely two weeks, and here they are getting married!"

"Well," said Broun philosophically, "it's one way of getting acquainted." — E. E. Edgar

"Waiter," said a diner who had just sampled his dinner, "these veal chops don't seem very tender to me."

"Sir," replied the waiter, "I used to be a butcher, and I can tell you that less than a month ago those chops were chasing after a cow."

"That may be," replied the man, "but not for milk!" — *Topnotcher*

Two nursemaids were wheeling their infant charges in the park, when one asked the other: "Are you going to the dance tonight?"

"I'd love to," the other replied, "but to tell the truth I'm afraid to leave the baby with its mother."
— *Commerce Magazine*

A tourist was introduced at Albuquerque to an Indian with a reputedly perfect memory. Skeptical, the tourist asked: "What did you have for breakfast on October 4, 1913?" The Indian answered, "Eggs." The man scoffed. "Everyone eats eggs for breakfast. He's a fraud."

Eight years later the traveler's train stopped again at Albuquerque, and he saw the same Indian lounging on the platform. The tourist went up to him and said jovially, "How!"

The Indian answered, "Scrambled."
— Leonard Lyons

The young father-to-be, registering his wife in the maternity ward, asked anxiously, "Darling, are you positive that you want to go through with this?" — *The Ship's Log*

On a quiet evening at home, a wife suggested to her husband: "Dear, why don't you read to me while I sew?"

The husband obviously didn't warm to the idea, stammered a bit,

then said: "I tell you what — you sew to me while I read."
— *The Christian Science Monitor*

Upon entering a room in a Washington hotel, a woman recognized a well-known Government official pacing up and down and asked what he was doing there.

"I am going to deliver a speech," he said.

"Do you usually get very nervous before addressing a large audience?"

"Nervous?" he replied. "No, I never get nervous."

"In that case," demanded the lady, "what are you doing in the Ladies' Room?" — *Floorcraft*

In Their Anecdotage

A guest at a Hollywood luncheon of gag writers was startled when one writer yelled "60," and everybody snickered. Another cried "42," and a ripple of laughter ensued. Then a third cried "94" — and a stout party in the corner practically went into convulsions.

"What on earth is all this laughing at numbers?" the visitor asked.

"These jokesters," explained the host, "know every gag in the world. They've given a number to each joke. When anybody calls out a number, they all laugh just as hard as if he had told the actual story."

"But what about that fat lad who is still choking with laughter because somebody yelled '94'?" asked the guest.

"Oh, him," came the answer. "I guess he never heard that gag before." — Bennett Cerf

The boss returned in a good humor from lunch and called the whole staff in to listen to a couple of jokes he had picked up. Everybody but one girl laughed uproariously. "What's the matter?" grumbled the boss. "Haven't you got a sense of humor?"

"I don't have to laugh," said the girl. "I'm leaving Friday anyhow."
— Bennett Cerf, *Laughing Stock* (Grosset & Dunlap)

> If he can remember so many jokes,
> With all the details that mold them,
> Why can't he recall with equal skill,
> How many times he's told them?
> — Lee Arvin in *Post Scripts: A Collection of Humor
> from The Saturday Evening Post* (Whittlesey)

A Definition of Marriage

Condensed from
The Saturday Evening Post
Ogden Nash

Just as I know that there are two Hagens, Walter and Copen,

I know that marriage is a legal and religious alliance entered into by a man who can't sleep with the window shut and a woman who can't sleep with the window open,

Also he can't sleep until he has read the last hundred pages to find out whether his suspicions of the murdered eccentric recluse's avaricious secretary were right,

Moreover, just as I am unsure of the difference between flora and fauna, and flotsam and jetsam,

I am quite sure that marriage is the alliance of two people, one of whom never remembers birthdays and the other never forgetsam,

And the one refuses to believe there is a leak in the water pipe or the gas pipe, and the other is convinced she is about to asphyxiate or drown,

And the other says, "Quick, get up and get my hairbrushes off the window sill; it's raining in," and the one replies, "Oh, they're all right; it's only raining straight down."

That is why marriage is so much more interesting than divorce,

Because it's the only known example of the happy meeting of the immovable object and the irresistible force.

So I hope husbands and wives will continue to debate and combat over everything debatable and combatable,

Because I believe a little incompatibility is the spice of life, particularly if he has income and she is pattable.

Childish Notions

"Mummy," asked the ten-year-old daughter of an English friend, "how did Princess Elizabeth *know* she was going to have a baby?"

Before the mother could reply, her younger daughter, aged five, piped up scornfully, "Well, she can *read*, can't she? It was in all the papers."
— Mrs. E. M. Darlaston in *John Bull*

At a wedding not long after the war, the groom, only recently back from overseas, had hardly glimpsed his bride before the ceremony. Therefore when time came for the kiss it was a long one, lasting on and on until a child's voice rang out in the silence of the church:

"Mummy, is he spreading the pollen on her now?" — E. P. Goodnow

Shortly after our neighbors had a new baby, my five-year-old daughter Lisa and her friend Claire sat on the front porch discussing what fun it would be if they, too, could become mothers. At length Lisa asked earnestly, "Claire, do you think you'll have a baby soon?"

Claire's expressive eyes widened. "Have a baby!" she exclaimed. "I can't even tell time yet!"
— J. T. B.

Zanies All

Jones was waiting for a bus when a stranger approached and asked the time. Jones ignored him. The stranger repeated the request. Jones continued to ignore him. When the stranger finally walked away, another waiting passenger said curiously:

"That was a perfectly reasonable question. Why didn't you tell him what time it was?"

"Why?" said Jones. "Listen, I'm standing here minding my own business and this guy wants to know what time it is. So maybe I tell him what time it is. Then what? We get to talking, and this guy says, 'How about a drink?' So we have a drink. Then we have some more drinks. So after a while I say, 'How about coming up to my house for a bite to eat?' So we go up to my house, and we're eating ham and cheese in the kitchen when my daughter comes in, and my daughter's a very good-looking girl. So she falls for this guy and he falls for her. Then they get married, and any guy that can't afford a watch I don't want him in my family."   — Herbert Asbury

The author of a famous book on economics received a phone call from a stranger recently. "I question your statistics on the high cost of living today," said the stranger. "My wife and I eat everything our hearts desire and we get it for exactly 68 cents a week."

"Sixty-eight cents a week!" echoed the economist. "I can't believe it! Won't you tell me how? And to make sure I get your story straight, please speak louder."

"I can't speak louder," said the stranger. "I'm a goldfish."
— Bennett Cerf in *The Saturday Review of Literature*

A drunk, armed with nickels, entered an Automat, stopped in front of the slot marked "Ham Sandwich." He dropped in two nickels and got a sandwich. He dropped in two more nickels and out came another sandwich. After he'd collected 20 ham sandwiches, someone suggested: "Hey, don't you think you've had enough?"

"I should quit now?" replied the drunk. "Now — when I'm on a winning streak?"   — Leonard Lyons

At the circus in Chicago last year a man was observed near the camels. He picked up a straw, placed it squarely on a camel's back and waited. Nothing happened. "Wrong straw," he muttered, and hurried off.   — June Provines in Chicago *Tribune*

A man who had a cello with a single string used to bow on it for hours at a time, always holding his finger in the same place. His wife endured this for months. Finally in desperation she said, "I have observed that when others play that instrument there are four strings, and the players move their fingers about continuously."

"Of course the others have four strings and move their fingers about constantly," he explained patiently. "They are looking for the place. I've found it!"   — William Saroyan, *Fables* (Harcourt, Brace)

The Day the Dam Broke

Condensed from "My Life and Hard Times"

James Thurber

Two Thousand People Were in Full Flight

My memories of what my family and I went through during the 1913 flood in Ohio I would gladly forget. And yet neither the hardships we endured nor the turmoil and confusion we experienced can alter my feeling toward my native state and city. I am having a fine time now and wish Columbus were here, but if anyone ever wished a city was in hell it was during that frightful and perilous afternoon in 1913 when the dam broke, or, to be more exact, when everybody in town thought that the dam broke. We were both ennobled and demoralized by the experience. Grandfather especially rose to magnificent heights which can never lose their splendor for me, even though his reactions to the flood were based upon a profound misconception; namely, that Nathan Bedford Forrest's cavalry was the menace we were called upon to face. The only possible means of escape for us was to flee the house, a step which Grandfather sternly forbade, brandishing his old army saber in his hand. "Let the sons —— —— come!" he roared. Meanwhile hundreds of people were streaming by our house in wild panic, screaming "Go east! Go east!" We had to stun Grandfather with the ironing board. Impeded as we were by the inert form of the old gentleman — he was taller than six feet and weighed almost 170 pounds — we were passed, in the first half-mile, by practically everybody else in the city. Had

Grandfather not come to, at the corner of Parsons Avenue and Town Street, we would unquestionably have been overtaken and engulfed by the roaring waters — that is, if there had *been* any roaring waters. Later, when the panic had died down and people had gone rather sheepishly back to their homes and their offices, minimizing the distances they had run and offering various reasons for running, city engineers pointed out that, even if the dam had broken, the water level would not have risen more than two additional inches in the West Side. The West Side was, at the time of the dam scare, under 30 feet of water — as, indeed, were all Ohio river towns during the great spring floods of 20 years ago. The East Side (where we lived and where all the running occurred) had never been in any danger at all. Only a rise of some 95 feet could have caused the flood waters to flow over High Street and engulf the East Side.

The fact that we were all as safe as kittens under a cookstove did not, however, assuage in the least the fine despair and the grotesque desperation which seized upon the residents of the East Side when the cry spread like a grass fire that the dam had given way. Some of the most dignified, staid, cynical and clear-thinking men in town abandoned their wives, stenographers, homes and offices and ran east. There are few alarms in the world more terrifying than "The dam has broken!"

The broken-dam rumor began, as I recall it, about noon of March 12, 1913. High Street, the main canyon of trade, was loud with the placid hum of business. Suddenly somebody began to run. It may be that he had simply remembered, all of a moment, an engagement to meet his wife, for which he was now frightfully late. Whatever it was, he ran east on Broad Street (probably toward the Maramor Restaurant, a favorite place for a man to meet his wife). Somebody else began to run, perhaps a newsboy in high spirits. Another man, a portly gentleman of affairs, broke into a trot. Inside of ten minutes, everybody on High Street, from the Union Depot to the Courthouse, was running. A loud mumble gradually crystallized into the dread word "dam." "The dam has broke!" The fear was put into words by a little old lady in an electric, or by a traffic cop, or by a small boy: nobody knows who, nor does it now really matter. Two thousand people were abruptly in full flight. "Go east!" was the cry that arose — east away from the river, east to safety. "Go east! Go east! Go east!"

Black streams of people flowed eastward down all the streets leading in that direction; these streams, whose headwaters were in the dry-goods stores, office buildings, harness shops, movie theaters, were fed by trickles of housewives, children, cripples, servants, dogs and cats, slipping out of the houses past which the main streams flowed, shouting and screaming. People ran out leaving fires burning and food cooking and doors wide open. I remember, however, that my mother turned out all the fires and that she took with her a dozen eggs and two loaves of bread. It was her plan to make Memorial Hall, just two blocks away, and take refuge somewhere in the top of it, in one of the dusty rooms where war veterans met and where old battle flags and stage scenery were stored. But the seething throngs, shouting "Go east!" drew her along and the rest of us with her. When Grandfather regained full consciousness, at Parsons Avenue, he turned upon the retreating mob like a vengeful prophet and exhorted the men to form ranks and stand off the rebel dogs, but at length he, too, got the idea that the dam had broken and, roaring "Go east!" in his powerful voice, he caught up in one arm a small child and in the other a slight clerkish man of perhaps 42 and we slowly began to gain on those ahead of us.

A scattering of firemen, policemen, and army officers in dress uniforms — there had been a review at Fort Hayes, in the northern part of town — added color to the surging billows of people. "Go east!" cried a little child in a piping voice, as she ran past a porch on which drowsed a lieutenant colonel of infantry. Used to quick decisions, trained to immediate obedience, the officer bounded off the porch and, running at full tilt, soon passed the child, bawling "Go east!" The two of them emptied rapidly the houses of the little street they were on. "What is

it? What is it?" demanded a fat, waddling man who intercepted the colonel. The officer dropped behind and asked the little child what it was. "The dam has broke!" gasped the girl. "The dam has broke!" roared the colonel. "Go east! Go east! Go east!"

Nobody has ever been able to compute with any exactness how many people took part in the great rout of 1913, for the panic ended as abruptly as it began and the bobtail and ragtag and velvet-gowned groups of refugees melted away and slunk home, leaving the streets peaceful and deserted. The shouting, weeping, tangled evacuation of the city lasted not more than two hours in all. Some few people got as far east as Reynoldsburg, 12 miles away; 50 or more reached the Country Club, eight miles away; most of the others gave up, exhausted, or climbed trees in Franklin Park, four miles out. Order was restored and fear dispelled finally by means of militiamen riding about in motor lorries bawling through megaphones: "The dam has *not* broken!" At first this tended only to add to the confusion and increase the panic, for many stampeders thought the soldiers were bellowing "The dam has now broken!" thus setting an official seal of authentication on the calamity.

"I ran east on Town Street," my Aunt Edith has written me. "A tall spare woman with grim eyes and a determined chin ran past me down the middle of the street. I was still uncertain as to what was the matter, in spite of all the shouting. I drew up alongside the woman with some effort, for, although she was in her late 50's, she had a beautiful easy running form and seemed to be in excellent condition. 'What is it?' I puffed. She gave me a quick glance and then looked ahead again, stepping up her pace a trifle. 'Don't ask me, ask God!' she said.

"When I reached Grant Avenue, I was so spent that Dr. H. R. Mallory — you remember Dr. Mallory, the man with the white beard who looks like Robert Browning? — well, Dr. Mallory, whom I had drawn away from at the corner of Fifth and Town, passed me. 'It's got us!' he shouted, and I felt sure that whatever it was *did* have us, for you know what conviction Dr. Mallory's statements always carried. I didn't know at the time what he meant, but I found out later. There was a boy behind him on roller skates, and Dr. Mallory mistook the swishing of the skates for the sound of rushing water. He eventually reached the Columbus School for Girls, at the corner of Parsons Avenue and Town Street, where he collapsed, expecting the cold frothing waters of the Scioto to sweep him into oblivion. The boy on the skates whirled past him, and Dr. Mallory realized for the first time what he had been running from. Looking back up the street, he could see no signs of water, but nevertheless, after resting a few minutes, he jogged on east again. He caught up with me at Ohio Avenue, where we rested together. I should say that about 700 people passed us. A funny thing was that all of them were on foot. Nobody seemed to have had the courage to stop and start his car; but as I remember it, all cars had to be cranked in those days, which is probably the reason."

The next day, the city went about its business as if nothing had happened, but there was no joking. It was two years or more before you dared treat the breaking of the dam lightly. And even now, 20 years after, there are a few persons, like Dr. Mallory, who will shut up like a clam if you mention the Afternoon of the Great Run.

Self-Composed Epitaphs

Ilka Chase: I've finally gotten to the bottom of things.   — Ade Kahn

Dorothy Parker: Involved in a plot.   — Louis Sobol, King Features

Clive Brook: Excuse me for not rising.

Lionel Barrymore: Well, I've played everything but a harp.

Walter Winchell: Here lies Walter Winchell in the dirt he loved so well.
          — Above items from Homer Croy, *The Last Word* (Specialist)

Embarrassing Moments

When Anne Morrow Lindbergh was a little girl, J. P. Morgan, the elder, was coming to tea at the Dwight Morrows'. Fearing the frankness of childhood, Mrs. Morrow talked to Anne beforehand.

"I need not tell you," she said, "that it is rude to comment on anything peculiar about people you meet, so, of course, if you notice that Mr. Morgan's nose is different you won't say anything about it."

Upon meeting the famous guest Anne fixed her eyes relentlessly on the celebrated nose. Her mother noticed this with trepidation and tried, not too obviously, to speed her departure. At last the child was gone — safely gone.

Mrs. Morrow breathed a sigh of relief and, pouring a cup of tea, she asked her visitor with a new complacence, "And now, Mr. Morgan, will you have cream or lemon in your nose?" — O. O. McIntyre

The first Mrs. Richard Harding Davis was one day riding in a Long Island train when an important-looking woman took a seat across the aisle from her. Mrs. Davis remembered that somewhere she had met the newcomer, but what her name was she could not recall. To make the situation acutely embarrassing, the lady nodded pleasantly and said, "Won't you come sit with me, Mrs. Davis?"

Mrs. Davis changed her seat, and then began a mental struggle to recall the eluding name. Presently what she hoped was a clue disclosed itself. The lady mentioned a brother. "Oh, yes. Your brother." Mrs. Davis grasped at the straw. "What is he doing now?"

"Oh, he's still President of the United States," said Mrs. Douglas Robinson, sister of Theodore Roosevelt.   — Joseph Cummings Chase

Ethel Merman was having lunch in an open-air café in Central Park. Her dachshund, Hansel, kept begging for food, but Miss Merman was dining on salad and there wasn't a thing for him. But when the man at the adjoining table departed, Ethel saw a whole lamb chop left on his plate. Unable to resist the temptation, she filched it and gave it to the rapturous Hansel. He was busy finishing off the bone, when the man returned to his lunch. He had been called to the telephone.
            — *Everywoman's Magazine*

The most embarrassing moment in the life of Jane Wyman happened when she was entertaining very special guests. After looking over all the appointments carefully, she put a note on the guest towels, "If you use these I will murder you." It was meant for her husband. In the excitement she forgot to remove the note. After the guests had departed, the towels were discovered still in perfect order, as well as the note itself.   — *Woman's Home Companion*

Some years ago, one of the bright young men who represented Standard Oil in China returned to America for a vacation, in the course of which he met and married a lovely girl from his home town.

"You'll just love Shanghai," he assured her again and again on the way out, "particularly my Number One Boy, Ling. You won't have to lift a finger. Ling runs the household."

They arrived in Shanghai, the bride met Ling and approved. The next morning her husband kissed her good-bye before reporting back on the job. "Sleep as long as you like, darling," he told her. "Ling will take care of everything."

A few hours later she awoke again, to find herself being shaken ever so gently by the Number One Boy. "Time to get dressed and go home now, Missy," he said.   — Bennett Cerf, *Try and Stop Me* (Simon & Schuster)

An exhausted shopper — a stout matron in mink — found herself pushed to the rear of a crowded department-store elevator. Glancing back over her shoulder, she was delighted to see a small, round brown seat in the corner. She sank down onto it thankfully, but it emitted an immediate roar. It seemed that it was a small boy in a brown beret.

— Katharine Brush, *Out of My Mind* (Doubleday)

With Malice Toward Some

An English lady, self-appointed supervisor of village morals, accused a workman of having reverted to drink because "with her own eyes" she had seen his wheelbarrow standing outside a public house. The accused made no defense, but that evening placed his wheelbarrow outside her door and left it there all night. — *The Countryman*

Next door to the quiet Smiths in a Los Angeles apartment building live the Joneses, who are addicted to boisterous Saturday-night parties. The Smiths suffered in silence until recently, when an air duct in the wall common to the living rooms of both apartments gave Smith an idea for suitable reprisal.

On Saturday he removed the grille where the duct entered his living room and, reaching in, placed the microphone of his home recording machine at the point where a patch of light marked the grille in the Joneses' living room. That night he recorded an hour of the hilarity next door at its peak. The following night, when he could tell that the Joneses were retiring early, he placed the loudspeaker of his machine against the wall between his and the Joneses' bedrooms and, with the volume turned up, blasted the Joneses with a canned broadcast of their own revelry. The Smiths' Saturday nights have been quite peaceful lately. — Robert E. Proctor, Jr.

A Detroit schoolteacher was given a ticket for driving through a stop light which called for her appearance in traffic court the following Monday. She went at once to the judge, explained that she had to teach on Monday, and asked for immediate disposal of her case. "So you're a schoolteacher," said the judge. "Madam, your presence here fulfills a long-standing ambition of mine. You sit right down at that table and write '*I went through a stop sign*' 500 times." — *Kablegram*

Fare Exchange

"You ain't got no cause to worry, lady," the taxi driver assured me as I picked myself up from the floor and straightened my hat while the taxi continued to swerve and skid down Butte's icy Main Street one wintry day. "I ain't goin' to land back in no hospital now after 18 months in one overseas."

"How dreadful," I murmured sympathetically. "You must have been seriously wounded."

"Nope," he replied cheerfully, "never got a scratch. I was a mental case!"

— Mollie O'Meara

In a Los Angeles taxicab, I spotted a neatly wrapped little box in the corner of the seat. Handing it to the driver, I said, "Looks like one of your passengers forgot something."

With a nonchalant "Thanks" he opened the glove compartment

and tossed in the package, which looked as though it had come from a jewelry shop. I noticed several similar packages in the compartment. Then he explained: "These boxes are just props for a little game of psychology I play with my customers. I've found that four out of five men will return the package. But I guess women are just too curious or covetous. About four out of five can't resist."

"What's in the box?" I asked.

"Nothing but a little note," he answered. "It says, 'Crime Does Not Pay.'"

— James Hodgson

A man who had been waiting 15 minutes on a Chicago street finally hailed a cab. Just as it drew up to the curb, a befurred dowager waddled up to the cab and climbed in triumphantly.

The gentleman, maintaining a cold calm, addressed the driver: "Did you come to the curb on my signal?"

"I certainly did."

"Then take this money," said the gentleman, "and drive around the block as long as it lasts."

The cab rolled away. After circling the block three times it stopped where the gentleman stood waiting. The dowager bounced out in a rage; the gentleman gallantly doffed his hat, entered the cab and drove off.

— Dale Harrison in Chicago *Sun*

A taxi driver whose fixed fee is 20 cents for the trip from the Mayflower Hotel in Washington to the Navy Building received just that amount from a prosperous-looking customer.

"That's correct, isn't it?" the man asked as the cabby stared at the two dimes.

"It's correct," answered the cabby cryptically, "but it ain't right."

— *This Week Magazine*

The actress Leonora Corbett sent the following note of apology to a friend:

"Dear Gerald: Do you remember the day we met outside my front door? I had not seen you for quite a while. You came toward me with outstretched hands and beaming smile. I was in a dreadful hurry.

'Oh, Gerald,' I said, 'I wish you were a taxi.' You laughed and said how funny I always was, but your arms dropped rather quickly to your sides.

"Months have passed since then. Gerald, will you forgive that naughty jest of mine if I tell you that this morning as I left my house an empty cab slowly passed me by, and half aloud I whispered, 'Oh, taxi, how I wish you were Gerald!' ' "

A taxi was creeping slowly through the New York rush-hour traffic and the passenger was in a hurry. "Please," he said to the driver, "can't you go any faster?"

"Sure I can," the cabby replied. "But I ain't allowed to leave the taxi."
                                                — *The American Legion Magazine*

As a New York taxi dodged daringly through congested traffic, the driver startled my friend by saying, "I've been watching you in the mirror ever since you got in."

"Yes?" she responded uncertainly.

"Yep. And what I want to say, ma'am," he continued gallantly, "you certainly ride a taxi well!"
                                                — Ray Mackland

Spiced Tongue

Observations: Of all the labor-saving devices ever invented for women, none has ever been so popular as a devoted man (Louise Paine Benjamin) . . . Modern marriage needs fewer eternal triangles and more cotton ones (Kathleen O'Dell) . . . People with time to spare usually spend it with someone who hasn't (*Collier's*) . . . I do the hardest work of my whole day before breakfast — getting up! (Bob Crosby)

Child's review: This book tells more about penguins than I am interested in knowing.

Barbara Stanwyck, after a dull party: "It was a fête worse than death." (Harrison Carroll, King Features)

Enjoying the signery: On a convalescent home in New York, "For the sick and tired of the Episcopal Church" (Roy Fitch) . . . On a country road, "NO HUNTING" — penciled beneath, "You're telling me!" (Mrs. Ellsworth Browning) . . . A Harlem barbershop has the casing of a 16-inch shell in its window, with a sign reading, "Rust in Peace" (*This Week Magazine*) . . . In a Delaware chemical plant, "If you insist on smoking, please tell us where to send the ashes" (Hy Gardner)

Epitaph for a waiter: God finally caught his eye. (Edith Gwynn)

The sort of man with whom to eat, drink and be wary (Phyllis Kiel)

. . . He's the type of person who keeps the conversation ho-humming (Dorothy Parker)

Old saws sharpened: A chrysanthemum by any other name would be easier to spell (William J. Johnston) . . . Money doesn't grow on trees but limbs have a way of attracting it (*Halt!*) . . . Opportunity knocks only once but temptation bangs on the door for years (*The Montana Farmer*)

A hearse in Norwich, Conn., has this gentle reminder as a license number plate: U-2.

After two days in the hospital I took a turn for the nurse (W. C. Fields) . . . My garden is a little jewel — 14 carrots (Bob Burns)

A pat on the back develops character, if administered young enough, often enough, and low enough. (Russell County *News*)

Weather reports: In the spring a young man's fancy, but a young woman's fancier (Richard Armour) . . . Tomorrow: snow, followed by little boys with sleds (Portland *Oregonian*)

Variations on a theme: Hick town — one where there is no place to go where you shouldn't be (Robert Quillen) . . . Hick town — one where, if you see a girl dining with a man old enough to be her father, he is (*The William Feather Magazine*)

Nautically Speaking

A young ensign, very insistent he must have leave, was asked the reason by his commanding officer.

"My wife is expecting a baby," he replied.

"Listen, young man, remember this — you are only necessary at the laying of the keel. For the launching you are entirely superfluous."
— Margaret Johnston

During the war Steve Trumbull, a salty, old-time newspaperman, was commissioned in the Navy only to find himself in Indoctrination School among students and instructors many years his junior. Thoroughly bored, he was dozing through a class in Navy correspondence when he was startled into wakefulness by the instructor: "Lieutenant Trumbull, you are to imagine you must report on the following incident: Yesterday, a mine layer was refueling at a pier when a mine somehow went off. The ship exploded and set fire to the pier and other ships tied up there. An ammunition shed blew up. Much damage was incurred. To whom would you address your report?"

Not knowing the correct answer, Lieutenant Trumbull hedged. "This seems important enough to send directly to Frank Knox, Secretary of the Navy."

The instructor replied that, although it wasn't the answer he had in mind, perhaps the incident justified his course. "Very well, Lieutenant. Now how would you begin your report?"

Trumbull started dictating, "My God, Frank, you should have been here last Sunday!"
— Dorothy Billheimer in *The Saturday Evening Post*

Franklin Roosevelt once told of a young Navy ensign whose marks in navigation had not been all that might have been desired, and who was once set at the task of shooting the sun to determine the ship's position. The vessel was on cruise, and was somewhere west of Penzance.

After a while the ensign delivered to the captain the result of his calculations.

Shortly afterward, the captain sent for the ensign. "Young man," said the officer, "remove your cap. We are now upon a hallowed spot."

"Beg your pardon, Captain?"

"Yes, sir," said the captain. "If you have calculated accurately we are now right smack in the middle of Westminster Abbey." — *Collier's*

Admiral Sir Andrew Cunningham was aboard his flagship in a Mediterranean port when a cruiser made a sloppy job of tying up to her berth.

The cruiser's captain, dreading the message he knew would come from his commander in chief, was relieved, if puzzled, when it was delivered. It consisted of the one word, "Good."

Fifteen minutes later, the captain was interrupted in his bath with a supplement reading, "To previous message please add the word 'God.'"
— Boston *Globe*

Jests for Fun

One of the famous umpires of the past was Joe Cantillion and one of the players who rode umpires to the limit was Dick Cooley. Their arguments went on for years until one day Cooley slashed a long drive deep into center field. The ball looked like a cinch to clear the center fielder, and Cooley rounded first with his head down, intent on scoring an inside-the-park homer.

Cantillion raced with him on the infield side. "Touch second!" he yelled. "Touch second, or I'll call you out!" Cooley rounded second and headed for third. "Be sure to touch third!" shouted Cantillion. Cooley touched third and headed for home. Cantillion was still right with him, screaming: "Touch home when you slide! Touch home and don't spike the catcher!"

Cooley went across home plate with a beautiful headfirst dive. He got up, brushed himself off and waited for the fans' applause. But Cantillion walked up to him and said: "Sit down, you big stiff — you're out on a fly ball to center field." — Douglas Moore in *Collier's*

An editor of *Good Housekeeping* had been fretting over his expanding girth. One day he got a terrific jolt when his overcoat wouldn't button in the middle. Later he discovered that two of his assistants had carefully moved all the buttons two inches to the right.

— Bennett Cerf in *The Saturday Review of Literature*

Norman Ross, Chicago ex-long-distance Olympic swimmer, was swimming far out in Lake Michigan. Eventually he started back to shore and when he got fairly close noticed that a big crowd was watching him from the beach. This sort of thing had happened before; Ross knew that when he got to the beach he'd be asked a lot of silly questions. So he swam into the shallow water, stood up, shook himself and asked: "What city is this?" Everybody hollered: "Chicago."

"Oh, hell, I wanted Milwaukee," said Ross, as he dived back into the lake and swam away.   — *Tide*

A pilot on one of the major air lines, when the going gets bumpy, strolls through the cabin with a book under his arm. The title, which he keeps prominently displayed, is *How to Fly in 20 Lessons.*

— George Dixon, King Features

Waldo Peirce, the artist-poet, one day gave the concierge at his Paris hotel a tiny turtle — about as big as the end of your thumb. She was fascinated by her pet. A few days later, Peirce substituted a turtle a size larger. On a following day the turtle grew another two inches. This went on until the delighted lady had an enormous turtle.

Then Peirce reversed the process. The turtle grew smaller day by day. The worried concierge stayed up nights, scarcely leaving her pet long enough for the American to substitute a smaller turtle. She was on the verge of insanity when Peirce, moved at last by pity, told all.

— H. Allen Smith in New York *World-Telegram*

New at the Game

Victor Moore, the comedian, invited on a deer hunt, came back to camp pale and perspiring after two hours in the forest, found his host and demanded: "Are all the others out of the woods yet?"

"Yup!"

"Well, then," sighed Victor, "I've shot a deer."

— Grace Perkins Oursler

Not long ago, the Toledo, Ohio, Junior League attempted to raise money by putting on a horse show. The socialite who was in charge of the affair fell ill the day before it was to open, and another girl, new to the ways of horseflesh, was put in command. Shortly before the event, she received an anxious telephone call from a man who had several horses entered. "I know this is for charity," he said apologetically, "and I'm sorry to have to ask you to do this, but can you scratch one of my horses for me?"

"Surely," said the Leaguer pleasantly. "Where?"

— Cleveland Amory in *The Saturday Evening Post*

At Jack Dempsey's café one prize fighter bragged to another: "Once I fought Jack and had him awfully worried in the third round — he thought he'd killed me!"
— Hy Gardner in *Parade*

A young broker, after a particularly brutal session in a sand trap, sought to relieve the uncomfortable silence by cheerily declaring to his caddy: "Funny game, golf." The boy morosely replied: " 'Tain't meant to be."
— *The Wall Street Journal*

On the ski slope at a New Hampshire winter resort, I watched an instructor show a group of novices the proper technique in executing turns. Most of his pupils, attempting to imitate him, failed miserably — their skis spread out and they slid along in a sitting position for a few feet. After one middle-aged woman did this, the instructor lifted her to her feet, and with masterly tact remarked: "Very good, madame. Now all you must do is eliminate the middle track."
— Clifford C. Cooper, Jr.

Classified Classics

Ad in *Your Weekly Guide to Cape Cod:* "ATTENTION all skiers! When you break an arm or leg, have your friends write their names on your cast. When removed, send cast to me. I will transform it into a beautiful, indestructible vase, lamp or umbrella rack. A treasured heirloom possession."

From the Abilene, Tex., *Reporter-News:* "$10 reward for south side apartment. Large enough to keep young wife from going home to mother. Small enough to keep mother from coming here."

Advertisement in a New York paper: "Young man who gets paid on Monday and is broke by Wednesday would like to exchange small loans with a young man who gets paid on Wednesday and is broke by Monday."

From the *Ohio State Lantern:* "Just broke with my girl friend. Want someone to finish Argyle socks."

From Middletown, Conn., *Wesleyan Argus:* "Lost — One upper dental plate by an alumnus in vicinity of Psi Upsilon over the week-end. Finder please return to Psi U asth thoon asth pothible."

From a Vermont Development Commission advertisement of a local farm for sale: "If purchased before the next heavy windstorm a barn is included."

— UP

From the Anderson, Ind., *Daily Bulletin:* "Will the party who picked up the black cocker spaniel puppy Saturday on Wendell Road either return him or come back and get three-year-old boy he belongs to?"

From the Houston *Post:* "Cowboy wanted for resort ranch; must be able to sing and play guitar. We'll teach you how to ride. Apply Lost Valley Ranch."

Where the West Begins

At the rodeo, my eyes wandered from the spectacle of bucking horses to the line of watchers on the fence and were caught by a tall lean chap in jeans and cowboy boots who held a very young baby cradled in his arms. A baby's bottle stuck out of his hip pocket, and he was whooping and waving his hat at a performer in the ring. The rider looked so young and showed such reckless courage that several times I turned away shuddering. I edged closer to the man on the rail.

"Your friend is very brave," I said.

"Heck," said the cowboy, "that's my wife."

— Dorothea Baker

At the ranch we were visiting in Wyoming — where they say that men are men and smell like horses — the first love of the handsomest cowboy of them all was Major, his coal-black horse. Now he had fallen bashfully and hopelessly for the prettiest of the dudes. He made the final gesture when he offered to let her ride Major.

"Oh, I couldn't," she fluttered. "I'd be afraid."

"Ma'am," he drawled, "in Wyoming, when a man offers you his horse you needn't be afraid of either one. Major is lady-broke, and so am I."

— Eva Fortier

A cowboy boarded our air liner at Santa Fe, N. Mex., on a day when gusty mountain winds made flying pretty rough. In spite of the hostess's numerous requests, he refused to fasten his seat belt.

"Young lady," he snorted, "for 30 years I've rode everything I ever mounted, and I ain't about to be saddle tied now. Let 'er buck! I'll ride 'er."

— Norman Meyer

The traditions of the Old West still live, as I discovered when I went to teach school in southern Nebraska. My pupils came to school on horseback, and spent much time demonstrating their ability to ride. Long after I had become acquainted with most of the families I discovered that two of my best pupils had a little brother. He was just pre-school age, an adorable youngster, and I thought it odd that neither his brother nor sister had ever mentioned him. Finally, I said to the boy, "How does it happen that you never told me you had a little brother at home?"

The boy looked at me in a rather embarrassed manner, scuffled his feet, and answered, "Aw, teacher, we don't talk about him. He fell off of a horse."

— Lulu Joy

An insurance agent, writing a policy for a cowpuncher, asked if he had ever had any accidents.

"No," said the cowboy, then added, trying to be helpful, "a bronc kicked in a couple of my ribs and a rattlesnake bit me a couple of years ago."

"Well!" said the agent. "Don't you call those accidents?"

"No," replied the knight of the branding iron, "they done it a-purpose."

— Grit

Cowboy commentators: Clarence Budington Kelland, the novelist, noticed a cowboy enjoying a cup of coffee outside a ranch house and asked if he could have one too. The cowboy held out his own cup: "Here, take this one. It's all saucered and blowed." (*The American Magazine*) . . . Asked how many children he had, the rodeo rider replied, "Three buckin' and one in the chute."

Department Stories

Shopping in Dallas's swank Neiman Marcus store one morning, I noticed a tall cowboy with a ten-gallon hat, faded Levis and high-heeled boots, typical of our West Texas stockmen. As I watched, a salesgirl asked if she might help him.

"No, ma'am, I reckon not," was his reply. "I ain't never seen so many things I could do without."

— Mrs. W. H. Venable, Jr.

During the Christmas rush, a girl, shopping for a gift for her brother, noticed an attractive pair of men's pajamas and asked the price.

"$42.50," answered the clerk.

"For $42.50," announced the girl, as she headed for the necktie department, "they should have a man in them!"

— Arthur Caylor in San Francisco *Daily News*

A customer in a Copenhagen department store complained to the management about the attendant in the ladies' rest room, who had given her a frosty stare when she failed to leave a generous tip.

"Why, we have no attendant in the ladies' room," said the manager. A check revealed that the "attendant" was a woman who had wandered in for a rest a year ago. While relaxing with her knitting the woman had received coins from patrons who thought she was the attendant. Recognizing opportunity when it knocked, the woman had come in regularly ever since, netting while she knitted.

— Walter Kiernan, WJZ

Clerk to sweet young thing in form-fitting sweater: "Would you like to step outside and try it for whistles before you decide?"

— Dave Gerard cartoon in *True*

A sign at the entrance of the women's clothing section of a Detroit department store read: "Ladies Ready to Wear Clothes." Underneath in bold masculine handwriting, someone had added: "It's about time!"

— Don A. Andreozzi

Upon his arrival at the office, a Los Angeles businessman learned that he must catch a noon train to Fresno. His wife had friends there and he knew that she would want to accompany him. To find her was the problem, since she had gone shopping and didn't expect to be home before evening.

Then he remembered that she had charge accounts at several department stores. He dialed the merchants' credit association and requested that they have all retail members suspend his wife's accounts immediately. In less than an hour his wife was phoning him in tears. He squared things by telling her to pack her bags and meet him at the station.

— *Telephony*

Customer to complaint-department clerk refunding money: "But you're not refunding it cheerfully."

— Homer cartoon in *This Week Magazine*

The Man's Glossary *of Unfamiliar Words and Phrases*

As Used by Advertising Writers
to Describe Female Apparel and Appurtenances

From a pre-Christmas ad by Macy's, the New York department store

lapin
French beaver
erminette
squirreline
polar seal
} Just a bunny, honey, made to look like much more money.

knickknack — Any little thing.

bibelot — Any little thing that costs more.

sequins — Female armor (not impregnable).

glamorous — Anything plus a sequin.

crocodile
alligator
} One has a bigger mouth but you can't tell the difference in the end.

swish net — Hammock for the hair.

mink — when a woman turns around to look at another woman — that's mink.

sable — When a woman in mink turns around to look at another woman.

negligee — What she hopes she'll have on when the house burns down.

bathrobe — Live alone and lump it.

wedges — vamps on ramps.

gossamer — The nearest thing to nothing — and better in black.

marabou — It's better to sneeze than to freeze.

new — Adjective for anything.

chic — Adjective for anything with a hat to match.

bois de rose
shocking
dusty
petal
} What do you think? Pink!

Maid's Eye View

A charwoman in a New York bank was telling of her prowess in polishing floors. "When I started to work here the floors was in bad shape. But since I've been doing them," she said with quiet pride, "three ladies has fell down."

— *Treasury of Modern Humor*, edited by Martha Lupton (Droke)

My friend's weekly cleaning woman failed to show up one day, but the mail brought a message. It was a condolence card, reading: "WITH DEEPEST SYMPATHY FOR YOU."

Scrawled in almost illegible handwriting at the bottom was: "My sister sick. I not come. Mary." — Mrs. D. J. Nilson

The Richard Himbers were being interviewed by a maid who explained that she left her last position because she couldn't stand the way the master and mistress were always quarreling. "That must have been unpleasant," remarked Himber.

"Yes, sir," the girl declared, "they was at it all the time. When it wasn't me and him, it was me and her!" — Sid Ascher in *Caravan*

Mrs. Smythe was making final arrangements for an elaborate reception. "Nora," she said to her veteran servant, "for the first half-hour I want you to stand at the drawing-room door and call the guests' names as they arrive."

Nora's face lit up. "Thank you, ma'am," she replied. "I've been wanting to do that to some of your friends for the last 20 years." — Neal O'Hara, McNaught Syndicate

We once had a very capable Negro woman working for us. Her husband, however, was a happy-go-lucky fellow who, although very likable, never seemed able to keep a job and seldom bothered to try. One day I asked her why she put up with him. Without hesitating she said, "It's like this, Mis'. I makes de livin' and he makes de livin' worthwhile." — Alvada Pope

Our new cook seemed to be a find. We had agreed on hours, wages and days off. "My husband is very punctual," I said. "But sometimes," I added apologetically, "he brings home unexpected guests for dinner. I would suggest you always be prepared for such an emergency."

"Yes, ma'am," Elinor nodded. "I'll keep my bags packed." — Christine Nason

Cartoon Quips

Dignified young man pulling away from ardent siren: "Please, Miss Swanson, you're steaming my glasses."
— Pearson in *The Saturday Evening Post*

Mother snatching up toddler who has just smashed a lamp: "*That* settles it! You're going to be an only child!" — Hank Ketcham in *Collier's*

Bank teller to man at window: "Sorry, Mr. Cotter. Your wife beat you to the draw."
— Leo Garel in *Esquire*

Girl to her date in a night club: "I think I'll have another drink. It makes you so witty."
— Bill King in *Collier's*

Small girl, commenting to friend on passing boy and girl: "Goodness, she's old enough to be his sitter." — Harry Mace in *This Week Magazine*

Meek little man in a florist shop: "I'd like something in the nature of a peace feeler for my wife."
— Angelo in *Esquire*

Radio announcer: "And now, a word from our sponsor, who has made this program impossible." — Carl Fleischmann, McNaught Syndicate

Transcontinental air lines passenger: "I hate riding locals. We've stopped at Denver, Chicago and now Pittsburgh!"
— Tom Blakley in *Collier's*

One girl to another: "If I could combine their qualities I'd be the happiest girl in the world. Ronald is gay, debonair, rich, handsome, witty, and Clarence wants to marry me." — Irwin Caplan in *Collier's*

Lawyer, reading client's last will and testament to circle of expectant relatives: "And so, being of sound mind, I spent every damn cent I had before I died." — Bill King in *This Week Magazine*

Personal Glimpses

Potter Palmer, the rich Chicagoan who built the famous Palmer House, had a beautiful and extravagant wife to whom he was devoted. In his will he left her most of his money, with no conditions attached. When his lawyer pointed out that she might marry again, he answered, "If she does, he'll need the money."

— Ernest Poole, *Giants Gone: Men Who Made Chicago* (Whittlesey)

In *My Own Story*, Marie Dressler wrote: During my first visit to Paris, when my French was extremely sketchy, I wanted to find the house of a friend. The taximan did his best to explain to me that the address of my friend was just *behind* the Hotel Continental where I was stopping. "*C'est derrière L'Hôtel Continental*," he kept repeating. I got it all but the *derrière*. I demanded, "*Que signifie derrière?*" The wearied cabby, who was watching me back out of his decrepit vehicle, lifted a shoulder and spread his hands. "If," he said, "Madame does not know the meaning of *derrière*, nobody does!"

— Published by Little, Brown

Even as a young officer in Panama, Dwight D. Eisenhower was preparing himself for future events. One hot afternoon he remarked to a friend: "It's very quiet here now, and I've been thinking I should go into the hospital to have my appendix out."

"Has it been bothering you?" the friend asked.

"Oh, no," Eisenhower replied. "But it might rear up and put me out of action sometime when things aren't so quiet."

— Demaree Bess in *The Saturday Evening Post*

"I don't mind being a grandfather," Senator Arthur H. Vandenberg remarked to his wife when informed of the birth of his first grandchild, "but I'm a little dubious about being married to a grandmother."

— Harlan Miller in Washington *Post*

At Sagamore Hill, Theodore Roosevelt and I used to play a little game together. After an evening of talk, we would go out on the lawn and search the skies until we found the faint spot of light-mist beyond the lower left-hand corner of the Great Square of Pegasus. Then one or the other of us would recite:

That is the Spiral Galaxy in Andromeda.
It is as large as our Milky Way.
It is one of a hundred million galaxies.
It consists of one hundred billion suns, each larger than our sun.

Then Roosevelt would grin and say: "Now I think we are small enough! Let's go to bed." — William Beebe, *The Book of Naturalists* (Knopf)

Having completed a biography of Cordell Hull, an author submitted the manuscript to the statesman for approval. On a section telling of a time during the Spanish-American War when young Cordell won all the money in his company at poker, only one correction had been made when the manuscript was returned. In Cordell Hull's own handwriting, the word "company" had been stricken out and the word "regiment" written in. — Jonathan Daniels, *Frontier on the Potomac* (Macmillan)

Sir Harry Lauder has never been one to toss his money about recklessly. At one time, after an American tour, William Morris, Sr., suggested that Lauder take a week's vacation in Florida and made accommodations for him at a swank Miami hotel. The daily rates were fabulous. After one night at the place, Lauder telegraphed that he was returning to New York. "Why don't you stay on and enjoy a well-earned rest?" Morris wired back.

"I never earned this kind of rest," replied Lauder, and caught the next train north. — Irving Hoffman in *The Hollywood Reporter*

Inn Detail

Shortly after my mother's second novel, *Tomorrow Will Be Better*, was published, I was traveling with her on a personal appearance tour and we stopped unexpectedly in Washington, D. C., where we had no hotel reservation. Mother had always used her first book, *A Tree Grows in Brooklyn*, as identification, so she said to the hotel clerk, "I'm Betty Smith, 'Tomorrow Will Be Better,' I'd like a room."

"I'm Mr. Fiske," he replied. "Peace, it's wonderful, we're all filled up." — Mary Smith Carroll

A man who lives in a Nob Hill hotel noticed that the contents of a bottle of fine bourbon were dropping at a rapid rate. So he made a tiny pencil mark on the label opposite the current level. Returning home that night, he found a note from the chambermaid: "Please don't put a pencil mark on the bottle, because I don't want to put water in such good whisky." — Herb Caen in San Francisco *Chronicle*

Joe E. Lewis once spent a night at Saratoga's old Grand Union Hotel. The railroad station was directly below, and a switching engine kept shunting cars back and forth incessantly. Finally Joe summoned the night clerk. "Maybe you can tell me," he suggested, "what time this hotel reaches Chicago!"— Bennett Cerf in *The Saturday Review of Literature*

Guests in a Cairo hotel, hearing a scream in the corridor, discovered a damsel in negligee being pursued by a gentleman who was, to put it bluntly, nude. Later it developed that the impetuous Romeo was an English major, who was promptly court-martialed. His lawyer won him an acquittal, however, by virtue of the following paragraph in the army manual: "It is not compulsory for an officer to wear a uniform at all times, as long as he is suitably garbed for the sport in which he is engaged." — Mabel Dana Lyon, quoted by Bennett Cerf in *The Saturday Review of Literature*

While stationed at the Army Air Base in Jacksonville, Fla., I got a week-end pass, and wired my wife to join me, telling her to travel light. Exhibiting unusual obedience, she showed up wearing an all-purpose suit and carrying only a slightly oversized pocketbook.

At the hotel, I realized my mistake. I had completely forgotten a recent ruling which demanded that all service men produce evidence to show that the women they took into hotels were really their wives. With neither luggage nor a marriage certificate, we were sunk. "Orders are orders," the desk clerk repeated flatly.

Then my wife lit into me. She pointed out my stupidity and my lack of forethought. As she warmed to her subject, I glanced back to see if the clerk was watching. He was, and he was also holding out a key. "Room 804," he said. "They don't talk that way unless they're married!" — John H. Newton, Jr., in *The Saturday Evening Post*

The Body Beautiful

Condensed from The American Mercury

Cornelia Otis Skinner

When a woman goes to try on a dress, she often finds herself before one of those mirrors with hinged side panels which suggest a primitive triptych — that is, if she has sufficient imagination to turn the triple reflection of herself clad in a pink slip into a trio of medieval saints. Such mirrors reflect many seldom-beheld angles and the sudden sight of them is a shock. You find you're staring at yourself rather than at the clothes you're buying. Your profile somehow isn't at all the way you'd remembered it; and your eye is arrested not without horror by that portion of the anatomy of which you catch a good glimpse only on these sartorial occasions. Since the last shopping trip it appears to have taken on distressing prominence, and you reach the grim conclusion that it's almost too late for clothes to matter.

Such a recently beheld panorama of myself filled me with panic. I felt I must do something immediately. I consulted one of my better-shaped acquaintances, who sent me with my troubles and my protuberances to a small but impressive "slimming" establishment. The façade was what is known as "moderne." Instead of the usual show window, it had portholes in which terra-cotta dryads danced amid bottles of perfume. In the reception room a marquise disguised as a saleswoman was sitting behind the sort of table at which Madame de Sévigné must have written her letters. The marquise asked if there were anything she could do for me and I said, "Yes, reduce my rear." This shocked her very much, but being of the aristocracy she managed to smile politely and ask, "Have you an appointment for consultation with Mme. Alberta?"

"I don't think I need any consultation," I said. "I just want to reduce my . . ." Her eyebrows flickered ever so slightly and I ended lamely, "I just want to lose a few inches."

"All our clients have a consultation first with Mme. Alberta," she replied; and she directed me up a mauve carpeted stair. I wondered whether Mme. Alberta would greet me with a stethoscope or would be discovered gazing into a crystal. She proved to be a youngish woman, frighteningly smart, seated at another period table. Her accent was so determined to be English that it broadened every *a*, even in such words as *hand* and *ankle*.

She listened to the story of my proportions as if it were a case his-

tory. On a card resembling a hospital chart she wrote my name and address and details of personal history that struck me as singularly irrelevant in the matter of hip reduction.

"Now, we'll see about your weight."

"I know what I weigh," I said, adding recklessly: "And I don't care. All I'm after is to reduce my . . ."

"Weight and measurements must be taken at every treatment," Mme. Alberta interrupted me with polite asperity. "There's the dressing room, madam. Will you disrobe kindly?"

I went to what seemed to be a daintily furnished sentry box and disrobed kindly. I felt somehow I was up for a woman's branch of the Army. A trim mulatto brought me a sheet and a pair of paper slippers. I tried to drape the sheet so I'd look like a Tanagra figurine but it wouldn't work so I arranged it along the more simple lines of a Navajo blanket. When I emerged Mme. Alberta led me down a corridor. Behind a screen she whisked off my sheet in the manner of a mayor unveiling a statue and placed me on a scale. When I protested that I already knew my weight, she shed on me the indulgent smile a night nurse might give a psychopathic patient.

"Now for those measurements," she said. "Miss Jones, will you please come here?" Miss Jones proved to be a lovely young thing in a wisp of a sky-blue tunic. She was of such bodily perfection one had the suspicion that "Miss Jones" was incognito for "Miss America." We were formally introduced — Miss Jones in her bright-blue suit, I in my bright-pink skin.

Then, as if she hadn't already sufficiently humiliated me, Mme. Alberta took a tape measure and began calling out my measurements to the world at large. She measured everything. "I hardly think you need go to all that trouble," I interposed. "It's just my . . ."

"We take all measurements," Mme. Alberta said somewhat acidly. She accompanied her work with a flow of exclamations that might be taken any way, "Well, *well!*" she'd murmur, or, "I *thought* so!" At times she shook her pretty head and went "tsk! tsk!"

After completing her survey she turned me over to Miss Jones, who led the way to a room that contained a mat, a gramophone and far too many mirrors. Here Miss Jones put me through twenty minutes of hard labor. I stretched and kicked. I jumped and pranced. I stood on my shoulders with my feet in the air;

that is, Miss Jones hoisted my feet into the air while I rose up onto a fast-breaking neck and screamed. I tried to take time out by distracting her with harmless chatter. But Miss Jones was very strict. Now and then when total collapse seemed imminent she'd play a lively record on the gramophone and call out "one *and* two *and* three *and* four" as if it were a battle cry.

Miss Jones herself was tireless. She'd do awful things such as picking up her ankle with one hand and holding her foot above her head like a semaphore. And she expected me to do likewise. She tells me I'm seriously hamstrung — a nasty expression that makes me feel they've been keeping me in the smokehouse all these years.

It's hard to feel cozy with Miss Jones. She is not only strict, she's exceptionally refined. What I call "middle" she calls "diaphragm," what I call "stomach" her whimsy turns to "tummy," and what I call something else she, with averted eyes, refers to as *derrière*.

Finally Miss Jones said I was a good girl and might go have my massage. I staggered into the capable arms of a Miss Svenson who looked like Flagstad dressed up as a nurse. She flung me onto a hard table and went to work on me as if I were the material in a taffy-pulling contest. She kneaded me, she rolled me with a hot rolling pin, she did to me what she called "cupping" — a beauty-parlor term for good old orthodox spanking. After she'd gotten me in shape for the oven she took me into a shower room and finished me up with the hose treatment used to subdue rioting prisoners.

Once I'd dressed and recaptured my breath I felt extraordinarily full of radiant health and rugged appetite. It was time for lunch and visions of beefsteak danced in my head.

But Mme. Alberta was lying in wait for me outside. "Here is your diet," she said.

It was a tasty little menu consisting of a dab of lean chop-meat, a few fruit juices and some lettuce garnished by a rousing dressing made with mineral oil.

Mme. Alberta's system includes a lot of extracurricular work. Now exercise in the privacy of one's domicile is a splendid idea provided one has a certain amount of domicile and a modicum of privacy. But the only reasonable space in my apartment is the living room, which is exposed to the hall by an open archway. For my exertions I generally gird myself in nothing more confining than a pair of old pink rayon bloomers. My child goes into fits of hysterics at the spectacle, and tries to bring in his buddies to "look at what Mummy's doing." Whenever the doorbell rings I am obliged to leap for sanctuary behind the sofa — and I don't always hear the bell, which makes it pretty fascinating for whoever comes to the door. Once in all innocence and seminudity I gave a private performance for the window cleaner — since when, if we have the misfortune to meet on the occasions of his monthly visit, we pass each other quickly with lowered eyes.

Reducing, if one follows the Mme. Alberta school, is a 24-hour job. You are shown contortions that can supposedly be indulged in anywhere, any time. You can straighten out your spine along the edge of the nearest door — which makes the casual observer think you are scratching an itching back. The thumps and double thumps especially recommended for reducing the — well, you know — can be done while leaning against any handy wall — say that of the elevator, thereby bringing a moment of diversion into the operator's monotonous life. Then there are a few less inconspicuous numbers such as standing on tiptoe and stretching up the hands ("Reaching for cherries" is Miss Jones's pretty term for it), and a movement dignified by the name of "abdominal control" which curiously resembles the beginnings of the *danse du ventre*. These you are expected to burst forth with at odd hours of the day and night even at the risk of starting the grim rumor that you're about to come down with St. Vitus's dance.

However, the more of a spectacle I make of myself in the eyes of other people, the less embarrassing I am in my own mirror. And Mme. Alberta is pleased with me. The last time she encircled me with her measuring tape she found "signs of considerable shrinkage."

Boston Bred

On Friday afternoons in autumn, Boston is rent by a great schism. The Red Sox are playing the season's crucial games at Fenway Park, the Boston Symphony is giving its opening concerts, and the natives must choose between sports and music. Last year, however, at Symphony Hall the twain met.

On one side of me sat an ill-at-ease young man who quickly identified himself as a prisoner in enemy territory: "I was dragged here by my wife and it's a crime, when I could be seeing the ball game." On my other side was an elderly dowager, in Queen Mary hat, pearl choker and fur tippet, who seemed in her element, leaning forward with a rapt expression. She spoke only once — after the baseball fan had asked me for the third time what I thought the score was.

"Please tell that young man," she whispered, "that the Red Sox are ahead six to two."

I relayed the message. "You're kidding," protested the young man. "How would *she* know?"

The lady nudged me and furtively pointed to a large knitting bag in her lap. In it was a miniature radio, and as Dr. Koussevitsky raised his baton to begin the last number on the program, to my astonishment I caught a muted voice from another world saying "Here's the pitch. . . ."

— Sherwood Rollins, Jr.

A Chicago banking house once asked a Boston investment firm for a letter of recommendation about a young Bostonian they were considering employing. The investment concern could not say enough for the young man. His father, they wrote, was a Cabot, his mother a Lowell; further back his background was a happy blend of Saltonstalls, Appletons, Peabodys, and others of Boston's First Families. The recommendation was given without hesitation.

Several days later came a curt acknowledgment from Chicago stating that the material supplied was inadequate. "We are not," the letter declared, "contemplating using the young man for breeding purposes."

— Cleveland Amory in *Harper's*

An old Boston family were persuaded to take a trip to California. Never previously had they considered it worth while to travel farther from home than Lexington, Concord, Dedham and other Boston suburbs.

When they arrived in Los Angeles, their friends inquired: "By which route did you come?"

The man turned to his wife and asked, "Darling, didn't we come by way of Dedham?"

— John Homer Miller

A distinguished Bostonian, stopping off in Salt Lake City on his way to the Pacific Coast, made the acquaintance of a little Mormon girl. "I'm from Boston," he said to her. "I suppose you do not know where Boston is?"

"Oh, yes, I do," answered the little girl eagerly. "Our Sunday school has a missionary there."

— *Listen to These*, edited by Thomas L. Masson (Doubleday)

A Boston lady was expressing her indignation at the indecent words being painted on the walls and sidewalks of the city.

"What will outsiders think of us?" she cried. "Why, some of the words aren't even spelled right!"

— Harold Helfer

On one occasion the delicate Boston *Transcript's* standing injunction against any reference to anatomy in its columns was ignored by a reporter who used the word "navel" in an article. The edition was already running before the managing editor spotted it. He stopped the presses with a stern order to chisel out the offensive word. Unhappily he had not had time to read the full context. The *Transcript* appeared on the streets that evening with the sinister information that a concert musician had been "in a state of repose as complete as that of a Buddhist regarding his   ."

When two midwestern sisters who arrived to marry Bostonians declared they were from Iowa, they received the astonishing rebuke, "In Boston we pronounce it Ohio."

— Above items from Cleveland Amory's *The Proper Bostonians* (Dutton)

Coping with the Public

The blizzard had turned Chicago's Michigan Avenue into a pedestrian hazard of churned-up slush. A pretty young thing, standing irresolutely at the crossing, extended a dainty foot and as hastily withdrew it. The big Irish traffic cop regarded her sympathetically. It took but a minute to blow his whistle, stride to the curb, gather her up in his arms, and deposit her carefully on the other side. Whereupon the

young lady, her eyes blazing, slapped him — hard. Without a word he once more swept her from her feet and bore her, kicking, back to her original position. Then he released the traffic.　　　— J. C. Graham

In Birmingham, Ala., cruising police cars got a radio call: "Car X-Y-3, car X-Y-3, go to Third Avenue and 14th Street — a nude woman running down the street. . . . All other cars remain on your beat. That is all."　　　— *Time*

An elderly woman strolled calmly out into the street after a cop had flagged her to stay on the sidewalk. "Lady," he roared, "don't you know what it means when I hold up my hand?"

"I ought to," she snapped. "For the last 25 years I've been a schoolteacher!"　　　— H. C. L. Jackson in Detroit *News*

A floorwalker, tired of his job, gave it up and joined the police force. Several months later a friend asked him how he liked being a policeman. "Well," he replied, "the pay and the hours are good, but what I like best is that the customer is always wrong." — *Sales Scrap Book*

"Time Brings All Things"

Excerpts from the Miscellany Department of Time

Fashion Note. In Chicago, a department store featured two brands of sheer nighties, found that "Sinners" outsold "Saints" three to one.

Stuck Pig. In Mobile, Ala., a housewife, short of cash, guiltily broke into her baby's piggy bank, found only a note inside: "IOU $5. [signed] Daddy."

Irate Citizen. In Jersey City, one Thomas unwisely reported the theft of his car to police, who discovered that it had been stolen once before — by Thomas.

Direct Action. In Brockton, Mass., a bartender who had refused to serve a drunk noticed at length that business was falling off, presently discovered that the offended customer had gone off to a hardware store, had come back, and padlocked the café's main door.

Apt Description. In Union City, N. J., a young woman whom Walter Blazeck had picked up robbed him of $150 and his car. When police asked him to describe her, he offered: "Overattractive."

Progressive Education. In Dartford, England, officials at an office-equipment exhibit discovered why the show was drawing so many small fry: they were doing their homework on the adding machines.

All Wet. In Kansas City, Mo., weather forecasters of the American Meteorological Society picked an "ideal day" for their annual picnic, were rained out.

Grievance. Near Winchester, Ind., a bull gored the auto of Jack Townsend, the county's artificial inseminator.

Century of Progress. In New Britain, Conn., manufacturers Landers, Frary & Clark proudly reported the sale of an electric blanket to a Sioux Indian.

Out of This World. In McCook, Neb., Ernest Olivier spun in a jitter-bugging step, reached for his jiving partner's hand, plunged out the second-story window of the dance hall.

Awful Truth. In Manhattan, New York *Post* columnist Leonard Lyons reported that in California a psychiatric patient was asked if he were Napoleon. He craftily said "No." A lie detector showed he was lying.

Yes Indeed. In Fort Worth, burglars lifted $2186 in cash and a 600-pound steel safe from the Helpy-Selfy Grocery and Market.

Doggone!

A haughty woman swept into a fashionable kennel shop.
"I want a collar for Alexander," she said.
Timidly, the clerk inquired, "What size, please?"
"You should know the size," the outraged customer exclaimed.
"Alexander buys all his clothes here!"
— Will Gerber

A woman who had been bitten by a dog was advised by her physician to write her last wishes, as she might soon succumb to hydrophobia. She spent so long with pencil and paper that the doctor finally asked whether it wasn't getting to be a pretty lengthy will.
"Will!" she snorted. "Nothing of the kind. I'm writing a list of the people I'm going to bite."
— Joseph W. Cochran

One day my elderly and unmarried aunt told me that her Pomeranian dog, Peggy, had been behaving most peculiarly. As I was a medical student at the time, she expected me to examine her pet and prescribe treatment. With some embarrassment I explained that it was spring, that animals — well, that Peggy needed a mate. Aunt Fanny ordered me to find Peggy a suitable one immediately.

After locating a fine Pomeranian at a nearby kennel, I described the dog to my aunt: its long pedigree, good coloring, record of healthy litters, all its fine qualifications. The fee, I added, would be $5.

Aunt Fanny told me to attend to the matter right away. Before starting off with Peggy, I explained that the kennel owner would probably require his fee in advance and since I was broke, asked her to give me the $5. Aunt Fanny was obviously startled. "Do you mean *Peggy* has to pay?" she gasped.
— Capt. H. L. Finsten

The gentle little lady who had been watching the antics of the Pekinese in the pet shop window came in to price them. "That bitch," said the salesman, pointing, "you can have for $30, or the one there for $35." The lady winced. "What's the matter," asked the salesman, "aren't you familiar with the term 'bitch'?" "Yes," she said haughtily, "but I've never before heard it applied to dogs."

Rustic Rejoinders

The members of a hunting party had been specifically requested to bring only male hounds. One indigent member, however, owned only a female, and out of courtesy was finally permitted to include her. The pack was off in a flash. In a matter of seconds they were completely out of sight. The confused hunters stopped to question a farmer in a nearby field, "Did you see some hounds go by here?"

"Yep," said the farmer.

"See where they went?"

"Nope," was the reply, "but it was the first time I ever see a fox runnin' fifth!"
— Leonora B. Wilson

In my small Connecticut town there is a man who repairs everything from leaky plumbing to rickety chairs, and each job is a masterpiece. One day I asked him what he would charge to refinish some small walnut tables badly marked with rings where glasses had been set down.

He looked at them carefully. "Have to be scraped down to the quick, and farther," he said thoughtfully. "It would cost $5 apiece. Take a couple of weeks. But I won't do it."

"You won't do it? But —"

He shook his head. "They'll be in the same shape a month later. Have to keep having 'em done, every month, six weeks, the rest of your life."

"But," I pleaded, "I'll buy more coasters. I'll put coasters *everywhere* —"

"Nope. It'd just be a waste of honest labor. More coasters won't do no good." He sighed. "When you got that kind of friends, ma'am, you got that kind of friends." — Anne Heywood Reid

On a hunting trip in the south my husband and I stopped with one of those Arkansas farmers who economize on speech. I asked him what he thought of my shooting outfit.

"Shoes too low," he opined. "Snakes."

Next day I bought a pair of boots that reached nearly to my knees. "Do you think the snakes will bite above these?" I asked anxiously.

"Nope. At least no *decent* snake would." — Elsie Willette

Weary and famished after a long day's trek through the North Woods, I begged shelter at a log cabin. It was a primitive affair of one room, in which was a stove, bed, table and chairs; a ladder led up to a loft under the roof. Despite such cramped quarters for a settler, his wife and four children, I was made welcome. With a hot meal under my belt, I began to nod. "Sorry to keep you up," the father said, "but we're kinda crowded so you'll have to wait till the little ones are out of the way." The children were put to bed early; then when the last one was asleep, the man took them up one by one and laid them side by side on the floor at the back of the room. Then he announced. "There she is, and she's all yours." I vigorously protested at robbing the youngsters of their comfort, but was told to think nothing of it. This procedure was usual whenever company came. Too tired to argue I turned in and knew no more until morning. When I awoke, I was lying on the floor with the kids; the settler and his wife were in the bed. — Rex Beach

A book agent came to sell one of the combination farmer-merchant-bankers of southeast Arkansas a set of books on scientific agriculture. The old man thumbed through them.

"No, I don't want to buy them."

"You ought to buy them, sir. If you had these books you could farm twice as good as you do now."

"Hell, son," he replied, "I don't farm half as good as I know how now." — Jonathan Daniels, *A Southerner Discovers the South* (Macmillan)

Motoring west one hot August, too weary to drive farther, we stopped for the night in a small country town. Neither of the two hotels looked particularly attractive, so we asked the garage attendant which one he would recommend. He hesitated. "Can't say I *recommend* the National House," he said slowly. "But I do say the folks who come for their cars after staying at the National aren't quite so mad as those from the Commercial." — R. D. Jones

The Coolidge Character

When Calvin Coolidge was in the Massachusetts legislature, another member asked him whether the people where he came from said, "A hen lays, or a hen lies."

"The people where I come from," Mr. Coolidge replied, "lift her up to see." — William Lyon Phelps

Richard Washburn Child, former ambassador to Italy, tells this story of a visit to the White House when Calvin Coolidge was President: "After dinner the President, saying he had something to show me, took me to one of the smaller rooms. Opening the door, he reached in and turned on the light. On the opposite wall hung a portrait of himself. I thought it so very bad I could think of nothing to say. For a long silent moment we stood there on the threshold. Then Coolidge snapped off the light and closed the door. 'So do I,' he said." — George Palmer Putnam, *Wide Margins* (Harcourt, Brace)

President Coolidge told me this story about his son Calvin. "He was working in a tobacco field the day I was made President. Some of the boys said: 'If my father were President I wouldn't be working in a tobacco field in the Connecticut Valley!' Calvin said: 'If my father were your father you would!' "

— William Allen White, *A Puritan in Babylon* (Macmillan)

Calvin Coolidge had humor and sense enough to escape that exaggeration of the ego which afflicts a good many of our Presidents. I once intercepted him taking a cat nap in the middle of a presidential executive day.

When he opened his eyes, he grinned and asked: "Is the country still here?"

— William Hard in *The Atlantic Monthly*

During my teaching days, I had Coolidge's sons as pupils. The President occasionally visited the school, and one evening at the headmaster's we sat around the fire talking. Reminiscing about his student days at Amherst College, Mr. Coolidge told us that he well remembered when the members of his class voted on the One Most Likely to Succeed. "Nearly all of them voted for Dwight Morrow," he said.

"For whom did you vote, Mr. Coolidge?" I asked.

"I voted for myself," said Cal.

— Archibald Rutledge

President Coolidge once invited some Vermont friends to dine at the White House. They were worried about their table manners, so decided to do everything Coolidge did. The meal passed smoothly until coffee was served and Coolidge poured his into a saucer. The guests followed suit. Then he added sugar and cream. The visitors did likewise. Then Coolidge leaned over and gave his to the cat.

— Henry Charles Suter

Shortly after Calvin Coolidge left the White House he was called upon to fill out a card to accompany the payment of his annual dues to the National Press Club.

Mr. Coolidge filled in his name and address, and then on the line provided for "Occupation" wrote simply "Retired." After a moment's thought, in the space headed "Remarks," the ex-President added the terse comment: "Glad of it."   — *The Christian Science Monitor*

That's Off Their Chests

In a Paducah, Ky., city election one independent citizen voted for no one, but wrote across his ballot, "God Pity Paducah."

— Louisville *Courier-Journal*

A sign in front of a shoe repair shop pictured several styles of rubber heels and a beautiful girl who was saying, "I'm in love with America's Number 1 heel." Underneath in small feminine handwriting, someone had added, "Too bad, sister! I married him." — Vera W. Postel

Among my pupils in a high school chemistry class was a lad who had a tendency to monopolize discussions. I decided that such a troublesome habit should be called to the attention of his parents. On his report card I wrote: "Allan is a good student but he talks too much."

Several days later the report was returned. Underneath my comment the boy's father had added: "You should meet his mother."

— Harold R. Maurer

In Northampton, Mass., a Smith College freshman scrawled as her denominational preference: "I like to be called Betty." — *Time*

A woman leafing through Dorothy Parker's *Enough Rope* at the Public Library found this remark penciled in a feminine hand under the crack about men seldom making passes at girls who wear glasses: "That's what SHE thinks!" — *PM*

On the front window of a Louisville, Ky., grocery store was written: "Boy Wanted." Below was scribbled: "I want one, too, Jeanne."

— Helyne S. Pincus

A young lady applying for a position in a large establishment was given a lengthy application to fill out. On the last page was a boxed space reserved for the employing official to fill in the salary. Above it were the words: "DO NOT WRITE IN THIS SPACE." The applicant, endowed with a sense of humor, wrote in: "DO RIGHT IN THIS SPACE." She got the job. — F. P. Pitzer

On the Job

On vacation from school, I had been making the rounds of Los Angeles business houses one day vainly looking for a summer job. Finally I decided to tackle just one more establishment and really sell myself. I proceeded to enact the part of a live wire — oozed confidence and vitality, talked fast and assuredly, then searched my mind for a final punch line. "In short," I concluded, "do you have an opening for an enterprising young man?"

"Yes, young man, I do," said the manager wearily, "and close it gently as you go out!"

— Paul C. Amis

A married couple of my acquaintance, returning from Europe, became interested in an attractive, red-cheeked Finnish girl in the steerage. They found that she was coming to America to look for work, and decided to offer her employment. "Can you cook?" they asked.

"No," said the girl, "I can't cook. My mother always did the cooking."

"Well," they said, "then you can do the housework?"

"No," she said, "I don't know how. My oldest sister always did the housework."

"Well, then we could let you take care of the children."

"No, I couldn't do that. My youngest sister always took care of the children."

"Well, you can do the sewing."

"No," said the girl, "my aunt always did the sewing."

"What *can* you do?" cried the despairing couple.

The girl was quite bright and cheerful as she volunteered, "I can milk reindeer."

— Donald Culross Peattie

An employer, interviewing an applicant, remarked: "You ask high wages for a man with no experience."

"Well," the prospect replied, "it's so much harder work when you don't know anything about it."

— Willow Grove, Pa., *Guide*

Waiting in a steamship office to be interviewed for a job as wireless operator, a group of applicants filled the room with such a buzz of conversation that they were oblivious to the dots and dashes which began coming over a loudspeaker. About that time another man entered and sat down quietly by himself. Suddenly he snapped to attention, walked into the private office, came out smiling.

"Say," one of the group called out, "how'd you get in ahead of us? We were here first."

"One of you would have got the job," he replied, "if you'd listened to the message from the loudspeaker."

"What message?" they asked in surprise.

"Why, the code," the stranger answered. "It said: 'The man I need must always be on the alert. The first man who gets this message and comes directly into my private office will be placed on one of my ships as operator.'"

— Walter C. Mello

At the Treasury Department they tell the story of the sweet young thing who applied for a job. "What're your qualifications?" asked the personnel man.

"Well," said the girl, "I've always liked to handle money."

— Joseph Young in Washington *Evening Star*

Quotable Quotes

Social tact is making your company feel at home, even though you wish they were.

Whenever I hear people discussing birth control, I always remember that I was the fifth.   — Clarence Darrow

America's best buy for a nickel is a telephone call to the right man.
                                                          — Ilka Chase

Many people's tombstones should read: "Died at 30. Buried at 60."
                                                — Nicholas Murray Butler

Before I got married I had six theories about bringing up children. Now I have six children — and no theories.   — Lord Rochester

You can't kiss a girl unexpectedly — only sooner than she thought you would.   — Jack Seaman in *The Saturday Evening Post*

Why must we have enough memory to recall to the tiniest detail what has happened to us, and not have enough to remember how many times we have told it to the same person?   — La Rochefoucauld

A tree is an object that will stand in one place for years, then jump in front of a lady driver.   — Ruth Lemezis

The only perfect climate is bed.   — Frank Crowninshield

Keep your temper. Do not quarrel with an angry person, but give him a soft answer. It is commanded by the Holy Writ and, furthermore, it makes him madder than anything else you could say. — Anon.

The Men Who Came to Dinner

The late Leonard Liebling, editor of *Musical Courier*, always remembered the day during his youth when a visitor arrived just as the family was about to sit down to dinner. Mr. Liebling, Sr., annoyed that anyone should choose the dinner hour as visiting time, had the maid ask the guest to wait. After an unhurried dinner, Mr. Liebling greeted his friend, "Sorry to keep you waiting, but we always eat at seven."

"That's what I thought," replied the friend, "when you asked me to come to dinner tonight."   — Abraham Mandelstam in *Pageant*

It happened on a Vermont week-end. As the party was breaking up, I said good-bye to one of the guests, a sad-faced, elderly man who had kept us laughing all through dinner and for several hours afterward. After he left, I asked my hostess, "Who is that man? He's the most entertaining fellow I've ever met."

"Why, I really don't know," she said. "He came to fix the furnace this morning, and he's been here ever since."—H.W. Young

A lecturer of some renown was asked to speak at a nudist camp. He was greeted by ladies and gentlemen with no more on than nature saw fit to bestow upon them. They suggested that he would probably like to get ready for dinner. He went upstairs realizing that he must disrobe like the rest of them. He paced the floor in an agonized panic of indecision. The dinner bell rang. With the courage of utter desperation he stripped, and in Adamite splendor descended the staircase — only to find that all the guests had put on evening clothes to do him honor.

— Donald Culross Peattie

At a dinner for a child star who was a big box-office attraction, a movie producer got up, patted the little girl on the head, and said, "We wish to pay homage to our little star." Then, placing his hand on the shoulder of the star's mother, he continued, "But we don't want to forget the goose that laid the golden egg."

— Joe Laurie, Jr., Press Features

At a dinner some years ago in honor of the newly elected president of the University of Chicago, Dr. Robert M. Hutchins, a visiting educator who did not know the young president remarked to the lady at his side, "So *that* is the new president!"

"I beg your pardon, but do you know who I am?" the lady asked stiffly. The visiting dean admitted that he did not. "Well," she remarked icily, "I am Mrs. Hutchins."

The stranger was stricken dumb for a moment, then said, "I'm sorry. Do you know who I am?" Mrs. Hutchins shook her head.

"Thank God," the dean responded weakly.

— Milton Bacon

Barbed Wires

A comedian sent a wire to a lifelong rival on the latter's opening night, reading, "I CAN'T BE THERE IN SPIRIT SO I'M COMING IN PERSON."

— Bennett Cerf

A member of the National Board of the YWCA, traveling in the West and finding some of her plans suddenly altered, decided to return at once to her home in Chicago. Accordingly she left the train at Reno and sent from there a telegram to her husband: "HAVE SUDDENLY CHANGED PLANS, RETURNING HOME AT ONCE. LOVE." She handed this to the young woman operator who read it thoughtfully and then said, "I hope you won't mind my saying it, madam, but it does do me a lot of good to send a message like this *once in a while*."

— D. Elton Trueblood

Sir Arthur Conan Doyle once sent a telegram to each of 12 friends, all men of great virtue and of considerable position in society. The message was worded: "FLY AT ONCE; ALL IS DISCOVERED." Within 24 hours, the story runs, all 12 had left the country.

— F. L. Wellman, *Gentlemen of the Jury* (Macmillan)

When the Lunt-Fontanne comedy, *O Mistress Mine*, was playing on Broadway, a man in Washington, D. C., wired a New York friend to get him a pair of tickets for the following Saturday night. This the friend was able to do, and promptly wired: "MISTRESS OKAY FOR SATURDAY."

The Washington man read the wire and chuckled. Penciled below the message were the words: "Western Union prefers not to transmit this type of message." — *This Week Magazine*

John Rosenfield is the moving spirit in the flourishing Dallas Symphony. On his last birthday, the 80 members of the orchestra sent him individual wires of congratulation. After 77 had been delivered, he opened one that read, "THANK GOD THIS WILL SOON BE OVER. (SIGNED) WESTERN UNION." — Bennett Cerf in *The Saturday Review of Literature*

Washington—Hubbub the Universe

Washington is the only place where sound travels faster than light (C. V. R. Thompson) . . . The District of Columbia is a territory bounded on all sides by the United States of America (Irving D. Tressler) . . . There are three major parties in the United States — the Democratic Party, the Republican Party and the cocktail party (J. Maurice Trimmer) . . . I love to go to Washington — if only to be near my money (Bob Hope) . . . Some politicians repair their fences by hedging (Hawley R. Everhart)

There's nothing so permanent as a temporary job in Washington (George Allen) . . . There's a current report that an important document that was to have been published by a columnist has come into the hands of the State Department (London *Punch*)

A large car skidded to the curb in front of the Capitol in Washington, and a well-dressed tourist couple hurriedly got out. After quickly surveying the surrounding scene, the man said: "All right, dear, you do the outside and I'll take the inside. We should be through in a half hour."
— Harold Helfer

During a cold snap a pretty secretary at the Army and Navy Munitions Board reported for work dressed in woolen snuggies. The office didn't observe the wartime 65-degree heat limit and, as the temperature soared, life became unbearable for the woolen-clad miss. Finally she grabbed a large manila envelope, retired to the ladies' room and removed her snuggies. She placed the envelope with the woolies on her desk, and shortly afterward it disappeared.

Hours later the snuggies were intercepted, but not until after they had made the rounds of the board. The envelope not only was addressed to the secretary's boss, a commander, but printed on it in large red letters was, "All Naval Officers — Circulate and Initial."
— Jerry Kluttz in Washington *Post*

Two men working side by side in the War Production Board in Washington never spoke, but each watched the other. One man quit work daily at four o'clock, while the other always worked till six or later. Finally the harder worker approached the other. "I beg your pardon," he said. "Do you mind telling me how you clean up all your work every day at four o'clock?"

"Not at all. When I come to a tough piece of detail, I mark it 'Refer to Commander Smith.' I figure that in an outfit as large as this there is sure to be a Commander Smith, and I must be right. None of those papers come back to me."

"Brother," said the hard worker, removing his coat, "prepare for action. I'm Commander Smith."
— Boston News Bureau

An efficiency expert stalked up to two clerks in a Government office in Washington. "What do you do here?" he asked one. The clerk, fed up with red tape, buck-passing, forms, office politics and, above all, efficiency experts, growled: "I don't do a thing!"

The interrogator nodded, made a note, then turned to the other clerk. "And you, what's your job here?" The second man, following his fellow worker's lead, replied, "I don't do a thing either."

The efficiency expert's face lighted up. "Hmmmm," he said knowingly, "duplication!" — *Pathfinder*

An official of the State Department encountered a member of the Polish Embassy accoutered with raincoat and umbrella. "Are you expecting rain?" asked the official.

"No," the Pole replied, "but we just got word that it's raining in Moscow." — Robert S. Allen in *Collier's*

Near a big Government building a Washington bureaucrat's car was parked in a lot whose sign read: "All day parking 35 cents." At lunchtime he asked the boy at the gate if he could drive his car away to lunch, bring it back after an hour and not pay a second time. The attendant's reply was wholly Washington:

"Suh, each car comes in has to pay 35 cents, and don' argue with me. I'se not on the policy-making level." — Barbara C. McNamee

One of the Mexican show places visited by President Truman was the new fiery Paricutín volcano. As he viewed it with keen interest, President Alemán asked what he thought of it. "It's quite a volcano," replied Truman, "but it's nothing compared to the one I'm sitting on in Washington." — Robert S. Allen in *Liberty*

South of the Border

A young couple from the States were temporarily living in São Paulo. One morning the wife telephoned the manager of their apartment house to ask that somebody come up with a passkey; her husband had left for work, taking both keys by mistake, and she was locked in. A half hour passed. She called again, pleading to be let out.

Almost in tears after two hours of repeated futile calls, she phoned her husband's place of business. Hurrying home, he confronted the manager and demanded an explanation. "But that is the *Senhor's* affair," was the manager's bland reply. "If the *Senhor* wants his wife locked in, she will stay locked in." — J. Howard Campbell

A fetching young lady from New York was tripping down a street in Bogotá, Colombia, minding her own business when a star-struck *bogotano* picked up her trail. He followed her for a block or two, breathing gentle compliments. She became angrier each moment, and at the end of the third block flounced over to a traffic policeman. "That man on the corner has been following me!" she announced indignantly.

The cop looked at the man, then surveyed the seething young lady. He took off his cap and bowed. "*Señorita*, if I were not on duty, I would follow you, too." — *Inter-American*

Simón Bolívar, the great South American liberator, was scheduled to pass the night in a small Peruvian town. His aide sent word to the local innkeeper, asking that "a room be prepared with special accommodations, food, etc., etc., etc."

Arriving in the village, Bolívar was shown the best room in the hotel. After he had expressed approval, the great man was conducted into an adjoining room where sat three lovely *señoritas*. "And who are these young ladies?" Bolívar asked.

"The three et ceteras," replied his host. — *South American Digest*

Lewis Cotlow of the Adventurers' Club wondered why Mexican peons ride burros while their wives walk. When he asked the reason, a Mexican replied, "But, *señor*, my wife doesn't own a burro."
— *This Week Magazine*

Animal Crackers

A Collection of Cartoon Quips

One circus elephant to another: "I'm getting sick and tired of working for peanuts." — Soriano in *Collier's*

Bear, standing at the door of his cave, reminds a bird: "Remember now — call us about half past April." — Ed Nofziger in *PM*

One very angry skunk to another skunk: "So do you!" — Hank Ketcham in *Liberty*

Mother rabbit to her small child: "A magician pulled you out of a hat — now stop asking questions!" — Franklin Folger in *Esquire*

"Would you mind if I asked Herbert to stay for lunch?" — Harry Mace in *Gourmet*

— Ray Helle in *This Week Magazine*

Tales of Kaufman

Once playwright George S. Kaufman, whose bridge is nearly as good as his dialogue, drew a particularly poor partner. After the first hand he asked her, "Do you mind if I inquire when you learned to play?" And before she could answer he added: "Oh, I know it was today. But I mean, what time today?"

— Lee Hazen, as told to Thomas H. Wolf, in *Collier's*

Describing a new play to George Kaufman, Ruth Gordon explained, "There's no scenery at all. In the first scene, I'm on the left side of the stage and the audience has to imagine I'm eating dinner in a restaurant. Then in scene two, I run over to the right side of the stage, and the audience imagines I'm in my drawing room."

"And the second night," nodded Kaufman, "*you* have to imagine there's an audience out front."   — Bennett Cerf in *Liberty*

Herbert Bayard Swope, who dines at hours that seem very peculiar to his more rational friends, called George Kaufman one evening at 9:30 and inquired, "What are you doing for dinner tonight?" Kaufman told him, "I'm digesting it."

— Bennett Cerf, *Shake Well Before Using* (Simon & Schuster)

Beatrice Kaufman's introduction to the literary and theatrical set came when her husband and Franklin P. Adams took her to a cocktail party, introduced her to numerous persons and deposited her on a cane-bottom chair in the corner. The cane bottom collapsed and Mrs. Kaufman found herself imprisoned in the framework, her posterior drooping to the floor. As everybody turned to stare, Adams remarked, "I've told you a hundred times, Beatrice, that's not funny!"   — Bennett Cerf in *Liberty*

When George Kaufman's daughter told him that a friend of hers at Vassar had eloped, he remarked, "Ah! She put the heart before the course!"   — Bennett Cerf, *Try and Stop Me* (Simon & Schuster)

"The Pun Is the Lowest Form of Humor— When You Don't Think of It First"

— Oscar Levant

After Fannie Hurst had acquired a beautiful figure by means of a rigorous diet, the late Irvin Cobb followed her down Fifth Avenue for six blocks without recognizing her. Finally she said to him: "Aren't you going to talk to me?" "Good Lord," said Cobb, "it's Fannie Hurst!" "The same Fannie Hurst," she agreed laughingly. "Not quite," said Cobb. "It may be the same Hurst — but it certainly isn't the same Fannie!" — Bennett Cerf in *The Saturday Review of Literature*

After an arduous session of the Supreme Court, the Justices once decided on a three-day boat trip for relaxation. On the second day out the late Justice Cardozo, somewhat the worse for *mal de mer*, was leaning over the rail of the boat which was rocking badly, when Chief Justice Hughes sauntered along. "Can I do anything for you?" said the Chief Justice. "Yes," answered Judge Cardozo, "overrule the motion." — Mrs. B. Greensburg

A professor of Greek tore his suit and took it to a tailor named Acidopolus, from Athens. Mr. Acidopolus examined the suit, and asked, "Euripides?" "Yes," said the professor. "Eumenides?" — Carlyn Coffin, quoted by Bennett Cerf in *The Saturday Review of Literature*

In the Viking Press office, Marshall Best looked out at a near-hurricane and remarked, "It's raining cats and dogs."

"Don't I know it," agreed the unquenchable Ben Huebsch. "I just stepped into a poodle." — Bennett Cerf in *The Saturday Review of Literature*

Mary Boland rushed into Kenneth Hopkins' hat salon for a new hat. "How about a dashing sailor?" suggested Kenneth. "Wonderful," said Mary, "but don't you think a retired admiral is more my type?" — Erskine Johnson, NEA

Young Ideas

During a spelling bee at a Long Island public school every child in the third grade went down on the same word: does. They spelled it D-U-Z. — *Newsweek*

Rudolph had heard a great deal about his little cousin Peter, but had never met him. So when he learned Peter was coming for a visit, the youngster was overjoyed. But when his cousin arrived, he took one look at him and burst into tears. "I thought," he wailed, "that Peter was a rabbit!"
— Mary C. Thomson in *Today's Woman*

One evening when I was having dinner with friends, the father in the family suggested to his ten-year-old son that he ought to give up something for Lent — something that would really hurt, such as candy. The boy hesitated, and finally asked what his father was giving up.

"Both your mother and I are giving up liquor," the father replied.

"But before dinner you were drinking something."

"Yes," acknowledged the father. "That was sherry. We gave up hard liquor." The boy thought a minute, then said, "Well, I think I'll give up hard candy."
— Richard K. Stevens

Michael had taken a strong dislike to kindergarten. All persuasion failed, and finally his mother, in desperation, told him firmly that he would *have* to go. "All right, Mother," retorted Michael. "If you want me to grow up into a damn bead-stringer, I'll go."
— *Parents' Magazine*

A mother had been lecturing her small son, stressing that we are in this world to help others. He considered this, then asked somberly: "What are the others here for?"
— Grace Perkins Oursler

From a harassed teacher comes this tale: Initiating my young pupils into the mysteries of the French language, I explained that "Madame" was used in speaking of a married woman; "Mademoiselle," an unmarried woman; and "Monsieur," a gentleman. To see if the children understood, I turned to a boy who seemed rather bored and asked: "What is the difference between 'Madame' and 'Mademoiselle'?"

"Monsieur," came his prompt reply.
— "Samuel Pepys Teucer" in Hamilton, Bermuda, *Royal Gazette and Crown Daily*

Repentance was perhaps best defined by a small girl: "It's to be sorry enough to quit."
— C. H. Kilmer in *The New Illustrator*

A small boy returned home from school and told his father that he was second in his class. Top place was held by a girl. "Surely, John," said the father, "you're not going to be beaten by a mere girl!"

"Well, you see, Father," explained John, "girls are not nearly so mere as they used to be."

— *Independent Forester*

The nine-year-old son of the Commander of the Nantucket American Legion Post listened open-eyed to his Sunday school teacher's vivid description of the nailing of Christ to the Cross.

In the ensuing pause, with flushed face and clenched fists the excited youngster shouted: "Well, where in hell were the Marines?"

— Dr. Joseph L. Cochran

Church Bulletins

A New York minister invited a contingent of Coast Guard Women's Reserve stationed near his church to a Sunday evening service. Five hundred and fifty uniformed women marched in that night, settled down to hear a sermon on the life of Saint Paul. When the minister came to the shipwreck scene, he raised his arms dramatically and asked: "Have you ever considered how different the history of the world might now be had not Paul clung to a spar all night?"

The SPARs say the minister still doesn't know why they all broke out into gales of laughter.

— The Rev. Carl Bihldorff

A Negro preacher began his sermon by saying: "Brethren and sisters, here you is comin' to pray for rain. I'd like to ask you just one question — where is yo' umbrellas?"

— Harper Garcia Smyth, *Let's Adventure in Personality* (Tower Press)

In one southern town, there are two churches across the street from each other. "Couldn't those churches be combined?" a visitor asked.

"Not very well," was the reply. "That church over there says, 'There ain't no hell,' and this one says, 'The hell there ain't.' "

— Marvin F. Engel

When I, with four other Americans, was received in audience by the late Pope Pius XI, the Rome correspondent for the United Press instructed us in Vatican protocol — which, in the matter of apparel, is rigorous. The men wear full dress suits with black waistcoats; the ladies wear a covering for the head, a high-neck dress and long sleeves.

The UP man — himself a devout Catholic — remarked when he saw us properly attired: "I've always believed it would be much easier and less expensive to blindfold the Pope."

— Stanley High

One day the telephone rang in the Rector's office of the Washington church which President Franklin Roosevelt attended. An eager voice inquired, "Tell me, do you expect the President to be in church this Sunday?"

"That," the Rector explained patiently, "I cannot promise. But we expect God to be there, and we fancy that will be incentive enough for a reasonably large attendance."

— John T. Watson

After Sunday morning services in a Boston church, a woman stayed to chat with a friend, leaving her purse on the seat. When she returned for her purse, it was gone, but she quickly found it in the possession of the clergyman himself.

"I thought I had better hold it," he said. "You must remember that there are some in the congregation so simple that they might consider it an answer to prayer."

— Ellen Lucinda Burnap

A sexton cleaning up the pulpit after Sunday service took a peek at the preacher's manuscript. Along the left margin were instructions such as: "Pause here," "Wipe brow here," "Use angry fist gesture," "Look upward."

Near the end was a long paragraph of texts, opposite which the preacher had marked in large capital letters: "ARGUMENT WEAK HERE. YELL LIKE HELL!"

— Alex F. Osborn

A young Scottish preacher lived seven miles up the river from his church. There came a Sunday when the snowdrifts made the road impassable, and he skated down the river to his church service. Haled before the bar of his presbytery for breaking the Sabbath, his defense was that skating was the only way he could get there. "Young man," said the moderator, "there is just one question. Did ye, or did ye not, enjoy the skatin'?"

— C. F. Wishart

Scotch and Wry

A Scotsman leaned against a midtown bar holding his stomach and moaning piteously. "Sick?" asked a sympathetic stranger.

"Verra, verra sick," said the Scotsman. "I am afraid I've got yoors."

"What's 'yoors'?" asked the stranger.

The Scotsman brightened immediately. "Make it a scotch and soda," he said.

— Bennett Cerf, *Laughing Stock* (Grosset & Dunlap)

A traveling salesman, held up in the Orkney Islands by a bad storm, telegraphed to his firm in Aberdeen: "Marooned by storm. Wire instructions."

The reply came: "Start summer vacation as of yesterday." — *Cheers*

A Scotsman was told by his doctor that his wife should have had her tonsils taken out when she was a little girl. He had the operation performed — and sent the bill to his father-in-law!

— *Scotch*, edited by Gregory Hartswick (Simon & Schuster)

Although he had just won a new car in a raffle, a Scotsman seemed decidedly glum. "What's the matter, Jock?" asked a friend. "Mon," he answered, " 'tis this other ticket. Why I ever bought it, I canna' imagine."

— W. N. Mackey in Louisville *Courier-Journal*

A Londoner shared the train-carriage with an elderly Scot. At each stop the old man rushed out, ran down the platform, then rushed back, panting. The curious Londoner finally asked why. "Well," said the Scot, "I saw a specialist in London about my heart. He says I might drop dead anytime; so I'm just booking from station to station."

— Leigh Mitchell Hodges

Spiced Tongue

Baby Talk: "And this is the bawl-room," she said, showing the nursery (Russell E. Bullock) . . . The baby wakes up in the wee wee hours of the morning (Robert Robbins) . . . Eventually most parents develop wails-resistance (Marcelene Cox) . . . Training a child is more or less a matter of pot luck (Rod Maclean)

All the things I really like to do are either immoral, illegal or fattening (Alexander Woollcott)

A man picks a wife the same way an apple picks a farmer (John W. Raper)

She skated for hours on end (Wes Pattersie) . . . The puppy greeted us with leaks and bounds . . . That called for intestinal fortitude with a capital G (Henry McLemore)

Some people get up to say good-bye and it seems to them they have gone (*Farm Journal*) . . . The question nowadays isn't so much who's who in society as who's whose . . . A boy becomes a man when he walks around a puddle of water instead of through it (Hoosier *Kiwanian*) . . . If all the automobiles in the world were placed end to end it would be Sunday afternoon.

Deft definitions: Canapés — a sandwich cut into 24 pieces (Billy Rose) . . . A girdle is a device to keep an unfortunate situation from spreading . . . Economy — a way of spending money without getting any fun out of it . . . Vacation folder — a trip tease . . . Radio commercial — the pause that depresses (Decatur, Ill., *Herald and Review*) . . . A good husband is one who feels in his pockets every time he passes a mailbox (*Bedside Examiner*)

Some people get results, others get consequences . . . He reads just enough to keep himself misinformed (Richmond, Va., *Times-Dispatch*)

There's many a slip: We want you to see the completemess of our hosiery department (H. Weil & Bros., Goldsboro, N. C.) . . . Irving Jones and Jessie Brown were married on Oct. 24. So ends a friendship that began in school days (Watertown, Mass., church bulletin) . . . The prosecutor did an excellent job of gumming up the case (Chicago, Ill., *Law Bulletin*) . . . Menu in Chicago restaurant, "Barely Soup" . . . Help wanted — maid to live on promises (Jackson, Miss., *Daily News*) . . . The song fest was hell at the Methodist church Wednesday (Bonner Springs, Kans., *Chieftain*) . . . At this point the gallery deserted Mrs. —— to watch Miss ——, whose shorts were dropping on the green with amazing regularity" (Synopsis)

We're getting a lot of government these days, but we'd probably be worse off if we were getting as much as we're paying for (Olin Miller)

She is vogue on the outside and vague on the inside (Helen E. Anderson)

Old saws sharpened: Where there's smoke, there's toast (Ruth H. Lane) . . . The longest way home is the quickest way to get married (Marcelene Cox) . . . Reducing slogan, "A word to the wide is sufficient" (Norman H. Kantor) . . . One touch of scandal makes the whole world chin . . . Give a husband enough rope — and he'll want to skip.

The kind of guy who would marry Hedy Lamarr for her money (George Loomis)

Ways and Means

Bargain-hunting for things to add to my collection of rare bric-a-brac, I stopped one day at the little curio shop of Sam Cohen, where from time to time I had picked up valuable pieces. Browsing around, I saw nothing of interest and was about to leave. Then, just inside the door, I noticed a cat lapping milk out of a saucer. One glance told me that the saucer was a priceless antique. With a wild hope that Sam was unaware of its value I said, "That's a nice cat you have there, Sam. Would you sell him to me?"

"Well," said Sam, "I'd be willing to sell him for five dollars, I guess."

I paid the five, put the cat under my arm, then added, "I'll just take the saucer along. The cat is probably used to eating from it."

"Oh, no," said Sam, "I can't give you the saucer."

"Well, then, I'll buy it."

"Oh, no," said Sam, "I can't sell it to you."

"That's ridiculous, Sam. Why can't you sell me this old saucer?"

"Because," replied Sam, "from that old saucer, I already sold 139 cats."

— Jules M. Smith

One evening James T. Powers, the comedian, and his wife were preparing to make a call. As they stepped from their apartment into the hall, Jimmie, turning to close the door, caught a glimpse of his wife. "My God!" he gasped. "What have you got on, a nightie?"

"It is," replied Mrs. Powers sweetly, "and now that you've noticed what I'm wearing, I'll go back and put on a dress."
— Joseph Cummings Chase, *My Friends Look Good to Me* (Sears)

A radio writer, well acquainted with the Hollywood brush-off, has developed a technique in telephoning. When a secretary asks, "What did you wish to speak to him about?" he replies in a very nasty tone, "I want to know what he's going to do about my wife!" He gets through immediately.
— Matt Weinstock, *My L.A.* (Current Books)

A busy hallway at the Navy's Radio Matériel School in Washington was being painted. All along the walls were large signs proclaiming, "Wet Paint," and in the corner of each sign was a dab of paint labeled "Test Here."
— H. H. Fuhrmann

In place of the annual church bazaar, the Vicar of St. Johns, Waterloo, England, billed expected patrons as follows, inviting them to let their consciences guide them in filling in amounts: "Bus fare to hall . . . Entrance fee . . . Wear and tear on clothes . . . Wear and tear on tempers . . . Afternoon tea . . . Side shows . . . Useless articles bought . . . Total . . . Please remit." Receipts were beyond all previous amounts.
— AP

Dorothy Parker and Robert Benchley once shared a microscopic office in the crumbly old building which still houses the Metropolitan Opera. There was just room in it for their two typewriters, their two chairs, and a guest chair. When both were supposed to be at work, merely having the other to talk to provided a splendid excuse for not working at all. But when Benchley would be off on some mischief of his own the guest chair became a problem. It afflicted Mrs. Parker because the office was then so new that not many of their friends had yet found a path to it. However, when the sign painter arrived to letter the names of the new tenants on the glass door, she hit upon a device which immediately assured her a steady stream of visitors. She merely bribed the painter to leave their names off the door entirely and print there instead the single word "Gentlemen."   — Alexander Woollcott

Max Schling, a New York florist, ran a whole advertisement in shorthand in the New York *Times*. Many a businessman cut it out and handed it to his secretary to translate. The ad asked secretaries to think of Schling when the boss wanted flowers for his wife.
                                                                — *Modern Selling*

A young mother was having great difficulty with her three-year-old son who had locked himself in the bathroom and either could not or would not unlock the door. Finally, in desperation, she called the fire department.

After a brief wait, a burly fire captain ran up the front steps with an axe in one hand, a fire extinguisher in the other. She explained her predicament, but instead of going back for a ladder, he asked her the sex of the child. When she had told him, he climbed the stairs and said in his most authoritative voice, "You come out, little girl!" Aroused at being called a little girl, the boy unlocked the door and marched out to confront the fireman. "It works just about every time," explained the grinning captain.   — Bernard G. Silberstein

When a young cousin was advised by Army doctors to spend his terminal leave at the seashore, we offered letters to some friends, but he refused them. "I'd rather borrow one of your bird dogs to take along," he said.

As he had never been particularly fond of dogs, I was really disturbed when he chose a setter puppy just weaned. I warned him that his charge would require care and be a general nuisance, but off they went.

Two weeks later, the pup was at the express office. Tacked to his crate was this note: "Have met all the girls on the beach, so won't need the pup any more. Thanks a lot!"   — Glenn Allan

For several years, a minister and a professor had regularly played golf together. They were very evenly matched, and there was a keen rivalry. Then one spring the professor's game suddenly improved so much that the minister was regularly beaten. The preacher's efforts to improve his own game were unsuccessful, but finally he came up with an idea. At a bookstore, he picked out three how-to-play-golf texts, and had them sent to the professor for a birthday present. It wasn't long before they were evenly matched again. — Havilah Babcock

And So to Press

Westbrook Pegler tells how his father once got a scoop on a story about an absconding bank president in Chicago: "He just walked into a meeting where examiners were going over the papers, laid his stick and gloves on the table and said, 'Well, gentlemen, let us get down to business.' Somehow the examiners thought he was the banker's lawyer, and the lawyers thought he was an examiner — until he got up to catch an edition. Then someone asked, 'And whom do you represent?' 'Hearst's Chicago *American*,' said my father, and bowed out." — *Time*

Horace Greeley, who always insisted that the word "news" was plural, once wired to a reporter: "Are there any news?"

The reply came back by wire: "Not a new." — *Christian Advocate*

The late Dexter Fellows, who was press agent for Ringling Brothers and Barnum & Bailey Combined, had magnificent faith in the overwhelming supremacy of his show. I first met him years ago when he came into a newspaper office in Kansas City.

"I am Dexter Fellows of the Circus," he announced, waving his cane, "and I am here to. . ."

"What circus?" I asked.

He was profoundly shocked. "Good lord, young man," he protested. "If you were in London and heard a man singing *God Save the King* would you interrupt him and ask 'What king?' " — Jerome Beatty

Reporter: I've got a perfect news story.
Editor: How come? Man bite a dog?
Reporter: No, but a hydrant sprinkled one.   — *The Yale Record*

A fair young graduate of the School of Journalism got a job as cub reporter on a Long Island daily. Her first story won the editor's approval, but he pointed out a few minor inaccuracies.

"Remember," he concluded, "it was Joseph Pulitzer, founder of the School of Journalism, who declared that accuracy is to a newspaper what virtue is to a woman."

"That in itself is not entirely accurate," said the girl triumphantly. "A newspaper can always print a retraction!"
— Bennett Cerf, *Shake Well Before Using* (Simon & Schuster)

Years ago, when Ernie Pyle was on the Washington *News* as a $30-a-week copyreader, he tagged a story with the headline: "Man Inherits Huge Fortune of $15,000."

"Where do you get the idea that $15,000 is a huge fortune?" his executive editor asked.

"If you were earning the same dough I am," Ernie replied, "you'd think so, too."   — Larry Boardman, quoted in *Editor and Publisher*

A midwestern newspaper heads the list of births, marriages and deaths briefly: "Hatched, matched, and detached."   — *Parade*

Mark Twain, in his reporting days, was instructed by an editor never to state anything as a fact that he could not verify from personal knowledge. Sent out to cover an important social event soon afterward, he turned in the following story: "A woman giving the name of Mrs. James Jones, who is reported to be one of the society leaders of the city, is said to have given what purported to be a party yesterday to a number of alleged ladies. The hostess claims to be the wife of a reputed attorney."

— *Counter points*

Taking It Literally

The metal strips used to band birds are inscribed: "Notify Fish and Wild Life Service, Washington, D. C." They used to read "Washington Biological Survey," abbreviated to "Wash. Biol. Surv." This was changed after an Alberta farmer shot a crow and disgustedly wrote the U. S. Government: "Dear Sirs: I shot one of your pet crows the other day and followed instruction attached to it. I washed it and biled it and surved it. It was turrible. You should stop trying to fool the people with things like this. . . ."

— Hugh Newton in *Liberty*

When Will Smith applied for a driver's license in Detroit's crowded License Bureau, an officer hastily thrust a paper across the desk. "Write your last name first and your first name last," he said hurriedly.

"How's that again, sir?" asked Smith, somewhat confused.

"Like I said," replied the cop. "*Backwards.*"

Smith shrugged his shoulders. After all, he thought, they knew what they wanted. Laboriously he wrote: "lliW htimS." — Detroit *Free Press*

When he was Secretary of Defense, the late James Forrestal received a letter from a New England farmer who said that he had read in an agricultural publication that the farmers around Hiroshima and Nagasaki had discovered that the atomic bomb had materially enriched their soil. The farmer complained that his soil was pretty well worn-out and requested the Secretary to drop an atomic bomb on his farm. He added a P.S. which said that he would require 24 hours' notice because he didn't want to be around and, please, don't tell his neighbors. — Sumner Blossom

Seating herself in the dentist's chair, she pulled from her finger a wedding ring of heavy gold with a delicately chased design. "I'd like to use this for filling my teeth, please," she said.

The dentist examined the ring. "Why I suppose that could be done. But this is an expensive ring, madam. Are you sure you wouldn't rather let me use our regular gold?"

"I'm afraid not," the patient said regretfully. "You see, I promised my first husband, before his death three years ago, that I would always wear his wedding ring. I'm getting married again next week, and the man I'm going to marry has made me promise that I'll wear only *his* ring after the ceremony. This is the only way I can keep my promise to both of them." — Arnold E. Batho

When a politician inquired about public sentiment in a rural community, one of the natives replied: "Still goin' strong — there were 16 cars parked in my lane last night." — Quoted by John A. Williams

During a performance at the California Laguna Beach Playhouse, a sweet little old lady, obviously unaccustomed to legitimate theater, started to leave immediately after the first act. "My, but I did enjoy the play," she told the hostess.

"Can't you stay to see the rest?"

The little lady smiled sadly. "There wouldn't be much use. Look," she pointed to the program, "it says here — Act II, same as Act I." — Neil Thayer in *This Week in Laguna*

A young physician and his wife had considerable difficulty teaching a new maid to answer the telephone properly. In spite of repeated instructions she persisted in answering: "Hello," instead of "Dr. Jones' residence." After many practice sessions, everything seemed to be all right. Then one morning the extension in the bedroom rang, and the maid, busy making the bed, grabbed the phone and blurted: "Dr. Jones' bedroom." — J. M. Rosbrow

Calling All Doctors

I had been sitting in the doctor's waiting room a long time. Every chair was filled and some patients were standing. There was desultory conversation, but after a while a silence fell and we sat waiting — waiting — waiting. Finally an old man stood up wearily and remarked, "Well, guess I'll go home and die a natural death." — Mrs. Paul B. Davis

Mrs. Brown was complaining to her doctor that his bill was unreasonably high. "Don't forget," he reminded her, "that I made 11 visits to your home while your son had the measles."

"And don't you forget," she countered, "that he infected the whole school." — *Commerce Magazine*

Dr. Maurice Ernest of London, founder of the Centenarian Club designed to help people reach 100, believes in thoroughly enjoying life. His favorite story is about the man who wanted to be a centenarian and was advised by his doctor to give up drinking, smoking and women. "Will I live to be 100 then?" asked the patient.

"No," said the doctor, "but it will seem like it." — UP

The patient, a middle-aged Yankee, had been wheeled into the operating room. Just before the anesthetic was started, he asked how long his incision would be. The surgeon gave him a noncommittal answer. "Well, Doc," said the patient, "I have just one request. My wife's incision is four and a half inches long, and her sister's is four inches. I want you to make mine longer than both of them put together, so I won't have to listen to any more nonsense." — W. O. M.

A bee stung our pup on the nose, and before long his muzzle was swollen, his eyes almost shut, his breathing labored. In a frenzy I phoned the vet. "Just bathe his muzzle in warm soda water," he said. "He'll be better soon."

"But, Doctor," I pleaded, "isn't there something more I can do? He's suffering. Would an aspirin help?"

"Yes," the doctor answered, "an aspirin might calm him. Give him one — and you take two." — Emily C. Hawkins

In Transit

A chap we know shared a commuter's seat the other day with a brisk, informative little man who said he was a butler at a Libertyville estate. "Oh," said our friend, "you work for Mr. Jones?"

The brisk little man drew himself up haughtily. "Certainly not. Mr. Jones is working for me. He gets up at seven every morning and goes down to that dirty, stinking city to make enough money to keep this place and me going."
— Marcia Winn in Chicago *Tribune*

A friend of mine who commutes to New York always avoids the smoking car — can't stand smoking himself and doesn't like other people to smoke. One day he took a seat as usual in a nonsmoking car, but to his dismay a man came in, sat down facing him, and lighted up a cigar. Not wanting to make a scene, my friend waited till the conductor came around to punch his 26-trip ticket. As he handed it to the conductor, he nudged him and nodded at the brazen smoker. The conductor nodded back, punched the ticket again, and went on.
— Irving Hoffman

On a crowded streetcar, a passenger apologetically handed the conductor a five-dollar bill, saying, "I'm afraid I haven't a nickel."

"Don't worry," the conductor assured him grimly. "In a minute you'll have 99."
— *Forum and Column Review*

On a Haverhill bus a fellow sitting beside a demure old lady, who was knitting, pulled out a cigarette and lit it. When the first puff of smoke drifted into the woman's eyes, she just shook her head and said nothing. But as the draft carried every mouthful of smoke in her direction, she politely pointed to the "No Smoking" sign and asked him to stop. The man ignored her. Her lips formed a straight line of determination, and she reached into her knitting bag. Then, while the smoker was gazing out the window, she snipped off the lighted end of his cigarette with a small pair of scissors.
— Joe Harrington in Boston *Post*

The Seeing Eye dog boarded the crowded streetcar with his master and led him to the only available space on the seat running the length of the car. It was too small to accommodate even a child, but the dog began pushing the passengers on each side farther apart with his nose. Every other passenger in turn squeezed against his neighbor. When there was room enough to accommodate two people, the dog signaled his master to be seated. The passengers' pleased expressions dissolved into laughter when the dog climbed into the remaining space beside his master and relaxed with his head on the blind man's lap.   — Elna Cuthbertson

As water rushed along the gutters curb-high and five feet wide after a downpour in Minneapolis, a trolley stopped for three young things in high heels marooned on the sidewalk. At last two of them took the leap, going into water over their ankles. The third edged this way and that and looked desperate.

Just then a closed car rolled up in front of her and the driver invitingly opened both his back doors. Daintily the young lady stepped into the car, out again onto the trolley, and Sir Walter Raleigh of the machine age closed his doors and rolled on.
    — *The Christian Science Monitor*

"Did you get home all right last night, sir?" said the streetcar conductor one morning to one of his regular passengers.

"Of course. Why do you ask?"

"Well, when you got up and gave the lady your seat last night you were the only two people on the car."   — Toronto *Globe and Mail*

As I balanced myself in the crowded subway, my arms were full of bundles and my soul full of bitterness at all the comfortably seated males. But chivalry was not quite dead in the man seated in front of me. He lowered his paper and surveyed me with some solicitude. "Be alert at 42nd Street, girlie," he admonished. "That's where I get off."
    — Esther T. Riley

Severely jostled in the thundering herd of New York's subway rush hour, a fragile young lady was finally crammed among the standees. Her sense of humor was not impaired, however. She poked her face close to the ear of an adjoining male.

"Look," she demanded tartly, "my rib — is it crushing your elbow?"   — Seaman B. Jacobs

While on my way home by subway one evening I was approached by a naval officer who said, "Pardon me, miss, but I think you'll be interested in what I have to show you."

In his hand was a copy of The Reader's Digest. Rather uneasily I looked at the title to which he pointed — then understood why he had singled me out. This is what I read: "Pardon, your slip is showing."   — Marie Kolar

Pardon, Your Slip Is Showing

Advertisement for a radio program from the Rochester *Times-Union:* "Hear . . . *The Weatherman.* The complete dope on the weather!"

From a publicity circular put out by a Drum and Bugle Corps: "The Erie Girls Drum and Bulge Corps has put on exhibitions in Chicago, Cleveland, etc."

News item in the Muscatine, Ia., *Journal and News-Tribune:* "Local police are puzzled over the finding of a car parked outside the Methodist Church containing a full case of Scotch whiskey. So far they have found no trace of the owner, but Captain Casey is diligently working on the case."

From the society column of the Lewistown, Ill., *Evening Record:* "Mrs. Pike C. Ross left today for La Harpe and the Brookfield Zoo in Chicago to visit relatives."

The Olando, Ala., *Star* reported: "A precious little bungle of love arrived at the home of Mr. and Mrs. Gordon Peter, Wednesday morning, a nine-pound bouncing boy."
— Quoted in *Hobo News*

Headline from the Stamford, Conn., *Advocate:* "Audience Acclaims Dame May Whitty in *Nighty Must Fall.*"

From the El Paso *Times:* "The driver reported that he lost control of the bus in an effort to keep hitting an automobile on which he saw a front tire blow out."

Real Estate ad from the Newport News, Va., *Times-Herald:* "You can't heat this one — nine-room and two-bath home . . ."

A Jefferson City, Mo., paper reports: "Columbia, Tenn., which calls itself the largest outdoor mule market in the world, held a mule parade yesterday, headed by the governor."
— Quoted in *Successful Farming*

From a N. Y. *Herald Tribune* advertisement for "Happy Acres," a Connecticut resort: "Honeymoon Heaven . . . Try a Week-End First."

From the reports on 4-H Club activities in Mount Vernon, Ohio, *News:* "The seventh meeting of the Knox County Jersey Boosters was held at the home of Katherine and Maxine Cochran. The group inspected the girls' calves."

From the Hartford *Times:* "Early yellow peaches and apples are being marketed by local fruit growers. oGod prices are being received, farmers said."

From the society column of the Winfield, Kans., *Daily Courier:* "Mrs. John King entertained the members of the Friday Boob Club."

Legends of Lethargy

Tramping down the railroad track one hot Kansas day many years ago, I was hoping to catch a freight out of the next town. In the shade beneath a water tank, an old hobo sat. "Going east, son?" he asked.

"Yes," I said. "All the way."

"Don't do it."

"Why not?"

" 'Twon't do any good for me to tell you why not. Just take the advice of an older man: Don't do it. You'd not believe me if I told you. Even when you see it you won't believe it."

"What won't I believe?"

"You will see people *running* — to work!"   — Garet Garrett

Nathan's wife tells of his discomfiture the time the sheriff's funeral passed their gate. "It was a grand sight," she said. "Nathan was restin' in the hammick when it went by. I come out and told him who all was in the carriages and autymobiles, and his kinfolk wavin' to him. Nathan was kinda peeved. 'Just my luck,' he said, 't' be facin' th' other way.' "   — Robert Davis, *Booklet of the Vermont Historical Society*

A panhandler approached a prosperous-looking man and asked for a dime for a cup of coffee. "Is this all you have to do?" replied the prospect reprovingly. "Look at you — you sleep on park benches, your clothes are tattered, and you're hungry. Why don't you get a grip on yourself and go to work?"

"Go to work!" growled the bum in disgust. "What for — to support a bum like me?"   — Irving Hoffman in *The Hollywood Reporter*

I like work; it fascinates me. I can sit and look at it for hours.
        — Jerome K. Jerome

The filling-station attendant was the slowest-moving person I had ever seen. "Why do you do so much loafing?" I asked jokingly.

"Well, suh," he replied deliberately, "some folks does all their loafin' at one time. Ah jes' does mine as Ah goes along."— Richard Eloi

David Starr Jordan, trying to advise a difficult young man on choosing a career, finally asked in despair: "Isn't there anything on earth you'd like to be?"

"Why, yes," the young man drawled, "I'd like to be a retired businessman." — Albert Edward Wiggam, *The Marks of an Educated Man* (Harper)

I was spending the night with a Kentucky mountaineer and his 19-year-old son. They sat silently in front of the fire, smoking their pipes, crossing and uncrossing their legs. After a long period of silence, the father said, "Son, step outside and see if it's raining."

Without looking up, the son answered, "Aw, Pop, why don't ye jest call in the dog and see if he's wet?"   — W. K. Welch

When General Brehon Somervell retired after four years of seven-day weeks and 12-hour days as head of Army Service Forces, he was dog-tired. A friend asked him his plans. "I'm going to rest," Somervell said. "For six weeks I'm going to just sit on the porch. After that, I'm going to start rocking — slowly."   — Karl Detzer

Striking Examples

General Somervell, acting as WPA administrator in New York City, was plagued with union and Communist trouble. But, with a mixture of firmness and fairness, he established good working relations. During the wave of sit-down strikes, one left-wing WPA union "sat down" in a public building and refused to budge. Somervell did not call the cops. He merely locked all the toilets in the building. The strikers gradually straggled out.   — John Janney in *The American Magazine*

When a sit-down strike was called among 60 employes of an Indiana auto-accessory factory, the president decided to settle it quickly. "Boys, you might as well be comfortable here," he told the strikers; and sent for blankets and three cases of brandy. When the brandy was almost finished, he sent in 16 young ladies to amuse the strikers. At the height of festivities, he brought in the strikers' wives to view the Indiana version of a Bacchanalian revel. . . .

The strike was called off forthwith.   — Leonard Lyons

Battle of the Sexes

My wife and I have been happily married for years — not for us the quarrels and boredom that often beset man and wife. But one morning at breakfast she was cross and irritable.

"What's the trouble?" I asked.

At first she refused to tell, but she finally turned to me with tears in her eyes and sobbed: "If I ever dream again that you kissed another woman, I'll never speak to you as long as I live!"

— C. C. B. in Denver *Post*

A young lady after a broken engagement returned all the gent's letters marked, "Fourth Class Male."

— Willie D. Herbert

A surgeon was taking a walk with his wife when a young and vivid blonde greeted him gaily. The doctor's wife eyed him narrowly. "Where," she asked, "did you meet that person, my dear?"

"Just a young woman I met professionally," he explained.

"I see," murmured his wife. "Yours, or hers?"   — *Perfection Pointers*

Spike Jones tells about the irate wife of a movie star who had gone off fishing and left her alone. Asked where her husband might be, she replied, "Just go down to the bridge and look around until you find a pole with a worm on each end!"

— Jimmy Starr in Los Angeles *Herald and Express*

A Hollywood agent came home unexpectedly and caught one of his biggest clients making violent love to his wife. The agent's denunciations made no particular impression on the guilty client. "Stop sounding like a B picture, Joe," he said. "Let's treat this situation like adults. You love your wife and so do I. Let's play one game of gin rummy — and the winner gets her."

The agent considered for a moment and agreed. "Okay," he said slowly. "but what do you say we play for a nickel a point on the side just to make it interesting?"

— Bennett Cerf, *Anything for a Laugh* (Grosset & Dunlap)

Jack Carson tells about the husband and wife who suddenly met up with the husband's girl friend. The wife, acknowledging the introduction, murmured, "My husband has told me so little about you."

— Andrew B. Hecht

The wife plays a snappy game of bridge, while the husband boasts of knowing no rules. However, one evening, in an exuberant mood, he bid and made a grand slam, doubled and redoubled. Gleefully, he turned to his wife: "And you thought I couldn't do it!"

"Well, dear," she countered, "you *couldn't* have, if you'd played it right!" — Mrs. A. E. Fossum

Spectator Sports

One sweet young thing arrived at her first ball game during the fifth inning. "The score is nothing to nothing," she heard a fan say.

"Oh, good," she cooed to her escort. "Then we haven't missed a thing." — Walter Winchell

At an appearance in New Jersey, Frank Sinatra gripped the mike, rocked back and forth as he usually does, then, when hitting a tender note, let go the mike and gestured soulfully to the audience. At that a male in the audience shouted: "Look, everybody! No hands!"

— Jersey City *Journal*

In a New York fight club, one of the fans, disgusted with the lack of action in the ring, called out: "Hit him now, you bum. You got the wind with you!"

— Bob Considine in *Argosy*

A horse-race enthusiast, asked the results of his afternoon at the track, replied: "I broke even, and boy, did I need it!" — F.P.A. in New York *Post*

A clergyman and a Scotsman were watching a baseball game together. The Scotsman continually took nips from a bottle, and the clergyman, unable to restrain himself, finally said: "Sir, I'm 69 years old, and never in my life have I touched alcohol."

"Well, dinna worry yourself," replied the Scotsman with a pronounced burr, "you're nae ginna start noo." — Vancouver *Daily Province*

John Barrymore, watching a tense football game, was distracted by the man next to him, who bragged, "When I was in college I helped Harvard beat Yale three times in succession."

"That so?" snapped Barrymore. "Which team were you playing on?" — *Liberty*

Strictly Stinky

Jack Cluett in The American Legion Magazine

Recently the advertising boys have been doing their best to bowl over man's natural apathy toward perfumes by camouflaging them in mannish-looking containers, describing them in virile terms, and giving them masculine titles.

The *White Shirt* cologne bottle actually is dressed in a white shirt with buttons, but no tie. I wonder why the producer didn't go really virile and unbutton the shirt, exposing the hair on the chest of the rugged bottle? Another manufacturer has dressed his bottle in Harris tweeds; it's a beautifully tailored little number — in checks, wide stripes or herringbone. But the contents still smell like a girls' school.

The ads use descriptive phrases like "whistling-clean fragrance from a man's world of wind and northern pine," and "capturing the crisp freshness of the seven seas," and "essences that tingle with the excitement of rare cognac, cedar and Russian leather."

Show me a man who wants to smell of cognac, cedar and Russian leather — singly or in combination. If I want to smell of cognac I know a little place right off Broadway which can do a better job. Cedar's efficacy as a moth repellent is well known, but as an aftershave lotion I have my doubts. And I have no intention of going around exuding the odor of an old Morris chair.

Everyone, I suppose, is familiar with the titles of female perfumes: *Shocking, Havoc, Indiscreet*, and so on. In contrast the titles designed to give cosmetics a muscular appeal sound downright feeble: *Seaforth, Cargo, Timber, Sportsman, For Men Only, Buckskin* and *Commando*. All I can say for these come-on titles is that rose water by any other name smells just as sweet.

By this time next year you should be able to buy *Sandhog, Lumber Jack* and *Stevedore*, but don't be fooled, Mister — every last one of them will leave you smelling like a petunia bush in full bloom. And now, if you'll excuse me, I'll go wash my hands of the whole matter with a good, clean unscented five-cent cake of soap.

Variations on a Theme

Early risers are conceited in the morning and stupid in the afternoon.
— Rose Henniker Heaton, *The Perfect Hostess* (Dutton)

To do each day two things one dislikes is a precept I have followed scrupulously: every day I have got up and I have gone to bed.
— Somerset Maugham

When Bidú Sayão, the Brazilian coloratura, came to New York to sign an operatic contract, an American impresario all but had her signature on the contract. He was thwarted, however, by Mamma Sayão who kept whispering into Bidú's ear. The star consistently shook her head. The producer reluctantly raised his offer. Again Mamma, who spoke almost no English, whispered urgently. The American jumped his price again and again until his limit was reached.

"Miss Sayão," he sputtered, "that is my best offer; I simply cannot go higher. Either you sign at this figure or the contract is off."

"But certainly!" Bidú smiled. "Of course I sign."

Then Mamma plucked at her sleeve again. Bidú blushed and stammered, "My mother wants to know, please — where is the ladies' room?"
— Jack Harding, *I Like Brazil* (Bobbs-Merrill)

The owner of a small cabaret had asked me to print a sign reading "Gentlemen" for his establishment. Thinking to dress it up a bit, I added the French "*Messieurs*," the Spanish "*Señores*," the Italian "*Signori*." And from an old plate I copied some Chinese characters, sure no one would have any more idea than I of their meaning.

A few weeks later the proprietor informed me that a Chinese student had been convulsed with laughter upon seeing the sign. When translated, it read: "Chinese Relief."
— John Milton Heins

During the Bikini operations, a discussion arose as to what weapons would be used in the next war — atom bombs, germs, rockets.

"I don't know what weapons will be used in the next war," a young

Army lieutenant interrupted, "but in the war after the next one, surer than hell they'll be using spears." ——Joe Laitin in *Frontpage*

Not long ago, an upset citizen nervously asked a prominent astronomer whether it was possible for the atomic bomb to destroy the earth.

"Suppose it does," said the scientist with a casual shrug. "It isn't as if the earth were a major planet." ——AP

Private Lives

While in charge of war production for the Army, William Knudsen telephoned a vice-president of General Motors in Detroit asking him to come to Washington to help expedite military supplies. "I have a job here that I can't very well leave," was the reply.

"Tell your president that I must have you," Knudsen persisted.

The vice-president said that he'd have to think it over.

"Sure, sure," said Knudsen, "think it over. I'll hold the phone."
——Thomas H. Briggs

At a buffet supper in Washington, a careless waiter spilled something on Senator Leverett Saltonstall's knee. As the Massachusetts Senator rubbed the trouser leg vigorously, his supper partner commented: "That's good material; it won't spot badly."

"It should be good material," confided Senator Saltonstall. "These pants belonged to my father." ——Bulkley Griffin in Boston *Traveler*

Gregory Peck made his first visit to the Stork Club after he had appeared in a few movies. He wanted to sit in the Cub Room, but the tables were occupied and he was told that he'd have to wait. "Tell him who you are, Greg," Peck's companion whispered.

"If I have to tell 'em who I am," replied Peck, "then I ain't."
——Leonard Lyons

Tiptoeing down the hospital corridor, I found Dorothy Parker hard at work. Since she had given her address as Bedpan Alley, and represented herself as writing her way out, I was loath to intrude, but she, being entranced at any interruption, greeted me from her cot of pain, waved me to a chair, offered me a cigarette and rang a bell. I wondered if this could possibly be for drinks. "No," she said sadly, "it is supposed to bring the night nurse, so I ring it whenever I want an hour of uninterrupted privacy."

— Alexander Woollcott, *While Rome Burns* (Viking)

When Lord Halifax was a young man, he traveled one day from London to Bath, seated between two sober-faced spinsters. No one spoke during the long journey.

Just before reaching Bath the train entered a tunnel and young Halifax put the back of his hand to his lips and made loud kissing noises. As the train emerged into daylight he looked from one to the other of the startled old ladies, rose, tipped his hat and said with a mischievous twinkle, "To which of you two charming ladies am I indebted for that most delightful interlude?"

Then he stepped out, leaving the two oldsters glaring suspiciously at each other.

— Allan Michie

In *Past Imperfect*, Ilka Chase wrote:

A month after Julia Hoyt married my ex-husband I was going through a trunk and found a box of my calling cards engraved "Mrs. Louis Calhern." They were the best cards — thin parchment, highly embossed — and it seemed a pity to waste them, and so I mailed them to my successor. But aware of Louis' mercurial marital habits, I wrote on the top one, "Dear Julia, I hope these reach you in time."

— Published by Doubleday

Gilbert Stuart, the celebrated portrait painter, once met a lady in the street in Boston, who saluted him with, "Ah, Mr. Stuart, I have just seen your miniature and kissed it, because it was so much like you."

"And did it kiss you in return?"

"Why, no."

"Then," said Stuart, "it was not like me."

— *Encyclopedia of Wit and Wisdom*

Sweden's King Gustav was walking near his country home when two young girls spied him and were, of course, duly impressed. "But, my," gasped one, "he looks old and wrinkled!" At that the monarch turned and said benignly, "Yes, but he hears well!"   — *Nordstjernan*

Someone once asked Professor Charles Townsend Copeland of Harvard why he lived on the top floor of Hollis Hall in his small, dusty old rooms. "I shall always live here," he answered. "It is the only place in Cambridge where God alone is above me." Then, after a pause, "He's busy, but He's quiet."   — *Ladies' Home Journal*

A maiden lady was very proud of her collection of letters from prominent persons, which she took delight in showing to her friends. Although she had never met the playwright Moss Hart, she kept writing to him for a note to add to her album. Finally, in desperation, he yielded with this message:

"To Mildred from Moss Hart — in memory of the happy days we lay in each other's arms at Miami."

— Elinor Rice

Dedications With a Difference

For his dedication of *Unaccustomed As I Am*, Morrie Ryskind wrote: "To the Great American Democracy — May It Bring Me Royalty."

— Elinor Rice

Betty MacDonald inscribed *The Egg and I* to her sister Mary, "who has always believed I can do anything she puts her mind to."

Rosemary and Stephen Vincent Benét dedicated *A Book of Americans* to their children thus: "To Stephanie, Thomas and Rachel, our other works in collaboration."

An RKO director dedicated his first book: "To my wife, without whose absence this could not have been written." — San Francisco *Chronicle*

Franklin P. Adams sent a copy of his book *Nods and Becks* to his former boss, the New York *Post* editor, with this inscription: "To Ted Thackrey, who fired me with ambition." — Clip Boutell in New York *Post*

The Life of Edward Fitzgerald by A. M. Terhune has this dedication: "To Annabelle: Who toiled that I might spin my yarn."

The dedication for Inez Puckett McEwen's *So This Is Ranching* reads: "Dedicated to my infant grandson, William Craig — the only gent on whom I've ever been able to pin anything."

— Maude Robinson in Salt Lake *Tribune*

Mark Hellinger always had an unflagging zeal to avoid the conventional. The acknowledgments at the end of *The Ten Million* include: "To my wife — for permitting me to work, and for going out to the movies three times a week alone, I hope. To the Bing & Bing Construction Company — for not building anything near my apartment for the past six months. And to Saks & Co. — for underwear that does not bind while seated before a typewriter."

— George Frazier, *The One with the Mustache Is Costello* (Random House)

Quakers Feel Their Oats

A gentle Quaker, hearing a strange noise in his house one night, got up and discovered a burglar busily at work. So he went and got his gun, then came back and stood quietly in the doorway. "Friend," he said, "I would do thee no harm for the world, but thee standest where I am about to shoot."

— *The Kellogg Messenger*

A man who knew little about Friends' ways was a bit uneasy when he was invited to a Quaker home for dinner. "I needn't have worried at all," he reported afterward. "Everything was fine. There was a little awkward silence at the beginning of the meal, but I just told a funny story and broke the ice."

— Irvin and Ruth Poley, *Quaker Anecdotes* (Pendle Hill)

A prim old Quaker lady was driving her shiny new car in Philadelphia. Suddenly, at a cross street, a heavy truck was unable to stop until it had collided, crumpling a fender, breaking a window and gouging a hole in the side of her car. Infuriated, the lady managed to control herself only by remembering her Quaker upbringing. She got out and walked over to the truck driver.

"When thee gets home to thy kennel tonight," she said, "I hope thy mother bites thee."

— John R. McWilliam

Said a Quaker spinster who was asked why she had never married:
"It takes a mighty good husband to be better than none."
— Irvin and Ruth Poley, *Quaker Anecdotes* (Pendle Hill)

In the old and lovely Quaker hamlet of Sandy Spring, Md., the
elder families of the Plain Speech are being crowded back by new-
comers of different faith. In this situation one can understand the
fiery Quakerism of young Abner who was scolding his friend Eli for
association with small Mike O'Bunion. "He is not a Friend. Thee
cannot love him like one of us."

"But I do," Eli retorted hotly. "He is kind, he is strong, he plays
football wonderfully. Better even than thee."

The argument waxed, until Abner, losing his temper, doubled his
fists and screamed into Eli's face: "Oh! Thee little *you*, thee!"
— Arthur S. Riggs

Tit for Tat

Some years ago Sinclair Lewis got a fan letter from a Southern girl,
who offered first of all to be his secretary, since she was mad to meet
him, and secondly to do anything for him. "And when I say anything," she wrote, "I mean *anything*." Taking care of such mail was the
delight of his wife. In her answer she noted that Mr. Lewis was provided with a competent secretary, and that she herself did everything
else. "And when I say everything," wrote Mrs. Lewis, "I mean
everything." — *The Stage*

One day when nylons were on sale at Marshall Field's, a dignified
middle-aged gentleman decided to get his wife a pair. But he soon
found himself being buffeted and stabbed by frantic women. He stood
it as long as he could. Then with head lowered and arms flailing, he
plowed through the crowd. "You, there!" challenged a shrill voice.
"Can't you act like a gentleman?"

"Hell," he replied, still charging forward, "I've been acting like a
gentleman for an hour. From now on, I'm acting like a lady."
— Jack Coghlan

Walter Winchell's favorite story, which may be apocryphal, is about an editorial feud between the old New York *Sun* and *Post*, when both were conservative papers. One day the very proper and staid *Post* lost its temper and editorially called the *Sun* a yellow dog. The *Sun* replied in its starchiest manner: "The *Post* calls the *Sun* a yellow dog. The attitude of the *Sun*, however, will continue to be that of *any* dog toward *any* post."

— *Variety*

Charles Feldman, the producer, tells this story: I lost at gin rummy with Alexander Korda one evening, and mailed him a check next day. It was written in red ink, and accompanied by this note: "Dear Alex: You will see that this check is written in blood."

A few nights later Korda lost to me. The next day I received a check written in blue ink. The note clipped to it read "Dear Charlie: Here is my check. Please note it is also written in blood — but be sure to note the difference in color." Signed "SIR Alexander Korda."

— Quoted by Irving Hoffman in *Theatre Arts*

A man who had been commissioned received a wire from the medical board several days later. "Regret to inform you," it read, "that tests show you have tuberculosis and heart trouble." An hour later another wire came, saying, "Please disregard last wire. Your record confused with that of another candidate." The relieved officer wired back, "Sorry, but your correction came too late. I committed suicide 40 minutes ago!"

— Bennett Cerf in *The Saturday Review of Literature*

An actress congratulated Ilka Chase on her book, *Past Imperfect*. "I enjoyed it," she said. "Who wrote it for you?"

"Darling," clawed Ilka, "I'm so glad you liked it. Who read it to you?"

— Walter Winchell

Passing through the garment factory at Marquette Prison one morning, I noticed a prisoner sitting cross-legged, sewing a burlap covering on a bale of overalls. "Good morning," I said. "Sewing, eh?"

"No, Chaplain," he replied with a grim smile. "Reaping."

— Chaplain Arthur C. De Vries

A story is told of Noel Coward and Lady Diana Manners, who met at a dinner party in England at a time when they entertained no great liking for each other.

"Did you see my last play, *Private Lives*?" asked Mr. Coward.

"Yes," replied the actress.

"What did you think of it?"

"Not very amusing."

There was a pause.

"Mr. Coward, did you see me play the role of the Virgin in *The Miracle*?"

"Yes."

"And what did you think of it?"

"Very amusing," answered the playwright.

Stage Interludes

In the dazzling white armor of Lohengrin, Lauritz Melchior once sang his sad farewell to Elsa, moving step by step with the surging music toward the swan boat which would carry him away. But something happened off stage, and the mechanics pulled the swan into the wings before Melchior could step into it. Finishing his song, in a *sotto voce* plainly audible in the fifth row, he asked, "What time does the next swan leave?"   — Mona Gardner in *The Saturday Evening Post*

A few seasons ago Frederic March and his wife, Florence Eldridge, produced a play, *Yr Obedient Husband*, which closed after eight performances on Broadway. Next day New Yorkers chuckled at a small advertisement inserted above their names in all the dailies: "Oops, we're sorry."   — Ed Sullivan

During the reign of Queen Victoria, Sarah Bernhardt appeared on the London stage in the role of Cleopatra. On this particular night Bernhardt was at her best as Egypt's fiery queen. She stabbed the unfortunate slave who had brought the tidings of Anthony's defeat at Actium, raved, wrecked the palace and finally, as the curtain fell, dropped in a heap in the wreckage.

During a lull in the thunderous applause which followed, a middle-aged British matron was heard to remark in tones of great satisfaction to her companion, "How different, how very different, from the home life of our own dear queen!"   — *The Christian Science Monitor*

Elisabeth Bergner, while playing in *The Two Mrs. Carrolls*, commented on the reactions of women in the audience. "Every night," she said, "women scream in high tones of fright when Geoffrey Carroll, bent on murder, makes a dramatic entrance through my bedroom window. But at matinees, when the women are alone and have no husbands or other men to comfort their fears, there are no shrieks."
                          — Marjory Adams in Boston *Globe*

William Frith, the English painter, was chatting backstage in a theater with a scene-shifter who said he himself had been a player in the provinces. In fact, he had played the part of " 'Amlet."

"Very interesting," said Mr. Frith. "Tell me — what is your conception of Hamlet's relation to Ophelia? Did he, so to speak, love her not wisely but too well?"

"I don't know, sir, if 'Amlet did," was the unblushing answer, "but *I* did."   — Walter Sichel, *The Sands of Time*

Edward Everett Horton tells that when he was playing a matinee of *Springtime for Henry* in Cambridge, Mass., where people take their pleasures seriously, no one laughed. The audience seemed interested, appreciative, and on occasion smiled gravely. He and his company tried every known trick of comedy but there was never a rewarding ripple of laughter from the audience.

At the conclusion of the show a woman came backstage to tell him how very much she and all her friends had enjoyed the play. "Really, Mr. Horton," she concluded, "it was so funny that we could hardly keep from laughing."   — Mary Ann Sprague

One of America's most tempestuous actresses is Tallulah Bankhead. The author of a play in which she was rehearsing staggered away from one rehearsal and coined a phrase which threatens to become immortal in theatrical circles: "A day away from Tallulah is like a month in the country."   — Bennett Cerf, *Laughing Stock* (Grosset & Dunlap)

Monkey Business

Tallulah Bankhead tells about a pet monkey her uncle, Colonel Henry M. Bankhead, tried to housebreak when he was in the Philippines. Whenever the monkey misbehaved, Colonel Bankhead slapped its seat and immediately tossed it out the ground-floor window to the yard outside. After several repetitions, the monkey finally got the idea. Thereafter, it would misbehave, slap its own seat and leap through the window.   — Leonard Lyons

A famous biologist, having unsuccessfully tried to teach a monkey to play ball, decided as a last resort to leave the little creature alone in a room with a bat and ball. He closed the door and waited a few moments. Then, very quietly, he stooped and peered through the keyhole.

He found himself staring into an intent brown eye.   — *Bored Walk*

Patter

A resentful taxpayer addressed an envelope to "Collector of Taxes, Boston City Haul" (*PM*) . . . A visitor to the Income Tax Bureau in Washington explained his mission: "I just wanted to see the people I'm working for" (*The Victorian Magazine*)

Our country cottage: Five rooms and a path . . . They live in a beautiful little apartment overlooking the rent (W. H. Eddy, Jr.)

So embarrassed, she tripped over the roses in the rug (Margery Wilson) . . . Her ailment is not only chronic but chronicle (Edward Artin) . . . A personality like a dental drill (Dan Walker) . . . Mama's little yelper (Louisville *Courier-Journal*) . . . His monthly salary runs into three figures — his wife and two daughters (*Woman's Life*) . . . The kind of girl who likes to eat her cake and have yours, too (Virginia Gaertner)

Imaginuity: There's a brilliant future ahead for the boy who found a purse containing a ten dollar bill. He returned the money to the owner — but first changed the bill to ten ones (*CBC Bulletin*)

Woollcott speaking: "I must get out of these wet clothes and into a dry martini."

The longest word in the English language is the one following the phrase: "And now a word from our sponsor" (Hal Eaton)

Coney Island, where the surf is one-third water and two-thirds people (John Steinbeck) . . . A bathing beauty is a girl who has a lovely profile all the way down (*The Wall Street Journal*) . . . Those women at summer resorts — just so many stuffed shorts (Uncle Walter's Dog House, NBC) . . . Gals at the seashore pitching their curves (Robert Carson) . . . Commenting on a sunburn, "She got what she basked for" (*The Christian Science Monitor*)

Conscience gets a lot of credit that belongs to cold feet.

The only way of catching a train I have ever discovered is to miss the train before (G. K. Chesterton)

Some girls get orchids. All I get are forget-me-notes (Ruth E. Sydor) . . . Give a woman an inch and she thinks she's a ruler (*Stars and Stripes*)

Olds saws sharpened: Men often make passes at girls who drain glasses . . . A kiss is the shortest distance between two (Happy Felton)

"When he dances he's all feet and when he stops he's all hands" (Motion Picture, *Welcome Stranger*)

Birth announcements: The baby has its mother's features and father's fixtures . . . Announcement from the proud parents of a baby daughter: "We have skirted the issue" (Earl Wilson)

Nothing but the Tooth

Condensed from "Inside Benchley"
Robert Benchley

People never tire of talking about their teeth. They hugely enjoy explaining to each other their worst experiences in the dentist's chair.

But as a matter of fact the actual time in the chair is only a fraction of the gross suffering connected with the affair. Much worse is the preliminary period, dating from the discovery of the wayward tooth to the moment when the dentist places his foot on the automatic hoist which jacks you up into range. Giving gas for tooth extraction is all very humane, but the time for anesthetics is when the patient first decides he must go to the dentist.

There is probably no moment more appalling than that in which the tongue, running idly over the teeth in a moment of carefree play, comes suddenly upon the ragged edge of a space from which a filling has disappeared. The world stops and you look meditatively at the ceiling. Then quickly you draw your tongue away and try to laugh the affair off, saying to yourself:

"Nonsense, my good fellow! There is nothing the matter. Your nerves are upset after a hard day's work; that's all."

And slyly, with a poor attempt at casualness, you slide your tongue back along the teeth to check again.

But there it is! There can be no doubt about it this time. The tooth simply has got to be filled. You might as well call a dentist and make an appointment.

Let us say this resolve is made on Tuesday. That afternoon you look up the dentist's number in the telephone book. A wave of relief sweeps over you when you discover it isn't there. How can you be expected to make an appointment with a man who hasn't a phone? The thing is impossible!

On Wednesday there is a more insistent twinge. You decide you must get in touch with that dentist. But you know how those things are. First one thing and then another comes up, and by the time you have a minute to yourself it's five o'clock. And, anyway, the tooth doesn't bother you now. You wouldn't be surprised if you could get along until the end of the week, when you will have more time. A man has to think of his business, after all.

By Saturday you are fairly reconciled to going ahead, but it is only a half day and probably the dentist has no appointments left. Monday is really the time. After all, Monday is the logical day to start going to the dentist.

Bright and early Monday morning you make another try at the telephone book and find, to your horror, that some time between now and last Tuesday the dentist's name and number have been inserted. Fortunately the line is busy, which allows you to put it over until Tuesday. But on Tuesday luck is against you and you get a clear connection with the doctor himself. An appointment is arranged for Thursday afternoon at 3:30.

Thursday afternoon, and here it is only Tuesday morning! Almost anything may happen between now and then. But Wednesday goes by, and Thursday morning, and nothing does happen. The only thing left is for you to call him up and say you have just killed a man and are being arrested and can't possibly keep your appointment. But any dentist would see through that. No excuse you could possibly invent would deceive him. No, you might as well see the thing through now. Perhaps all he intends to do this time is to look at it, anyway. You might even suggest that. You could very easily come in again soon and have him do the actual work.

Three-thirty draws near. A horrible time of day, just when a man's vitality is lowest. As you enter the dentist's building you take one look at the happy people scurrying by in the street. Carefree children they are! What do they know of Life? Probably that man in the silly-looking hat never had trouble with so much as his baby teeth.

Into the elevator. The last hope

is gone as the door clangs, shutting you in. Of course there is always the chance that the elevator will fall, but that is too much to hope for. You feel a glow of heroic pride when you tell the operator the right floor number; you might as easily have told him a floor too high or too low, and caused delay.

Dentists' waiting rooms are all alike. The antiseptic smell, the ominous hum from the operating room, the ancient magazines, and the sullen group of waiting patients. As you sit looking, with unseeing eyes, through a large book entitled *The War in Pictures*, you would gladly change places with the most lowly of God's creatures. It is inconceivable that there should be anyone worse off than you, unless perhaps it is some of the poor wretches who are waiting with you.

That one over in the armchair, nervously tearing to shreds a copy of *The Dental Review and Practical Inlay Worker*. She may have something frightful the trouble with her. She couldn't possibly look more worried. Perhaps it is very, very painful. This thought cheers you up considerably. What cowards women are!

And then the nurse appears, and looks inquiringly at each one in the room. Each one evades her glance in one last, futile attempt to escape. But she spots you and nods pleasantly. God, how pleasantly she nods! There ought to be a law against people being as pleasant as that.

"The doctor will see you now," she says.

Smiling feebly, you totter into the delivery room, where amid a ghastly array of death masks of teeth, blue flames waving eerily from Bunsen burners, and the sound of perpetually running water, you sink into the chair and close your eyes.

But now let us consider the spiritual exaltation that comes when you are at last turned loose. It is all over, and what did it amount to? Why, nothing at all. A-ha-ha-ha-ha! Nothing at all. You suddenly develop a particular friendship for the dentist. A splendid fellow, really. You ask him about his instruments. What does he use this thing for? Well, well, to think a little thing like that could make all that trouble. A-ha-ha-ha-ha! And the dentist's family, how are they? Isn't that fine! Gaily you shake hands with him and straighten your tie.

As you pass out through the waiting room, you leer at the others unpleasantly. The poor fishes! Why can't they take their medicine like grown people and not sit there moping as if they were going to be shot?

When you step out into the bright, cheery street — a wonderful street, all full of nice people — you feel that life is sweet, after all. Forgotten is the fact that you have another appointment for Monday. There is no such thing as Monday. You are through for today, and all's right with the world.

Court Gestures

A visitor sightseeing in New York City fell into conversation with a Negro who began to point out places of interest with enthusiastic civic pride. As they approached a courthouse, the self-appointed guide proclaimed: "And that am the place where they dispense with justice!"

— Albert J. Pyle

Out in Nevada a mining claim was pending before a judge with a reputation for a free and easy brand of justice. One morning His Honor remarked:

"Gentlemen, this court has in hand a check from the plaintiff in this case for $10,000 and a check from the defendant for $15,000. The court will return $5000 to the defendant. Then we will try the case strictly on its merits."

— *The Wall Street Journal*

After a young lawyer had talked nearly five hours to a jury who felt like lynching him, his opponent in the case, a grizzled old veteran of the legal cockpit, rose, smiled sweetly at the judge and jurymen, and said:

"Your Honor, I will follow the example of my young friend who has just concluded, and will submit the case without argument."

— Montreal *Star*

In a New York court, "Action by one Bologna against one Weiner to compel specific performance of contract," elicited this from the judge, "I never sausage a case."

— Doron K. Antrim

"Why don't you settle the case out of court?" said an Irish judge to the litigants before him.

"Sure, that's what we were doin', my lord, when the police came and interfered."

Judge Kenesaw Mountain Landis once sentenced an old offender to five years in prison.

"But, Your Honor," the felon protested anxiously, "I'll be dead long before that! I'm a very sick man — I can't possibly do five years!"

Landis glared at him. "You can try, can't you?"

— Josef S. Chevalier in *Coronet*

The woman called to the stand was handsome but no longer young. The judge gallantly instructed, "Let the witness state her age, after which she may be sworn."   — Joe Harrington in Boston *Post*

In a Charlotte, N. C., domestic relations court, the judge listened intently to both sides in a case against an elderly man who was charged by his wife with nonsupport. After all the evidence was in, the judge told the defendant: "You haven't taken proper care of this good woman and I'm going to give her $25 a month."

The defendant beamed with pleasure. "That's mighty nice of Your Honor," he said, "and I'll give her a dollar or two from time to time myself."   — AP

A. S. Trude, the famed trial lawyer, and the distinguished Dr. Frank Billings lived next door to each other in Chicago. One day Billings testified as a medical expert against Trude. Trude's cross-examination of his eminent neighbor was brief. "Was Marshall Field one of your patients?" he began.

"Yes."

Trude asked, "Where is Mr. Field now?" and the doctor said "Dead." Trude named other patients of Billings — Mr. Armour, Mr. Pullman, Mr. Cudahy, all of whom had died natural deaths. Each time Trude asked: "Where is he now?" and each time Dr. Billings had to answer: "Dead."

"That's all, thank you," the lawyer concluded, and won his case.

— Leonard Lyons

Passing Moments

Protocol required Supreme Court Justice Hugo Black to attend the funeral of a man he had cordially detested for years. A colleague who was late for the services whispered in Justice Black's ear, "How far has the service gone?" Justice Black whispered back, "They just opened the defense."

— Bennett Cerf

After attending the funeral services for a business friend, a San Francisco man had planned to hurry back to his office, but his car got wedged in behind the hearse. He followed sedately in line toward the cemetery until he came to an intersection, where he ducked off and away.

About a half mile farther on he noticed, in the rear-view mirror, that the entire funeral parade was still tagging along behind him.

Seized with an understandable panic, he stepped on the gas, skidded around a turn, parked off the road and pretended he was an utter stranger changing a tire. The procession drove mournfully past and disappeared down the wrong road — where, he's never had the nerve to inquire.

— San Francisco *Examiner*

A New Hampshire farmer had been urged to attend the funeral of his neighbor's third wife. "But I'm not goin'," he announced to his own wife.

"Goodness sakes, why not?" she asked.

"Well, Mary, I'm beginnin' to feel kinda awkward about goin' so often without anything of the sort to ask him back to."

— Nashua *Cavalier*

Charles Dillingham and Florenz Ziegfeld were among the pallbearers at the funeral of Houdini, the Man of Mystery. As they lifted the elaborate casket to their shoulders, Dillingham whispered to Ziegfeld in a sepulchral tone:

"Suppose he isn't here!"

— Bob Davis

It was at the funeral of a woman who had been thoroughly disliked in our rural community — and for cause. With a sharply barbed tongue and a violently explosive disposition, she henpecked her husband, drove her children mercilessly and quarreled with her neighbors. Even the animals on the place wore a hunted look.

The day was sultry, and as the minister's voice droned on the sky grew darker and darker. Just as the service ended, the storm broke furiously. There was a blinding flash followed closely by a terrific thunder clap. In the stunned silence a voice was heard from the back row of the crowded room: "Waal, she's *got* there!"   — Harriet E. Meyer

Chauncey Depew, asked what kind of exercise he took, answered: "I get my exercise acting as a pallbearer to my friends who exercise."
— Portland *Sunday Telegram*

It's Human Nature

More than 100 Washington notables attended a party one night in honor of Titus Oates in the Hotel Statler's South American Room. The distinguished guests were milling around, sipping cocktails and looking for the guest of honor, when each was given a slip of paper which read:

"Mr. Oates regrets he will be unable to swill with us today. If you wish to know why, we refer you to page 1111 of Webster's *Biographical Dictionary* which states: 'Oates, Titus. 1649-1705. English imposter and fabricator of the Popish Plot.' " The paper went on to say that Oates' forgery of the plot, whereby Catholics were supposedly pledged to massacre Protestants, burn London, and assassinate the king, resulted in the death of about 35 persons. Sentenced to life imprisonment for perjury, he was later released by William of Orange.

The party was the idea of George Dixon, Washington newspaperman, who wanted to prove that people in Washington will attend a party for anyone.   — Harold Helfer

Composer Maurice Ravel was an enthusiastic collector of rare books and prints, fine porcelains, and other *objets d'art*. In his study, occupying a place of honor on a pedestal, stood his most treasured possession — a ball of smoked crystal, which he invariably pointed out to his friends with great pride.

"Maurice," his guests would whisper in awe, "where did you get it? It's exquisite!"

"You really think so?" he would answer modestly. "Well, it's just a burned-out electric bulb."   — E. E. Edgar

An Atlanta woman, riding home on a bus, suddenly realized she had left a "piggy bank" at the post office while mailing letters. She hurried back and found the bank on the counter, but noticed it had become heavier.

Generous Atlantans, thinking it was there for aiding some worthy cause, had put many coins in it.   — AP

A Seattle chest X-ray worker thought she saw a familiar face in the line of persons being X-rayed, asked the woman if she hadn't already had an X-ray.

"Certainly," replied the woman. "I've had three already. The first didn't help me, but after the second one I began feeling a lot better. I don't have to stop taking treatments, do I?"   — Seattle *Times*

About three weeks before an annual college-club dinner, a member received a letter from the club president, asking him to serve on the reception committee and be there at seven o'clock sharp. A scarlet ribbon marked RECEPTION COMMITTEE was enclosed. He hadn't meant to go. The dinners were usually a bore. But since he had been asked to be on the committee . . .

By the time he arrived, almost all 800 members of the club were there, each wearing a scarlet ribbon marked RECEPTION COMMITTEE.
                                                   — Rita Halle Kleeman

College Humor

The Proper Bostonian reserves his highest regard for something which is not located in Boston at all, but is a few miles up the Charles River in Cambridge, and which he calls Hahvud. Since all First Family sons repair there he wishes it to be recognized as the only college there is. "If a man's in there," one Bostonian used to say, tapping the catalogue of Harvard graduates, "that's who he is. If he isn't, who is he?"   — Cleveland Amory, *The Proper Bostonians* (Dutton)

In a restaurant at Columbia University, a refugee professor, speaking English with that acquired precision which so often shames the native-born, ordered "figs and cream." The waitress brought a dish of figs covered with cream. "I ordered figs *and* cream," the professor protested. "There they are," she retorted. "But this is figs *with* cream," he persisted. "But I don't see . . ." she began, bewildered. "Madam," said the professor, icily, "would you say a woman and child were the same as a woman with child?"

"Miss Jones," said the science professor, "would you care to tell the class what happens when a body is immersed in water?"

"Sure," said Miss Jones. "The telephone rings."

— Bennett Cerf, *Anything for a Laugh* (Grosset & Dunlap)

While my husband was teaching at a small state agricultural college a proposal was brought before the legislature to raise faculty salaries. The farm bloc was solidly against the measure — they couldn't see why the state should pay those college professors $5000 a year just for talking 12 or 15 hours a week. Faculty representatives made no headway with their arguments until one of them, who had had some farming experience, had an inspiration.

"Gentlemen," he told the lawmakers, "a college professor is a little like a bull. It's not the amount of time he spends. It's the importance of what he does!" The professors got their raise.   — R. H.

The poet Louis Untermeyer was attending a costume party one evening. He was looking his silliest in a ridiculous paper hat, tooting a horn for nobody's benefit. Just at that moment a young college girl walked up to him and looked him up and down scornfully. Then she turned on her heel. "Huh!" she snapped, "and you're Required Reading!"

— Neal O'Hara, McNaught Syndicate

Holding a Baby

Condensed from the Collected Edition of

Heywood Broun

It would be interesting to figure out just how many foot-pounds of energy men have saved themselves, since Adam delved and Eve span, by keeping up the pretense that a special knack is required for washing dishes and for dusting, and that the knack is wholly feminine.

Men build bridges and throw railroads across deserts, and yet they contend successfully that the job of sewing on a button is beyond them. Accordingly, they don't have to sew buttons. It might be said, of course, that the safety of suspension bridges is so much more important than that of suspenders that the division of labor is only fair, but many of us have never thrown a railroad in our lives and yet swagger in all the glory of masculine achievement without undertaking any of the drudgery of odd jobs.

Probably men alone could never have maintained the fallacy of masculine incapacity. As soon as that limited sphere once known as woman's place was established, women began to glorify and exaggerate its importance, and men gave eager assent.

There are other factors. Biology has been unscrupulous enough to distinguish markedly against women, and men have seized upon this advantage to press the belief that, since the bearing of children is exclusively the province of women, it must be that the caring for them belongs properly to the same sex. Yet how ridiculous this is. Most things which have to be done for children should tax the intelligence of no one. Men profess lack of ability to wash baby's face simply because they believe there's no great fun in the business, at either end of the sponge. Man even pretends that he doesn't know how to hold the baby. From this has grown the shockingly transparent fallacy that holding a baby correctly is one of the fine arts; or, perhaps, a wonderful intuition which has come down after centuries of effort to women only.

"The thing that surprised Richard most," says a woman novelist, "was the efficiency with which Eleanor handled Annabel. Her fingers seemed, of themselves, to curve into the places where they would fit the spineless bundle and give it support." Places indeed! Except that right side up is best, there is not much to learn about holding a baby. There are 152 distinctly different ways — and all are right! At least all will do. A baby is so soft that anybody with a firm grip can make places for an effective hold wherever he chooses. But, "If Richard tried to take up the bundle, his fingers fell away and the bundle collapsed. And Eleanor would smile gently and send him on some masculine errand, while she soothed Annabel's feelings." You may depend upon it that Richard also smiled as soon as he was safely embarked upon some such masculine errand as playing 18 holes of golf.

It is pretty generally held that all a woman needs to do to know all about children is to have some. This wisdom is attributed to instinct. Again and again we have been told by rapturous grandmothers that: "It isn't something which can be read in a book or taught in a school. Nature is the great teacher." This simply isn't true. There are many mothers who have learned far more from the manuals of Dr. Holt than from instinct — and Dr. Holt is a man. I have seen mothers give beer and spaghetti and Neapolitan ice cream to children in arms, and if they got that from instinct the only conclusion possible is that instinct is not what it used to be.

I believe in a rough equality of parenthood. In shirking all the business of caring for children we men have escaped much hard labor. But we have also missed much fun of a very special kind. Children mean nothing at long range. For our own sake we ought to throw off the pretense of incapacity and ask that we be given a half share in them. I hope that this can be done without sharing the dishes, also. I don't think there are any concealed joys in washing dishes. Washing children is quite different. A dish is an unresponsive thing. It gives back nothing. After you have washed somebody else's face you feel that you know him better. A child's face offers competitive possibilities. It is interesting to see just how high a polish can be achieved without making it cry.

There is also a distinct sense of elation in doing trifling practical things for children. When you have completed the rather difficult task of preparing a child for bed and actually getting him there, you have a sense of importance almost divine in its extent.

There is less to be said for dressing a child, from the point of view of recreation. This seems to us laborious and rather tiresome, both for father and child. Still, I know one man who managed to make an adventure of it. He was a skilled automobile mechanic, much in demand at races where tires are whisked on and off. He brought his technique into the home, and boasted that he had broken all world records for changing all or any part of a child's clothing. He was a silent man who habitually carried a mouthful of safety pins. He wasted no time in preliminary wheedlings but tossed the youngster on the floor and even before her head had bumped he would be hard at work. He endeavored always to have his task completed before the child could begin to cry. He never lost.

There is nothing dull in feeding a child. I doubt whether the world holds for anyone more soul-stirring surprise than the first adventure with ice cream. There is the immediate frightened rebellion against the coldness of it, and then the amazing sensation as the strange substance melts into magic of pleasant sweetness. Even golf is a trifling thing beside the privilege of taking a small son to the zoo and letting him see his first lion, his first tiger and, best of all, his first elephant. Probably he will think they are part of your own handiwork turned out for his pleasure.

To a child even the meanest of us may seem glamorous with magic and wisdom. It seems a pity not to take advantage of this before the opportunity is lost. There must come a day when the most nimble-witted father has to reply, "I don't know." On that day the child comes out of Eden and you are only a man again.

Punctuation with a Punch

Fred Flanagan and Stan Merritt in Printers' Ink

WRITING advertising has become increasingly difficult because of the feebleness of our system of punctuation. Even the exclamation point is often called upon to perform tasks which are beyond its capabilities. Take this typical headline: "Sudsi-wudsi for dandy dudsies!" How ineffectual the little exclamation point! Here is a headline that *sings* with excitement, that cries out for punctuation in keeping with its world-shaking message! So — we suggest what we call the *flabbergasterisk* (✳). Here we have a punctuation mark that really makes you sit up and take notice ✳

Occasionally we are called upon to express more intense heights of emotion, such as in the epic headline, "Everybody . . . yes <u>everybody</u>, chews CHEWIES!" Even the *flabbergasterisk* cannot express the full dramatic content of this epic caption. For such cases we have developed a still more powerful punctuation mark — the *stupendapoint* (⟨✳⟩). This last headline brings up another problem.

Note the underline beneath the word <u>everybody</u>. Completely unimaginative and inadequate ✳ To achieve the wanted impact we should use the more arresting *fluctustress* (〰〰〰〰). Working with new tools such as these, we can forge into written copy as much <u>meaning</u> as is possible to the radio announcer through the spoken word ✳ ✳

Teen-Age Trials

A worried father hurried to his teen-age son's hospital bedside. The lad had a broken leg and myriad cuts and bruises. "What happened, son?" asked the father. "Did you have an accident coming home from your girl's house?"

"No," the boy groaned.

"Well, how *did* it happen?" persisted the father.

"We were jitterbugging," the boy explained, "when her old man came in. He's deaf and couldn't hear the music — so he threw me out the window!" — Ken Norton in *Pageant*

A very sedate grandmother was rather perturbed when her 18-year-old granddaughter announced that she was going off to the lake with one of her suitors for an all-day picnic.

"In my day no nice girl would think of traipsing off with a man unless she was engaged to him!" said Grandma.

"Oh, that's all right," confided the girl. "Billy is one of my fiancés."
— Louisville *Courier-Journal*

A young Baltimore debutante handed over the list for her coming-out dance to the cousin who was giving the party. Looking over the neatly written pages he came to one which severely tried his composure. Headed "Divine Elderly Men," it consisted of friends of his whose venerable ages, he knew, ranged from 25 to 27.   — Mary Hughes

It's Sam Hoffenstein's story: A bobby-soxer was making telephone explanations concerning her loss of a current boy friend to a rival. "He may think it's love," she stated, "but it's only a passing fanny."
— Irving Hoffman in *The Hollywood Reporter*

When a young Coast Guardsman calling on my 16-year-old daughter remarked that he was from Brooklyn, I commented that my husband and I had lived there 18 years ago, when we were first married. I noticed a startled expression pass over the young people's faces. Next morning, my daughter said with disgust, "That certainly did it, Mother. I'd told him I was 18; so then of course I had to tell him I was illegitimate."
— L. K. Davis

In a Minneapolis drugstore, a 17-year-old, buying a lipstick as a present for his girl, was at a loss when asked the shade. Suddenly his face brightened; he whipped out his handkerchief and pointed to a crimson smear. "There," he exclaimed happily, "*that shade!*" — Enid Wold

Newman Levy, the author, has a 13-year-old daughter who spends blissful hours at the movies. "How did you enjoy the picture this afternoon?" he asked her one Saturday. "It was simply awful," she replied. "I could hardly sit through it the second time."
— Bennett Cerf, *Try and Stop Me*
(Simon & Schuster)

In her book *Smile Please*, Mildred Spurrier Topp recalls the day she and her sister decided to send a valentine, supposedly from their widowed mother, to a prominent judge who had shown marked, if discreet, signs of interest. Mildred wanted to use a new word she had heard in Sunday school. "I'm not sure what it means," she confessed to her sister, "but it's in the Bible, so it must be O.K. Besides, it was used about King Solomon, so it's bound to be romancy enough for a valentine."

That's how the judge came to receive a gaudy, lace-bedecked valentine that read:

> *If you will be my valentine,*
> *I will be your concubine. . . .*
> — Bennett Cerf in *The Saturday Review of Literature*

A bobby-soxer was extolling Gregory Peck to her father. When she had finished, Pop summed it up with, "Isn't he rather like Abraham Lincoln?"

"Well, somewhat," she answered, "but I think he has more character than Lincoln."
— L. L. Stevenson in Detroit *News*

Letter from a schoolboy recently received by the Library of Congress:
"Can you give me the name of a good book on aeronautics and one on sane sex life? I am more interested in aeronautics."   — *Newsweek*

Plane Talk

At a fashionable boarding school overlooking the Hudson River, a 19-year-old student, whose room opened conveniently onto a balcony removed from the eyes of the world, was cultivating a deep all-over sun tan. No textbooks, nothing more grueling to do than watch a small airplane which frequented the neighborhood. Her peace was abruptly broken one afternoon by the close approach of the plane. As it passed overhead a small missile landed accurately on the balcony. Wrapped around a small stone was a note which read: "I love you."
— Mrs. A. C. G.

The new air-line hostess taking over her first flight was more than a bit nervous. Soon after the big twin-engined plane was in the air the chief pilot's voice came over the intercom: "Hostess! Send the co-pilot forward, please." She made a quick search, reported back that he was nowhere to be found. "You weren't supposed to let me take off until you checked in the co-pilot," snapped the intercom. "Nothing to do now but proceed to the next station." A thoroughly frightened young lady patted pillows into place, served coffee and sandwiches with trembling hands.

Actually, the co-pilot had entered the plane through the cargo hatch in the nose of the ship, and was sitting just where he should be. When the plane rolled to a stop at the first station, the co-pilot broke open the cargo hatch, ducked under the air liner's belly, broke into a hard run that took him in a wide sweep to the side where the hostess was seeing off the last of her passengers. Up the ramp he staggered and fell panting into her arms.

"Lord, what a race!" he gasped. "Didn't think I'd make it."

— H. W. Hoover

When air lines were young and people were wary of flying, a promotion man suggested to one of the lines that they permit wives of businessmen to accompany their husbands free, just to prove that flying was safe. The idea was quickly adopted, and a record kept of the names of those who accepted the proposition. In due time the air line sent a letter to those wives, asking how they enjoyed the trip. From 90 percent of them came back a baffled reply, "*What* airplane trip?"

— Marguerite Lyon, *And So to Bedlam* (Bobbs-Merrill)

Hitchhiking home recently, I was on the outskirts of Victoria, Texas, when an elderly farmer stopped and said, "Goin' about 50 miles down the road, son." I got in and settled down, but we had gone only about a mile when, to my dismay, we turned off on a lonely country road and pulled up before a barn at the edge of a large pasture. He asked me to get my bag and I hesitantly followed him. As he opened the barn doors I saw a small plane. "Nice weather t'fly, eh son? Get in." He spun the propeller, ran the plane down the pasture once to scare the cows out of the way, turned into the wind, and we took to the air. — Alfred R. Smith

Stewardesses on Western Air Lines planes making regular flights to Wyoming's Grand Teton mountain region were embarrassed by passengers who wanted to know what "Grand Tetons" means in English. Airline officials instructed the girls to tell inquirers that the name can be translated "Sweater Girl Mountains." — *Business Week*

To celebrate Uncle Dudley's 75th birthday, an aviation enthusiast offered to take him for a plane ride over the little West Virginia town where he'd spent all his life.

Uncle Dudley accepted the offer.

Back on the ground, after circling over the town 20 minutes, his friend asked, "Were you scared, Uncle Dudley?"

"No-o-o," was the hesitant answer. "But I never did put my full weight down." — Ralph P. Norton

Lady traveling with friend to air-line pilot: "Now don't start going faster than sound. We want to talk." — B. Tobey cartoon in *This Week Magazine*

Sidney Skolsky, the Hollywood columnist and movie producer, is highly allergic to air travel but from time to time finds it necessary to get to New York in a thumping hurry. At such moments he drives to the airport, accompanied by his physician. Arranging himself comfortably in his seat, he fastens the safety belt and says, "Now." The physician jabs him in the arm with a needle containing a mild anesthetic. Fourteen hours later when Sidney opens his eyes and murmurs, "Where am I?" the porter replies, "La Guardia Field, sir. Will you be wanting a cab?"

This is probably the best solution to air travel yet devised by man. — Paul Gallico in *Esquire*

For the Love of Mike

A dramatist employed to write stories from the Bible in radio form was astonished, at the end of a broadcast, to hear the announcer say: "Will Cain kill Abel? Tune in at the same time tomorrow morning and find out."
— Albert R. Perkins in *Vogue*

Earl Wilson and Morton Downey passed their pal Ted Husing in a radio broadcasting booth one evening, where he was giving a long script his customary impassioned interpretation. Realizing that he couldn't interrupt his broadcast, they sneaked up behind him, took off his shirt, pants, shoes and socks, and left him there in his BVD's. "Be sure to drop in at Studio C," they told a group of sight-seers on the way out. "Husing is giving one of his most unusual performances."
— Bennett Cerf, *Shake Well Before Using* (Simon & Schuster)

A nice bit of radio ad-libbing is attributed to Juano Hernandez, who played De Lawd in *Green Pastures* for "Theater Guild on the Air." When a fellow actor forgot his lines and froze, Hernandez came to the rescue.

"Son," he said reassuringly, "you is nervous before me and I can understand that. But I is de Lord, and I knows what is on your mind." Whereupon he supplied the missing lines.
— Louis Berg in *This Week Magazine*

Paul Barnes, radio actor, tells of the receptionist at NBC in New York who was helping an aspiring actress fill out an audition blank. When the actress was asked her age she hesitated. The receptionist waited patiently while seconds ticked by, then she quipped, "Better hurry up. Every minute makes it worse!"
— Dutton-Lippold in *Coronet*

The radio program "Information Please" was once sued for $17.62. One night when Alice Marble was our guest, we men were adjured to shut our eyes and tell the colors of our neckties. A man driving through Boston, with his radio turned on, heard that query. He also closed his eyes, hit the car ahead of him and paid $17.62 for fender damage.
— Franklin P. Adams, *Nods and Becks* (Whittlesey)

After Tallulah Bankhead spent a nervous half-hour as quizmaster for the Quiz Kids, a press agent approached her and said soothingly, "The Quiz Kids were thrilled to death to meet you, Miss Bankhead. They've been reading up on your life all week."

"Heavens!" cried Tallulah. "What a thing for children to read!"

     — Eliza Merrill Hickok, *The Quiz Kids* (Houghton Mifflin)

The prize of all radio announcements I heard in California. A plummy-voiced gentleman was pleading for his sponsor, who built mausoleums: "Ladies and gentlemen," said he, in organ tones, "is seepage disturbing your loved ones?"

     — Peggy Wood, *How Young You Look* (Farrar & Rinehart)

Everybody's Business

A crowd in a small-town Michigan drugstore was listening intently to a broadcast of the World Series when a woman came in to the soda fountain. After considerable delay the soda jerk approached and in a hushed tone asked what she wanted. In the silence her voice boomed, "A chocolate milk shake."

Looking thoroughly annoyed, the clerk whispered, "Madam, I'll be glad to make you something like a soda or a sundae, but a milk shake is much too noisy and will interfere with the folks who are listening to the game."

     — Jeanne E. Keefe

A stout gentleman, determined to lose weight during a stay on his Vermont farm, hustled to the general store for a pair of overalls. He picked out a pair big enough for energetic exercise. Then a thought struck him. "Wait a minute," he told the clerk, "those fit me now but I expect to lose a lot — maybe I'd better buy a small pair."

The clerk shook his head. "Mister, if you can shrink as fast as these overalls can, you'll be doing pretty good," he said, and calmly went on wrapping the overalls.   — *Rockefeller Center Magazine*

A sign in a store window read: "Fishing Tickle." Noticing the error, a customer asked: "Hasn't anyone told you about it before?"

"Yes," replied the dealer. "Many have dropped in to tell me, and they always buy something." — Sam Holt in *Modern Retailing*

A farmer walked into the hardware store of a mid-western town and asked to see an axe. After carefully examining a half-dozen, he chose one and asked its price.

"It is $1.50," said the storekeeper.

Producing a page torn from a mail-order catalogue, the farmer said, "Here is the same axe for only $1.33."

The hardware man looked at the picture, pondered, then said, "If they can sell it for that, so can I."

"O.K. I'll take it," said the farmer.

The storekeeper picked up the axe, weighed it on a scale behind the counter and began to make out a sale bill, $1.33, plus 15 cents, total $1.48.

"Hey!" shouted the farmer. "What's that 15 cents for?"

"For postage. If you sent off for it you'd have to pay postage, wouldn't you?"

The farmer had to admit he would. He counted out the $1.48. The storekeeper wrapped up the axe — and calmly laid it on a shelf.

"Say, what is the big idea?" asked the farmer.

With a twinkle in his eye, the storekeeper replied, "Come back in three days and you can have it." — Ben Shatzman

For several seasons I had marveled that the owner of a general store on Cape Cod could supply his customers' needs, considering the chaotic condition of his merchandise. Last summer this sign appeared above the store entrance:

STORE OF THREE WONDERS

1 — YOU WONDER
If I Have It
2 — I WONDER
Where It Is
3 — EVERYBODY WONDERS
How I Find It

— Julia W. Kyle

The sun-dried old Connecticut storekeeper and I watched two city girls riding down the dusty road on their bicycles, clad in the briefest of shorts and halters. "The modern girl knows how to get her man better than her grandma did," I remarked.

The old man eyed the girls reflectively. "I don't know about that, mister," he said at length. "I never seen a successful merchant who put all his goods on display at once. The wise storekeeper shows one prize item at a time. . . . That's what their grandmas did," he concluded.
— Clifford W. Fitton

Sign in a Tulsa, Okla., secondhand store: "Nothing Sold on Credit — Damn Little for Cash" (Thelma H. Quast) . . . In York Village, Me., is the sign: "The General Store. Bill Gallagher & Son, Mgr.; Mrs. Gallagher, Boss" (Brooklyn *Eagle*) . . . On the door of a small restaurant outside Chicago: "Gone for the Week. Fishingpox" (Katharine Loudon)

Number, Please

One day Groucho Marx received a phone call from his brother Harpo. As they were talking, Harpo suddenly interrupted: "Wait a minute — someone's at the door." Groucho waited patiently, holding the phone.

Harpo rushed outside to his car, raced to Groucho's house, walked in, seated himself quietly near where Groucho was still holding the phone and said: "Now, as I was telling you . . ." — Leonard Lyons

Our phones in Dickens County, Texas, were all party lines, and neighbors listened in for miles. One night during a prolonged dry spell, old Ed, a shrewd cattle rancher, got a phone call from a Kansas

City buyer who said, "I understand you've got some steers to sell."

"Well, now," dickered Ed, "I'm not sure I want to sell right now —"

"Ed, for heaven's sake," broke in an agonized wail from the party line, "you sell them steers! You know you ain't got any grass!"

— George Pattullo

One evening, hearing the telephone ring, Mrs. Robert A. Millikan, wife of the world-famous physicist, went into the hall and found that her maid had already answered the telephone. "Yes, this is where Dr. Millikan lives," she heard her say. "But he's not the kind of doctor that does anybody any good."

— Jeptha Wade and David Cope

My mother lives in a small Arizona town of perhaps 500 inhabitants and a dozen telephones. She hasn't one, so when my sister had her first baby I put in a person-to-person call for Mother through the telephone office. "It'll take a while to get Mrs. Quinn here," my operator was told. "Her place is about a half mile down the road."

"Will there be a charge for messenger service?" asked my operator.

"No, indeed, ma'am, no charge at all. I'll just fire a shot down in that direction and when Mrs. Quinn looks up this way to see what's going on, I'll wave her in."

— Evelyn Anderson

In a gay and carefree mood, a man telephoned a friend at two o'clock in the morning. "I do hope I haven't disturbed you," he said cheerily.

"Oh, no," the friend replied, "that's quite all right. I had to get up to answer the telephone anyway."

— Carl Brandt

A New York bookstore was crowded with customers waiting for attention. The telephone rang in the mail-order department and a voice asked for certain books. "Just a moment," the clerk said, and returned with the news that all were in stock. "That'll be $8.50 c.o.d. To what name and address shall we send them?"

"Never mind sending them," said the voice on the telephone. "Just bring them to the front of the store — I'm in the public telephone booth there."

— E. H. Niehaus

A lady was alone in her home knitting peacefully when a telegram arrived, telling her a distant cousin had passed away and left her a million dollars. Half the thrill of getting news like that, of course, comes from telling others about it. The little lady dropped her knitting, ran to the telephone, and cried excitedly, "Hello, operator! Get me anybody!"

— Bennett Cerf

A minister in New York phoned a minister in California. "Is this a station-to-station call?" queried the operator. "No," replied the Reverend, "it's parson-to-parson."

— Bennett Cerf in *The Saturday Review of Literature*

Mrs. Rex Beach, phoning from her Manhattan hotel suite, was greeted by the switchboard operator with a cheery "Hotel Algonquin."

Replied Mrs. Beach, "Yes, I know."

Asked the operator, "Is this 1106?"

"No, it's 408, and I want to order breakfast."

"There's no room service except Sunday."

"Yes, there is; I've had breakfast up here every day — and furthermore it's Sunday."

Operator: "Sunday! My God, I'm not supposed to be here!"

— *Time*

A job as night disc jockey on a radio station involves many strange duties. One is deluged with telephone queries such as "Will it freeze tonight?" "How can I make my baby stop crying?" "Who composed Beethoven's Fifth Symphony?" and so on. I thought I had heard the book until one night the phone rang and I answered with the usual, "Good evening. KWKH."

"Oh, thank you," said a sultry feminine voice. "I just wanted to hear a man's voice before I went to sleep."

— Paul W. Beardsley

An angry subscriber, having trouble with the telephone, bellowed at an operator, "Am I crazy, or are you?"

"I'm sorry, sir," she replied in her sweetest institutional voice, "but we do not have that information."

— *Insults*, edited by Max Herzberg (Greystone)

Our New Telephone

Condensed from The Atlantic Monthly

Ruth Gordon

"You know I been thinking, Clinton," my mother said one evening as she and my father sat reading, "that everybody else has got one and we ought to have a telephone."

"Wouldn't have one if you gave it to me," declared my father, knocking the ashes from his pipe into the Dresden china cuspidor.

"Why, Clinton?" asked my mother. "What have you got against it?"

My father sat as still as a statue for a moment and then gave a loud sneeze. "Get that cat off the register," he demanded, blowing his nose with a groan. "Hot air coming up through cat fur'll give me back my old trouble. Get him off of there. I ain't going to have him lying around warming up all his germs."

"Punk's clean and hasn't any germs, Clinton," said my mother. "Please try not to be against a telephone."

"I ain't against it," said my father, "so long as we don't have to have one."

"But, Clinton," my mother went on, "Ruth's growing up, you know, and all the other girls have them, and it isn't as if we wanted to make a lot of outgoing calls to cost us money. It's so the young people can call up Ruth. And, Clinton, if you don't want to, you don't have to have a thing to do with it; it can just be Ruth's and mine."

"It can be Shem and Japheth's," said my father genially, "so long as I don't have to pay for it. But the way it'll turn out'll be, it *ain't* Shem and Japheth's but mine. And I won't have my name in the telephone book. I got no wish to call attention to myself."

"We won't use your name at all, Clinton. It can be in my name, and don't you trouble about the money because I can always get it from somewheres."

When our telephone was installed, my father ignored it unless he thought we were talking too long, and then he told us briefly to quit. Once it rang at nine o'clock, after we had gone to bed, and as I came upstairs again my father called out to me, "What's the matter? Is the house afire?"

"No," I said, "It was Richard DeNormandie."

"Oh," he said, "is DeNormandie's house afire?"

"No, Papa, nobody's house is afire," I said, feeling grown-up and important. "He just simply asked me to go to a dance."

"I knew it must have been some-

thing vital," my father said. "Anything to prevent him askin' you in
the daytime, or don't he get the
power of speech before night?"

There came a day when my father
was troubled. There was word at the
factory that Dan Weymouth was
going to retire on a pension, and it
frightened my father, for he thought
perhaps the retirement was compulsory. "Dan's only been there a
little longer than me, you know," he
reminded my mother.

"I know, Clinton," said my
mother, "but couldn't you just try
to eat supper?"

My father pushed back his chair
from the table and stood up. "No,"
he said, "I couldn't. I'm too troubled. If I knew Dan went and done
it of his own free will, that would be
all right."

"Well, Clinton, it's probably all
your imagination, but if it's going to
make you worry like this, won't you
please, just to make me happy, call
up Dan on the telephone and see
what he has to say?"

"Oh, no," said my father. "It
ain't as bad as all *that*."

"Think a minute, Clinton. Is
your peace of mind worth a nickel?"

My father looked moodily out the
window. "What the hell consolation
is it goin' to be? If it's good news
it'll still be good news tomorrow,
and if it's bad news we're payin' a
nickel to get it quicker."

My mother did not stop to hear
anything further but hurried to the
telephone book hanging beside the
instrument in the entry between the

cellar stairway and kitchen door.

My father sat down in his reading
chair and looked at the back of his
hands.

Soon my mother came back with
the book. "Here's Dan's number,
Clinton," she said.

My father resignedly went to the
phone, called the number and cleared
his throat several times, so as to be
ready. There was a click at the other
end of the line and my father became as stiff as a ramrod. "Hello,"
he said distinctly. "Is that you,
Dan?" He paused. "Yes, I thought

it was, it sounds like you. Can you hear me, or do you want me to be louder?"

Results were apparently satisfactory at Mr. Weymouth's end so my father continued. "Dan, I'd like to find out about what's goin' on in the factory, about you gettin' ready to leave."

A short pause followed, while my father listened. Suddenly his expression brightened and he said eagerly, "You done it because you wanted to. They didn't ask you to do it. Well, Dan, I'm glad to hear you say so.

I'm *damn* glad to hear you say it. That's all I had in my mind, Dan. So you can start to hang up now same as me. Good-bye."

My father took off his glasses and polished them.

"A telephone," he said, "is a very remarkable invention. I never said it wasn't. I could hear Dan just now as clear as if he was down in our cellar. Of course, what effect it's goin' to have on the next generation's powers of hearing, with all that clickin' and bell ringin', still remains to be seen."

Definitions

Meteorologist: A man who can look into a girl's eyes and tell whether.
— Bennett Cerf in *The Saturday Review of Literature*

Mal de mer: French for "You can't take it with you."
— Garry Moore

Intuition: The strange instinct that tells a woman she is right, whether she is or not.   — *Methodist Recorder*

Throw rug: A small rug that usually throws anyone who steps on it.   — Margaret Schooley

Etiquette: Learning to yawn with your mouth closed.
— *It Pays to Be Ignorant*, CBS

Diplomat: A man who can convince his wife a woman looks stout in a fur coat.   — *Northwestern Bell*

Television: Radio with eyestrain.
— Archie in *Duffy's Tavern*, NBC

A good storyteller: A person who has a good memory and hopes other people haven't.   — Irvin S. Cobb

Poise: The art of raising the eyebrows instead of the roof.
— Howard W. Newton in *Redbook Magazine*

Golf: A good walk spoiled.
— Mark Twain

Minor operation: One performed on somebody else.   — *Lutheran Men*

Platonic friendship: The interval between the introduction and the first kiss.   — Sophie Irene Loeb, *Epigrams of Eve*

Conscience: The still small voice that makes you feel still smaller.
— James A. Sanaker

A Word of Difference

A very pretty redhead window-shopping on Fifth Avenue was being followed by a smooth Latin type.

At Sloane's she turned on him, indignant. "You've been following me for three blocks — I saw you. You can stop right now. I'm not the type of girl you can pick up."

The Latin bowed, and smiled. "Madame," he said, "I am not picking you up. I am picking you *out*."

It worked!

— *PM*

Having heard much of the famous "corn likker" of the region, a party of tourists decided to stop at a shack in the Arkansas hills and try to buy some. An old man came to the door. "We heard you had some homemade liquor," they said. "Could we buy some?"

"Yep," said the mountaineer. "I got some. What kind d'ye want?"

"Why, it's called corn likker, isn't it?"

"Yeah, both kinds is corn likker. But which kind d'ye want — courtin' likker or fightin' likker?"

— H. Lloyd Clark

Oscar Wilde arrived at his club one evening, after witnessing a first production of a play that was a complete failure.

"Oscar, how did your play go tonight?" said a friend.

"Oh," was the lofty response, "the play was a great success, but the audience was a failure."

— Daniel Frohman, *Encore* (McLeod)

"Are you homesick?" her aunt asked a small girl, away for the first time overnight. "No," the child sobbed. "I'm here sick."

— S. M. L. in *Capper's Weekly*

The officers at Fort Dix, who were giving a dance, delegated a persuasive young second lieutenant to ask the dean of a strait-laced eastern women's college to allow some of the girls to attend. The dean promised to send a dozen of her best and most trustworthy students. The lieutenant hesitated. "Would it be possible," he finally asked, "to send half a dozen of that kind and half a dozen of the others?" — *Coronet*

An aspiring actor who was getting nowhere in Hollywood decided to see if a little publicity might help. Going to an office near one of the studios, he inquired of the receptionist about the different kinds of publicity. "We got two kinds, son," she replied. "Piety and notoriety. Which do you want?"

— Verda M. Ross

Filling out an application for dependents' aid, a colored soldier answered "no" to the question as to whether he had any dependents.

"You're married, aren't you?" an officer said.

"Yessir," the soldier replied, "but she ain't dependable."

— *Cannoneers Post*

Johnson, the man-of-all-work for a friend of mine in New Jersey, had sent a part of each month's salary to a small bank in his home town in the South. After two years of this, he went to New York for a gay week-end. He ran out of money, and induced a friend to cash a check for him.

About a week later the friend showed up with the check marked "Insufficient Funds." Johnson dug up the money to buy it back and immediately penned an angry letter to the bank, pointing out that he must have had infinitely more money in his account than the check called for.

He got this reply from the bank: "Dear Mr. Johnson: When we say 'Insufficient Funds' we don't necessarily mean *you* got insufficient funds. It could also mean *we* got insufficient funds."

— John McClain in New York *Sun*

Southern Exposure

A group of sight-seers visiting southern battlefields listened stoically to the comments of their native guide. "Here a handful of our southern boys routed 30,000 Yanks. Here one fine battalion from Georgia annihilated a corps of Yankee troops. Here two brave Virginia boys captured an entire regiment of Northerners."

Finally, one woman in the party spoke up with an unmistakable New England twang. "Didn't the North ever win a single victory?" she asked.

"No, ma'am," said the guide politely, "and they never will, as long as I'm running this bus."

— *The Saturday Evening Post*

A young breeder of race horses down South explained at some length to an attractive Northern visitor the intricacies of horse naming — one foal, for instance, was named *Carrot* because it was by *Caron* out of *Ottilia*. That evening, however, under a romantic full moon, the breeder forgot his horses and concentrated on the girl to such an extent that she promptly left for home. Arrived in New York, she wired the horseman: "Home, by Jove, out of Danger."

— Iles Brody

At an international banquet in London each guest was asked to rise, give his name, and the name of his country. After representatives from China, Russia, South Africa and Argentina had identified themselves, a tall, scholarly figure rose and in the soft accent of a Virginian drawled proudly, "Suh, Ah come from the southern end of Fauquier County."

— Mrs. Arthur B. Kinsolving

State College alumni attending a dinner in Raleigh, N. C., were asked to name their professions. One shy young undertaker, fearing the derision of the crowd when he told his calling, answered smoothly, "I'm a southern planter."

— Betty C. Waite

A hillbilly had been courting a mountain gal. At last her father spoke up: "You've been seeing Nellie for nigh onto a year. What are your intentions — honorable or dishonorable?"

The startled young blood replied: "You mean I got a choice?"

— Harry Hershfield

After a visit to the South, a Massachusetts man was pleased to get a letter from a courtly old planter he had met there. He momentarily ignored the typewritten enclosure, and turned to the letter proper. This began: "Out of courtesy to you, I write in my own hand, but to save your time and to spare you the annoyance of deciphering it, I also send a typewritten copy which I have had prepared for you."

— *The Christian Science Monitor*

A Southern beauty and her kind but ugly husband returned after several years to visit her home in Savannah. The children unfortunately "favored" their father. Aunt Chloe was exceedingly happy to have her darling home again, but she remarked to a confidante, "That Marse Edward, he's jess about ruined all Miss Sally's babies!"

— F. C. Smith

An ancient gentlewoman in Albemarle County, Va., frequently complains about the suffering and damage caused by the war. (Of course she is referring not to the last conflict but to "The War between the States.")

"We're still paying for that dreadful war," she exclaimed recently.

"But what made you think of that today?" she was asked.

"I'll tell you what made me think of it," she replied with spirit. "When those damyankees came through here they broke the hinges off our cellar door, and today the hogs got into the cellar and ate up all my butter."

— Agnes Rothery

Three newly inducted soldiers from the Ozarks approached the Information Desk at a St. Louis YMCA and asked what the "Y" offered. They were told they could write letters, read magazines, visit the game rooms. They didn't show much interest until they were told, "There's swimming also in the basement."

Then the trio moved a few feet away, engaged in animated argument. Finally one returned to the desk. "Did you say," he inquired earnestly, "that there wuz wimmen in the basement?"

— W. A. Chamberlin

A State Selective Service Headquarters in the South was being inspected by a brassy young officer from Washington. Noting that the number of typewriters and desks far exceeded the number of typists, he asked one of the girls, "What is the normal complement of this office?"

"Well, suh," she replied, "Ah reckon the most usual compliment is, 'Howdy, honey chile, you're sure luscious-lookin' this mawnin'.'"

— Lt. Col. H. P. Agnew

The Perfect Squelch

A retired Navy captain on the administrative staff of a southern university still clung to his rank. And when a young veteran named Brown said to him, "I'd like to talk with you about entering the university, Mr. Smith," he was enraged at being addressed "Mr."

"*Captain* Smith to you, young man!" he stormed.

Looking him straight in the eye, and standing at attention, the young veteran snapped back, "And in that event, *Colonel* Brown to you, sir!"

— Thelma Ann Reynold

One of the few instances in which George Bernard Shaw was "hoist by his own petard" came when he appealed to Mrs. Shaw for support of his contention that male judgment was superior to female judgment. "Of course, dear," Mrs. Shaw replied. "After all, you married me and I you."

— Herbert Adler

Many irate citizens are complaining to the Better Business Bureaus about having merchandise mailed to them that they have not ordered and do not want — and then being billed for it. Not long ago a Chicago physician received such a package with the following letter: "We are taking the liberty of sending you three exceptionally fine ties. Because these ties have the approval of thousands of discriminating dressers, we know you will like them. Please send $2."

The indignant doctor replied: "I am taking the liberty of sending you $2 worth of extra fine pills. These pills have helped thousands and I am sure you will appreciate my thoughtfulness in sending them. Please accept them in payment of the ties which you sent me recently."

— *The Report of the Chicago Better Business Bureau*

Sir C. Aubrey Smith, grand old gentleman of stage and screen, liked to dine quietly. Consequently he was rather put out when, in a Hollywood restaurant, he happened to be seated near a noisy diner who kept yelling for the waiter. "What do you have to do," demanded the pest finally, "to get a glass of water in this dump?"

The sedate, polished Sir Aubrey turned to the noisy one and quietly said: "Why don't you try setting yourself on fire?"

— Joe Laurie, Jr., Press Features

Dr. Alfred Adler, the psychiatrist, was lecturing on the theory that people with handicaps often specialize on their handicapped functions. Thus, short-winded boys tend to train themselves into being distance runners, people with weak eyes tend to become painters, and so forth. Adler finished his exposition and asked for questions.

Immediately this one was pitched at him from the back of the auditorium: "Dr. Adler, wouldn't your theory mean that weak-minded people tend to become psychiatrists?"

— J. C. Furnas in *The Saturday Evening Post*

Turning to the best player of the bridge foursome, the novice asked, "How would you have played that last hand of mine?"

"Under an assumed name," was the prompt answer.

— *Hawaii Farm and Home*

Bill Greenfield, famous fictioneer of the Adirondack lumber camps, was telling how he had been hunting in a forest so thick that he had had to pass sideways among the trees, when all at once he saw a buck, full-antlered, running through the wood. . . .

"Hold on, Bill!" said one of the listeners. "How could that buck run through the forest that way if you had to turn sideways to get through?"

Bill stared contemptuously, "Why, the buck had to pull in his horns — the way some of you have to do sometimes."

— Harold W. Thompson, *Body, Boots & Britches* (Lippincott)

At a dinner party several doting mothers were discussing their children's illnesses with the guest of honor, a noted pediatrician. One mother asked, "Doctor, what do you find to be the principal ailment of children?"

The doctor considered the question, then answered gravely, "Mothers, madam."

— Jay J. Dugan

Mother's Day

Not long ago a Princeton student was very short of cash. Since it was only the third of the month, he didn't dare ask his parents for money. The only solution was to sell something. So the next issue of the *Princetonian* carried the following ad: "For sale: One good-looking sport coat. $25. Size 41. A superior coat, and I need money. Apply 312 Walker Hall."

Two days later a special delivery letter arrived from New York, containing the advertisement, a check for $25 and the terse comment: "I'll buy the dern coat. Love, Mother."   — Charles T. Coyle

On a jammed Boston streetcar, a man stood beside a woman having difficulty keeping her balance in the swaying crowd. Before them sat a husky youth of 14 or 15, oblivious to her plight. Eyeing him with mounting indignation, the man finally said, "I'll give you a quarter for that seat." When the boy promptly accepted the coin, the man indicated that the woman was to take the seat.

"Oh, no," was her startled reply, "you take it."

"Madam, I don't want to sit down. I merely wish to give this boy a lesson in manners."

The woman sat down gingerly, casting a troubled look at the boy and her benefactor. Then she beamed and settled back contentedly, saying, "Benny, thank the gentleman for his quarter."

"I already did, Ma," came the reply.   — Thomas C. Higgins

"Where's Henry?" asked a neighbor boy.

"I'm not sure," replied Henry's mother. "If the ice is as thick as he thinks it is, he's skating. If it's as thin as I think it is, he's swimming."
— Mrs. Fiske in *Woman's World*

Little Claude's mother had reluctantly allowed her precious child to attend public school. She gave the teacher a long list of instructions. "My Claude is so sensitive," she explained. "Don't ever punish him. Just slap the boy next to him. That will frighten Claude."
— Philadelphia *Bulletin*

A young couple sent a friend of theirs — an Australian woman living in this country — a playpen upon the arrival of her fourth child. When her thank-you note arrived, it left them somewhat astonished. "The pen is a perfect godsend," she wrote. "I sit in it every afternoon and

read — and the children can't get near me." — Rosamond Lee in *Baby Talk*

My son, who works an early morning shift at a commercial air line, always leaves before the rest of the household arises. Recently, on the occasion of his 24th birthday, his mother found the following note on her breakfast plate:

"Dear Mom: Twenty-four years ago I had lunch on you. Will you meet me downtown this noon and permit me to return the compliment? Love, Jack." — J. E. Ercanbrack

A friend of mine with three children in college was badly upset when her physician told her she was going to have another child. "I simply can't go through it again, Doctor!" she wailed.

"Did you have complications with your other pregnancies?" he asked sympathetically.

"Heavens, no! Having babies never bothered me a bit, physically. It's the PTA that gets me down!" — Marie Hamel

My wife called on a Blue Ridge Mountain woman who was the mother of nine children and was expecting the tenth within a few days. "I sure am tired of having babies," the woman complained.

"Then why don't you stop?" asked my wife.

"Only way I know of to keep the youngest from being spoiled," explained the woman. — Keith H. Palmer

At the Metropolitan Museum of Art in New York, a little girl, who was buying one of the ten-cent prints of famous paintings for her mother, could not find one that suited her.

"Would your mother like the yellow sunflowers?" asked the attendant.

"No."

"Would she like the blue sea? The pretty children?"

"No."

"Well, what does your mother like?" the attendant demanded.

"Men," said the little girl.   — *Time*

When Mary Roberts Rinehart, the well-known novelist, was covering World War I battle zones as a correspondent, her son Stanley was stranded behind the lines as an officer in the Services of Supply. He asked repeatedly for permission to visit the front, but was put off every time. What finally jolted his superiors into action was the reason the young officer assigned in asking for a short leave. "To go to the front," he wrote, "to visit my mother."   — *The Saturday Evening Post*

Readin' & Writin'

Some years ago, Mary Roberts Rinehart was walking with her granddaughter in the park. The little girl was extremely attractive and many passers-by paused to admire her. "And what is your name, darling?" one fluttery lady inquired.

The child, named after her grandmother, lisped, "My name is Mary Roberts Rinehart."

"Goodness me!" exclaimed the astonished questioner. "You don't say so! Why, I read a book of yours just the other day."

                              — *The Christian Science Monitor*

When Stephen Leacock was asked by ambitious would-be authors to impart his magic formula for writing success, he would reply, "It is not hard to write funny stuff. All you have to do is to procure a pen and paper, and some ink, and then sit down and write it as it occurs to you."

"Yes, yes," the would-be writer would prompt.

"The writing is not hard," Leacock would conclude, "but the occurring — that, my friend, is the difficulty."   — *The Wall Street Journal*

A famous author was autographing copies of his new novel in a Cleveland department store. One gentleman pleased him by bringing up not only his new book for signature, but reprint editions of his two previous ones as well.

"My wife likes your stuff," he remarked rather apologetically, "so I thought I'd give her these signed copies for a birthday present." "A surprise, eh?" hazarded the author. "I'll say," agreed the customer. "She's expecting a Cadillac."
          — Bennett Cerf, *Anything for a Laugh* (Grosset & Dunlap)

Two Chicago matrons stopped to look at a bookstore display. "There's a book on *How to Torture Your Husband*," said one.

"I don't need that," the other replied. "I have a system of my own."
          — Marcia Winn in Chicago *Tribune*

A few summers ago I visited Hannibal, Mo., the sleepy little river town where Mark Twain spent his boyhood. Stopping at a roadside stand one day, I asked the white-bearded old proprietor if he had known Mark Twain. The reply was prompt, long-suffering and a little indignant.

"Sure I did," he replied. "And I know just as many stories as he did, too. Only difference is, he writ 'em down."   — R. D. Campbell, Jr.

At an author's tea: "You write? What a coincidence! I read!"
          — Dan Koerner cartoon in New York *Times Book Review*

Bookstore clerk to couple: "Here's a practical book on child training written by an authority — a sitter."
          — Cartoon in New Orleans *Times-Picayune*

George Bernard Shaw was poring over a secondhand bookstall of volumes much marked down, when he came across a volume containing his own plays. The book was inscribed, moreover, to a friend, beneath whose name on the flyleaf G. B. S. saw, written in his own hand, "With the compliments of George Bernard Shaw." Buying the book, Mr. Shaw wrote under the inscription, "With renewed compliments. G. B. S.," and sent it back to the early recipient.

A short-story manuscript submitted to Whit Burnett at *Story Magazine* was a startling mélange of Hemingway, Dos Passos, Faulkner, Cain and Saroyan. "Tell me," asked Burnett in his letter of rejection, "was your father an anthology?"

— Bennett Cerf in *The Saturday Review of Literature*

Hollywood Round-Up

Told that a famous mind reader was planning to locate in Hollywood, Monty Woolley snapped: "It is my prediction that he will starve to death."

— Charles B. Rothman

The daughter of a wealthy producer was asked at school to write a story about a poor family. Her essay began: "Once upon a time there was a poor family. The mother was poor. The daddy was poor. The children were poor. The butler was poor. The chauffeur was poor. The maid was poor. The gardener was poor. Everybody was poor."

— Carleton Young, quoted by Erskine Johnson, NEA

Ruth Hussey tells about the actress who phoned a friend and wept: "I just heard my husband wants a divorce." "So what?" asked her unsympathetic pal. "Well," said the actress, "my psychiatrist is out of town and I just don't know what to *think!*"   — Erskine Johnson, NEA

A Hollywood producer's wife wanted her portrait painted by a local artist. "Nonsense," declared the producer when she told him about it. "I am sending you to Europe to have you painted by one of the old masters."

— Andrew B. Hecht

One of the godfathers at a Hollywood christening party became nervous just before the ceremony began. "What if they give me the baby to hold?" he asked.

"Don't worry," Walter Pidgeon told him soothingly. "Same grip as a cocktail shaker."   — Mona Gardner

A naïve young actress was being rushed by a not-so-young male star. "Don't you understand?" he urged. "I want to marry you. I want you to be the mother of my children."

"But how many do you have?" she asked.   — Andrew B. Hecht

When Gary Cooper completed *The Adventures of Marco Polo*, Hunt Stromberg, the producer, exercised his option on Cooper's services. Sam Goldwyn phoned Stromberg and said: "I don't mind your taking Cooper, but you could have been nicer about the way you did it. Now why didn't you call me up and say, 'Sam, I need Cooper right away, if it doesn't interfere with your plans.' Then I'd have said 'No.' "
— Leonard Lyons

Gene Fowler tells a story about a Hollywood mogul who met a young eyeful on Wilshire Boulevard and gushed, "Golly, it's good to see you again. It so happens there's going to be a marvelous party tonight, and I want you to come to it. I won't take no for an answer." "Where's it to be?" asked the girl. "At my house, darling. And I think it will be an all-time high for fun. Lots of liquor and music, and nobody knows when it ever will break up." "Who's going to be there?" asked the girl eagerly. "Oh," replied the prospective host, "just you and me."   — Bennett Cerf

When press agent Art Franklin got back from vacation one of his aides asked for a week off. "I was away for two weeks," Art stormed. "That was your vacation!"   — Earl Wilson, Post-Hall Syndicate

A few years ago a $1000-a-week Hollywood writer got in trouble with the front office. His contract had six months to go, but the bosses decided to get even by making him work out his contract as a messenger boy. One day the $1000-a-week messenger boy was asked to take some visitors — stockholders in the studio — on a tour of the lot. He gave them a very fine tour and when it was over one of them offered him a ten dollar tip.

This was the moment the writer had been waiting for. "Thanks very much," he said sweetly, "but I'm very well paid as a messenger boy. Look — here's one of my checks — $1000 a week."

There was hell to pay in the front office.   — Erskine Johnson, NEA

Sign Language

Sign in a Cleveland bookshop: "Curdle Up with a Good Murder Mystery."

Warning at a New Jersey intersection: "Cross Road — Better Humor It."   — *The American Magazine*

Sign in a New York night club: "Not responsible for dates left over ten minutes."

Sign in maternity department of a St. Louis hospital: "Ladies Ready to Bear Department."

Pawnbroker's sign: "See me at your earliest inconvenience."

Hotels in Rochester, Minn., home of the Mayo Clinic, have signs reading: "Please do not discuss your operation in the lobby."
— Danton Walker in
New York *Daily News*

A Philadelphia nut shop boasts: "If our peanuts were any fresher, they'd be insulting."
— A. J. Zimmerman

Sign in a Navy yard shop: "To Women War Workers: If your coveralls are too big, beware of the machines; if too tight, beware of the machinists."   — *Ship's Log*

Sign in the window of a second-hand bookshop in California: "We Buy Old Furniture and Books. We Sell Rare Antiques."
— Bennett Cerf in *The Saturday Review of Literature*

A sign on a New York bank building would have startled our grandfathers, but goes unnoticed in this age of taxes. Exhorting the citizenry to save, it ends up: "Remember, *part* of all you earn belongs to you."   — *This Week Magazine*

Sign on Los Angeles dance hall: "Good Clean Dancing Every Night But Sunday."

On a movie theater: "Children's Matinee Today. Adults Not Admitted Unless With Child."
— Hugh Dixon in Pittsburgh
Post-Gazette

Street Scenes

During a Shriners' convention in Los Angeles one of the downtown boulevards was roped off for a parade. Only official cars with large signs such as *Potentate* and *Past Potentate* were allowed there; all other traffic was halted or rerouted. But one ingenious Californian got by the police blockade and drove nonchalantly down the street. His placard read: *Past Participle*. — Milford P. Johnson

As I stepped aboard a bus in New York City I felt the back garter supporting one of my stockings snap. I didn't worry because I had faith in the remaining one, but when I left the bus the front one gave too, and my stocking slithered to my ankle.

Nearby a very correct chauffeur stood by a custom-made town car, talking to a doorman. Without a word he opened the rear door of the car, bowed me in with a courtly gesture and he and his friend discreetly turned their backs. When I had repaired the damage he received my thanks graciously and ushered me out ceremoniously. — Mrs. S. S. Brock

During San Antonio's Fiesta Week, when curbside vantage points for the parade are at a premium, a schoolteacher surrounded by some 20 small children marched down the main street and came to a halt beside a vacant parking space. Herding her charges into the small space, she made sure of their safety by passing a stout rope around the group, then dropped a nickel into the parking meter and settled back to wait. An irate policeman charged over and ordered them back to the sidewalk.

"Parking is allowed on this side of the street," the young teacher replied firmly. "The law doesn't say what *kind* of parking. I've paid my nickel and we're going to stay!"

The policeman walked off, grinning, amid shrill cheers from the Fifth Grade. — Helen L. Bond

Nothing annoyed one brisk and determined walker in our town more than the college girls' habit of linking themselves four or six abreast and strolling along the sidewalk. Finally he bought the loudest automobile horn he could find and kept it under his coat. Every time he found himself stymied by a chain gang, he'd walk quietly up behind them, let go a great blast and when the girls scattered, squealing, he'd march calmly ahead.   — Claire MacMurray, *Out on a Limbo* (Lippincott)

A vivacious brunette of about 40 was standing on the boardwalk at Virginia Beach when she heard an admiring whistle from a very young sailor. He ambled up purposefully with his cap pushed jauntily over one eye.

"Son," she reproved him gently, amused and flattered, "don't you flirt with me! I'm a grandmother."

"But, grandmother," replied the undismayed sailor, "what big eyes you have!"   — Mary Holt Woolfolk

An elderly, impeccably dressed gentleman was walking down Broadway when he noticed a spot on his tie. Without hesitation, he stepped to the nearest automobile, unscrewed the gas tank cap, dipped a handkerchief in, carefully rubbed out the spot, replaced the gas cap and proceeded on his way.   — Philip Cohen

The trolley on New York's 59th Street was blocked by an enormous truck parked diagonally at the curb, with the driver nowhere in sight. The conductor clanged his bell, cars choked the street behind, and the passengers began to worry about the delay.

"I'd like to show that driver a thing or two — leaving a truck practically in the middle of the street," said a fluffy little blonde in a fox jacket, a very tight skirt and extravagantly built-up platform shoes. "Conductor, let me out."

Carrying a handbag about the size of a sofa pillow, she marched to the truck and climbed in. Before he knew what was up, she was jockeying that ten-ton truck — the kind with five speeds forward — back and forth, edging closer and closer to the curb until she had it clear of the tracks. Everybody in sight cheered her as she came back to the trolley.

"Well, that's one thing I learned in the Navy," she said, tenderly patted her hair-do, and sat down. — Roma Rose

On a winter morning when the streets of New York were slick with ice, I saw a man sitting in the middle of the sidewalk. Thinking he must be hurt, I asked, "May I help you up?"

"No, thank you," he laughed. "I'm just sitting here to melt the ice on this particular spot." He moved aside for a moment. There under the ice was a five-dollar bill which he was hatching. — R. M. Geis

Thrift with a Capital T

At the grocery store I used to meet a quiet, middle-aged lady who was the thriftiest shopper I had ever seen, and one day I told her so. "I suppose it runs in the family," she said. "My grandmother brought me up on a farm in Vermont, and she would never cut the lettuce on a Sunday till she returned from church."

"Why?" I asked in surprise.

"Why? So the lettuce might grow a little more while Granny was at church!" — Charlotte Raman

A West Virginia man wrote the Rural Electrification Administration in Washington inquiring how to avoid burning his hands. Investigation revealed that although the man's home had been completely wired, he had only one light bulb, which he patiently screwed and unscrewed as he took it from room to room wherever it was needed.
— Neal O'Hara, McNaught Syndicate

Former Vice-President Garner had lost a ten-dollar bet on a Washington baseball game, and the winner asked him to autograph the bill. "I'm giving it to my grandson for a souvenir," he explained. "He wants to frame it and hang it in his room."

"You mean the money's not going to be spent?" asked the Texan.

"That's right."

"Well," said Garner, "then I'll just write you a check!"
— Milwaukee *Journal*

The daily patron of a Charleston, S. C., restaurant always has his coffee black. But he has an arrangement with the management whereby at the end of each month he gets a quart of cream free, to take home.
— Neal O'Hara, McNaught Syndicate

Wife modeling a new hat before husband: "It didn't cost a thing. It was marked down from $20 to $10, so I bought it with the $10 I saved!"   — Fritz Wilkinson cartoon in *The American Magazine*

Shortly before sailing to England some years ago, foreign correspondent Quentin Reynolds was received by President Roosevelt in his office at the White House. While he was there the President put through a transatlantic call to another eminent statesman, Winston Churchill. Mr. Reynolds was slightly startled when, after a conversation, the President said, "I'll have to hang up now. My three minutes are up!"   — *The Saturday Review of Literature*

Two Broadwayites started on a honeymoon trip to Hollywood six months after their marriage. "We've delayed," they explained, "because we wanted to see how the marriage worked out before spending the money."   — Earl Wilson, Post-Hall Syndicate

Merry Christmas!

The wife of a movie actor was telling Lucille Ball that she bought all her Christmas presents in October. "But how do you know in October," exclaimed Miss Ball, "who your friends are going to be in December?"   — Earl Wilson, Post-Hall Syndicate

During the last days of the Christmas rush in one of New York's largest department stores a frenzied clerk, overwhelmed by pushing women shoppers, was making out what she hoped would be the last sales check of the day. As the customer gave her name and address, the clerk, pushing her hair up from her damp forehead, remarked: "It's a madhouse, isn't it?"

"No," the customer replied pleasantly. "It's a private home."
— Nancy Fitzgerald Smith

Apparently even the often grim practice of dentistry is not above an occasional touch of whimsy. During the holiday season a friend had some dental work done. When it was all over the dentist picked up a different syringe from the one he had been using and gave his patient's mouth a good squirt with it. "That tastes very good," observed the patient. "What is it?"

"Oh," said the dentist casually, "that's rye whisky. I just use it at Christmas time." — *Montrealer*

One dreary December night a wet and bedraggled tramp appeared at the back door of a well-known restaurant in Springfield, Ohio. He blessed the occupants of the kitchen, wished them a Merry Christmas, and asked so appealingly for something to eat that they served him the chef's best. Finishing with relish, he thanked the waitress and praised the food. As he bowed his way out, she noticed a book sticking out of his ragged pocket. It was that national guide to fine restaurants, Duncan Hines' *Adventures in Good Eating*. — Ann Jones

We have traded with a mail-order house for years, and last Christmas had an unusually large order. Across the bottom of the order blank my wife wrote in her large, flowing handwriting, "Merry Christmas to all of you!"

Ten days later our packages arrived, mostly clothing for us and the five children. It was fun for the two of us, opening the packages after our family was asleep. But what really warmed our hearts was the notation at the very bottom of our returned order blank: "And a Merry Christmas to you, sizes 40, 38, 14, 12, 10, 8 and 6!" — A. J. Diener

My Christmas gifts included a sampler made by my little niece. She had patiently cross-stitched this misquotation: "Let me live in a house by the side of the road, and be friendly with men." — C. Lary

A Hastings, Neb., man sent his best girl this Christmas greeting: "You are a dear, sweet girl. May God bless you and keep you. I wish I could afford to" (AP) . . . Happy wife to husband on Christmas morning, "You angel! Just what I need to exchange for just what I wanted" (R. E. Dell cartoon in *True*)

During the Christmas rush in a large Philadelphia department store, I came on a booth arranged with special gift suggestions. One article fascinated me. It was an intricate little gadget, with no apparent use. I asked the salesgirl if she could tell me what it was for. She turned it this way and that, working each movable part. Then she looked up brightly and said, "I don't know, miss. I guess it's just a Christmas present."

— Catherine M. Norton

Feeling Game?

Highly Irregular

London's *New Statesman and Nation* conducts weekly "competitions" in epigrams, limericks, etc. In one contest readers were asked to play a game originated by Philosopher Bertrand Russell. On BBC's *Brains Trust* program he had humorously conjugated an "irregular verb" as "I am firm; you are obstinate; he is a pig-headed fool."

Among winners picked by the *New Statesman* were the following:

I am sparkling; you are unusually talkative; he is drunk.

I am righteously indignant; you are annoyed; he is making a fuss about nothing.

I am beautiful; you have quite good features; she isn't bad looking, if you like that type.

I have reconsidered it; you have changed your mind; he has gone back on his word.

I am an epicure; you are a gourmand; he has both feet in the trough.

I have the New Look; you have let down your hem; she has had that dress since 1934.

I am fastidious; you are fussy; he is an old woman.

I have about me something of the subtle, haunting, mysterious fragrance of the Orient; you rather overdo it, dear; she stinks.

— Adapted from *Time*

Try, Me.

Joseph Henry Jackson of San Francisco invented a new game — the idea is to think up fictitious place names that go with abbreviations of state names. For instance: Shapeless, Mass.; Ooola, La.; and Goodness,

Me. Pennsylvania offers a rich variety, ranging from Poison, Penn., to Grandpa, Pa. These days someone was bound to think of Income, Tex. Of those about Illinois, Mr. Jackson awarded first place to Deathly, Ill. He's fond of Hittor, Miss., and Praise, Ala. We like Proan, Conn.; Coco, Colo.; Either, Ore.; Rockand, R.I.; and Farmerina, Del.

These, however, go too far for us: Montmore, N. C.; Apples, Ida.; Squee, Mich. For the culture-minded, there is Paderoffs, Ky.; and Turge, Nev. And then there is always that model of simplicity: Bee, O.

— *The Pleasures of Publishing*

Sportin' Life

Sweeping up and down the gridiron all afternoon, a strong Ohio State team had completely overwhelmed the University of Virginia eleven. Both sides had sent in so many substitutes that the players weren't unusually worn out, but the referees were exhausted from racing after State's backs.

Late in the fourth quarter, with the score 68–0, one of the referees handed his whistle to a Virginia end and, gasping for breath, said, "Here, you referee for a while and let me play!" — A. Klinefelter

A complacent golfer teed his ball, looked away to the next green, and declared confidently, "That's good for one long drive and a putt." He swung the driver, tore up the sod, and managed to move the ball a few feet off the tee. Stepping forward, the caddy handed him the putter and suggested, "Now for a hell of a putt."

— Walter B. Cannon, M.D., *The Way of an Investigator* (Norton)

At a track in England some years ago, a mounted policeman was helping to get the race horses into starting position. At the cry, "They're off!" the policeman's horse broke with the field and the astonished bobby found himself desperately trying to pull in his mount. The best he could do, however, was to slow him down to third place. On the stretch, the horse began to fight it out with one of the official entries, and despite the policeman's efforts to pull out of the race, he came in second, a scant neck behind a horse ridden by Freddy Archer, one of England's greatest jockeys. — Dee Eckman in *Collier's*

One over-enthusiastic fisherman was haled into court, charged with catching 18 more black bass than the law allows. "Guilty or not guilty?" asked the judge.

"Guilty," the young man admitted.

"Ten dollars and costs," announced the judge.

The defendant paid the fine, then asked cheerfully, "And, now, Your Honor, may I have several typewritten copies of the court record made to take back and show my friends?" — *The Railroad Workers Journal*

An American League umpire named Jack Kerns had a phobia against calling games. No matter how dark it got, Kerns felt that a ball game was nine innings or more. One day in Washington's Griffith Stadium when Kerns refused to call a game, the pitcher in desperation huddled with his catcher and whispered, "Listen, you keep the ball in your mitt. I'll wind up and pretend to throw it. You pop it into your glove as though you'd caught it."

There were two strikes on the batter. The pitcher set himself and went through his motion: the catcher popped his mitt. "Strike three and out!" bellowed Kerns.

"Strike?" screamed the batter. "Why you blind so-and-so. That ball was two feet outside!" — Tom Van Dyke in *Salute*

Out duck hunting with a friend, Irvin Cobb was so anxious to shoot that he aimed his shotgun at the ducks the moment they settled on the water. "Irvin," protested his friend, "you mustn't shoot now. Wait until the ducks are on the rise, and give them a chance."

Cobb turned patiently toward the other hunter: "When I shoot, the ducks *always* have a chance." — John Newton Baker

After being badly outplayed during the first half of a football game, members of the team of Texas A. and M. College sat dejectedly around the locker rooms waiting for a tongue-lashing from their coach, Dana X. Bible. He entered on the signal for the second half, looked slowly around at each player, and turned to the door. Then he paused, looked back and said, "Well, girls, shall we go?" They won the game. — Stanley Gunn

In the early '30's, Louisiana State University had a six-foot-five heavyweight boxer named C. D. Blaylock, who had an extremely long reach. In one meet he was fighting a stocky opponent from Mississippi State. During the second round, Blaylock wound up with a round-house right that was labeled knockout if it landed. To avoid the blow, the Mississippi State heavy stepped in close, and his head hit Blaylock's right elbow. This acted as a lever and added power to the fist, which completely circled the shorter man's head, ending up on Blaylock's own jaw. Stunned by his own blow, the fighter grasped the rope and started groggily around the ring, then collapsed. He had knocked himself out. — G. A. Simes in *Collier's*

Frederick Stock, conductor of the Chicago Symphony Orchestra, was playing golf and not doing too well. In annoyance, he turned to his caddie and asked, "Can you tell me what's the matter?"

The caddie's diagnosis was immediate: "Mister, you ain't got rhythm!" — New York *Times*

Concert Pitch

The late Vladimir de Pachmann, most capricious of pianists, always fussed over his piano stool in full view of the audience. On one occasion, he fiddled and fumed and called for something to sit on. When a thick book was handed him, he tried it, shook his head. Then he carefully tore off a single page, tried it again, and smiled happily as he began his first number. — John Selby, quoted in *Cue*

In his early days as a concert pianist the thought of facing a huge audience often filled Vladimir Horowitz with a panicky horror akin to nausea. On one occasion he was in the wings about to go onstage when he was seized with the familiar malaise. "I'm ill," he told the manager. "I cannot play tonight."

"Well, if you can't, you can't," replied the irritated manager. "But for goodness' sake go out and excuse yourself to the audience."

Horowitz faltered to the center of the stage, gazed at the sea of faces, then — more panic-stricken at the thought of speaking than of playing — lunged gratefully at the piano and played as well as he had ever played in his life. — Howard Taubman in New York *Times Magazine*

Walking with a friend one day, Fritz Kreisler passed a large fish shop where a fine catch of codfish, with mouths open and eyes staring, were arranged in a row. Kreisler suddenly stopped, looked at them, and clutching his friend by the arm, exclaimed:

"Heavens! That reminds me — I should be playing at a concert!"
— Bernard Shore, *The Orchestra Speaks* (Longmans, Green)

At the first performance of George Antheil's ultra-modernistic *Ballet Mécanique*, the orchestra contained ten grand pianos, six xylophones, a fire-alarm siren, an airplane propeller, and several automobile horns. As the music mounted in volume, the audience became fidgety and continued to grow more restless and excitable. Finally, after eight minutes of the composition, a man in one of the front rows raised a white handkerchief tied to his cane, and the entire audience burst into laughter.
— Deems Taylor, quoted by Irving Hoffman in *The Hollywood Reporter*

The night Jascha Heifetz and his violin made a triumphant New York debut, the pianist Josef Hofmann and the violinist Mischa Elman were in the spellbound audience. As the music went on, Elman became increasingly fidgety, running his finger inside his collar and mopping his forehead. In the pause between two selections, he whispered to Hofmann, "Awfully hot in here, isn't it?" Hofmann whispered back, "Not for pianists."

— Edmund Fuller, *Thesaurus of Anecdotes* (Crown)

We were giving a concert in a hotel. After the last strains of Handel's *Largo* floated out, a fat, motherly woman near me leaned over and asked, "Won't you please play Handel's *Largo?*"

"But we've just finished playing it," I said.

The fat lady sank back in her chair. "Oh, I wish I'd known it," she sighed. "It's my *favorite* piece."

— Mary Browne

Punch Lines

Few of us can stand prosperity. Another man's, I mean.

— Mark Twain

Society would be delightful were all women married and all men single.

— Edgar Saltus, *The Pomps of Satan* (Coward-McCann)

Conscience: Something that feels terrible when everything else feels swell.

The worst thing about history is that every time it repeats itself the price goes up.

— *Pillar*

In three days guests, like fish, begin to stink.

— Benjamin Franklin

It costs something to reach for the check and pay it, but it gets you home at a reasonable hour.

— William Feather

The chain of wedlock is so heavy that it takes two to carry it — sometimes three.

— Dumas

A word of advice: don't give it.

— A. J. Volicos in *Flight Log*

A pink tea: Giggle — Gabble — Gobble — Git.

— Oliver Wendell Holmes

Women's styles may change, but their designs remain the same.

— Oscar Wilde

Modesty has ruined more kidneys than bad liquor.

— Dr. S. Morris

If you want a thing well done, don't do it yourself unless you know how.

— *Cutting Remarks*

"Make love to every woman you meet," my uncle advised me. "If you get five percent on your outlay, it's a good investment."

— Arnold Bennett

Millions long for immortality who do not know what to do with themselves on a rainy Sunday afternoon.

— Susan Ertz, *Anger in the Sky* (Harper)

I Hate Cocktail Parties!

Condensed from Liberty

Paul Gallico

I hate cocktail parties. To be invited to one is an insult; to be present is a bore. I must have attended more than a hundred in my lifetime and cannot remember once having had a good time.

Let it be made clear at the outset that I am not against the gathering of a few friends for drinks before dinner. I am referring only to that planned and staged shindy involving from 50 to 100 human beings crammed into a smoke-filled enclosure meant to hold 20, at which refreshments are limited to cocktails and trays of utterly revolting assortments of swill which pass under the name of canapés.

The reason for such a party is usually this: Somebody's little lady gets that look in her eyes and says, "Dear, there are so many people we ought to entertain. But most of them are such bores. Oh, I know what we'll do! We'll give a cocktail party and get rid of them *all* that way!"

When you arrive at the party, nobody pays the slightest attention to you. The hostess gives you a limp hand and a glassy look, as if trying to remember where she had encountered you before, murmurs, "So glad you could come. Have you met Mrs. Umph?" and abandons you.

While you flounder around thinking of something to say, you are faced with the party's real menace — not the cocktail but the canapé. Nobody ever got into greater difficulties from imbibing Martinis or Old-Fashioneds than to punch his best friend in the nose or attempt to go up the Empire State Building on the outside, whereas the wear and tear on the digestive system caused by those nasty little concoctions is simply incalculable.

There seem to be but three major foundations for the various smears, pastes or mucks that appear on toast, crackers or small slivers of disconsolate bread — these being cold cream, glue and hand lotion. These are used either singly or in combination, or laced with bird seed, cadmium green, rose madder, sawdust or lawn grass.

I have been exposed to the weary bit of salmon turned from pink to deep rouge with fatigue; the disillusioned sardel that has curled itself around its only friend, a lonely caper, and retired from the world; the antique graying slice of hard-boiled egg used as a display platform for three unhappy fish eggs masquerading as caviar. All of these more or less revolting items are bedded upon a type of cracker

(Liberty, June 22, '46)

which disintegrates at the first bite and scatters the remainder over your lap.

You can avoid the cracker altogether by confining yourself to the Thing on the End of a Toothpick. This varies from a small sausage gone cold and introspective to a large olive stuffed with melted cheese, peanut butter, petroleum jelly, ski wax or anything else that happens to be lying around the house, and presented in an overcoat of limp and greasy bacon. The more outrageous the things that are impaled on the end of the toothpick, the greater the kudos that falls to the hostess, and the sicker you will be the next day.

As a social function the cocktail party completely fails of its purpose, which is to promote good feeling and exchange of ideas and telephone numbers, or to enable one to meet new people and decide whether one would care to expand this meeting into an interesting friendship. For the first thing that happens is that the people who know each other immediately gravitate toward one another in self-defense and form tight, impenetrable little corporations which present nothing but hostile backs to the outside world.

If there is a main celebrity for whom the jamboree has been cooked up, the hostess will eventually pilot you to him and permit you to enjoy a squeeze of a cold and disinterested flipper and absorb a glare from him. If by some miracle a spark of interest develops and you embark upon conversation that might eventually lead to something of mutual advantage, down sweeps the wary hostess — "You wicked boy (girl)! I can't let you monopolize Mr. Big Shot. There are ever so many people simply dying to meet him. Now come along. I want to introduce you to Mrs. Oldstuff." She then deftly inserts a hip between you and the celebrity and before you know it you are stuck with some ancient battleaxe wearing a Queen Mary hat.

The only refuge at the cocktail party is liquor, as indicated by the bitter remark overheard at one recently when the Martinis were passed for the third time and a slightly fuzzy gentleman remarked, "Yes, thank you, I'll have another — I can still hear what people are saying. . . ."

Picnic

Upon this theme
I'll briefly touch:
Too far
To go
To eat
Too much.

— A. A. Lattimer in *Liberty*

Ego-Twists

A few seasons ago Notre Dame's star center, Frankie Szymanski, appeared in a South Bend court as a witness in a civil suit. "Are you on the Notre Dame football team this year?" queried the judge.

"Yes, your honor."

"What position?"

"Center, your honor."

"How good a center?"

Szymanski squirmed in his chair, but in confident tones admitted, "Sir, I'm the best center Notre Dame ever had."

Coach Frank Leahy, who was in the courtroom, was surprised because the lad had always been modest and unassuming. When proceedings were adjourned, the coach asked him why he had made such a statement. Szymanski blushed. "I hated to do it coach," he explained, "but after all, I was under oath."

— Des Moines *Register*

Bernard Shaw once remarked: "I often quote myself. It adds spice to my conversation."

On a CBS broadcast Hildegarde told Henry Daniell, "You were superb in *Lady Windermere's Fan*," and Mr. Daniell answered, "Oh, Hildegarde, I bet you tell that to everyone who's superb!"

Movie actress: "Now let's talk about you. What did *you* think of my picture?"

Orson Welles was browsing in a Beverly Hills bookstore when a clerk suggested Salvador Dali's autobiography. Orson angrily rejected the suggestion, indulging in flowing rhetoric for a sulphuric five minutes.

"But if you haven't read the book, why are you so vehement?" the clerk persisted.

In tones that attracted everyone's attention, Orson replied, "If there is one thing I loathe, it's an exhibitionist."

— Marshall Kester, quoted by
Erskine Johnson, NEA

I once asked Mrs. James Roosevelt, the president's mother, "What was Franklin like when he was a small boy?"

"Full of ideas," she replied. "He was always making boats or building

orts or collecting stamps or stuffing
irds or something. Once I told him
ot to order the other boys around
o much. 'But,' he protested, 'noth-
ng would get done if I didn't give
rders!' "　　— M. H. Halton in
　　　　　Toronto *Star Weekly*

A certain Welshman, the proud
ossessor of a very fine bass voice,
onfided one day to a friend that he
ad had a remarkable dream. "I was
n a mighty choir: 5000 sopranos,
000 altos, 5000 tenors — all singing
t once, double forte. Oh, magnifi-
ent! But suddenly," continued the
inger, "the conductor stopped the
ot, and turning to me said, 'Not
uite so loud in the bass, Mr.
ones.' "　　— *The Wall Street Journal*

Oscar Levant, after listening to
he late George Gershwin's mono-
ogue about himself, inquired:
'George, if you had it to do over,
would you fall in love with yourself
gain?" — Oscar Levant, *A Smattering of
Ignorance* (Doubleday)

Two actors were discussing a cer-
ain conceited Hollywood execu-
ive. One actor said to another,
"I hear that he's changing his faith."
"You mean," asked the other,
"he no longer believes he's God?"
　　　　　— Walter Winchell

The six-year-old son of a well-
known insurance man has inherited
his father's self-confidence and gift
of gab. One evening the father came
home to find sonny with a ball and
bat. "Hi, Dad!" shouted sonny.
"Watch me! I'm hitting 'em a
mile!"

The boy tossed the ball up, took
a swing and missed. "Strike one!"
he shouted gleefully. "But watch
this one, Dad. Boy, oh, boy, am I
going to knock the cover off this
one!"

Again he tossed the ball in the
air, took a poke at it, missed.
"Strrrike two!" he intoned. "Whata
you know! Well, it only takes one to
hit it. Am I going to clout this one!"

Carefully he took his stance, carefully he tossed his ball, mightily he
swung his bat — and missed.

"Strrrike three!" he announced.
"And out." Then, exultantly, "Gee,
Dad, am I a pitcher!"
　　　　　— Claire MacMurray in
　　　　　Cleveland *Plain Dealer*

Whee! The People

A young woman walked into a Pittsburgh police station and gave
the desk sergeant a detailed description of a man who had dragged her
by the hair down three flights of stairs, threatened to choke her to
death and finally beat her up.

"With that description, we'll have him arrested and put in jail in
practically no time," said the desk sergeant.

"But I don't want him arrested," the young woman protested. "Just find him for me. He promised to marry me."

— E. V. Durling, King Features

"Well, Uncle Joe," the real estate man said to an old Negro who had just paid the last installment on a small farm. "I'll make you a deed to the farm now it's been paid for."

"Boss," the Negro replied, "If it's all de same to you, I wish you'd give me a mo'gage to de place."

The surprised real estate man protested that Uncle Joe didn't seem to know the difference between a deed and a mortgage.

"Well, mebbe not," said the Negro. "But I owned a fahm once an' I had a deed an' de Fust National Bank had a mo'gage, an' de bank got de fahm!"

— *Banking*

In Washington they tell the story of the Government official who asked his secretary to look through the haphazard filing system in his office for some details on a case. "The name is Sawyer," he said.

The girl looked but told him she couldn't find the name. "Well," shouted the exasperated official, "what *do* you have filed under S?"

"Only the sandwich I'm having for lunch," she said.

— Washington *Star*

A distinguished gentleman came to Abercrombie and Fitch's in New York and asked to see shotguns. The clerk, sizing him up as a man of means, showed him a fine English model priced at $450. "That is a splendid gun," the gentleman said, "but a little expensive."

The clerk brought out a Belgian model priced at $275. "Still a little too expensive," observed the gentleman.

A bit discouraged, the clerk said: "Well, here is a Winchester mass production stock model at $17.50."

With that the gentleman brightened. "That will do nicely. After all, it's only a small wedding."

— Jennie Justin

The young volunteer receptionist at the Charlotte, N. C., Memorial Hospital had noticed an old gentleman who had been sitting in the lobby for about an hour. Finally he came over to her desk and asked whether Mr. C. E. Jones could receive visitors. The young lady consulted her card index and said, "No."

"How is Mr. Jones getting on?" asked the old gentleman, and was told that the patient's card showed he was progressing very nicely.

"I'm glad to know that," said the gentleman. "I've been up in that room ten days and couldn't find out a darn thing from the doctor. So I dressed and came down here to find out. I'm C. E. Jones."

— Harvey Wilson Moore

A mink coat, draped over the back of a chair in a New York night club, bore a huge inscription on the label: "Paid for by myself."

— Walter Winchell

Byfield Byplay

Ernie Byfield, whose Pump Room is a popular gathering place for celebrities in Chicago, was asked how he happened to go into the hotel business. "It was one of those quirks of fate," answered Byfield. "My father owned the Hotel Sherman. He bumped into me in the lobby one morning — and took a liking to me!"

— Bennett Cerf in *The Saturday Review of Literature*

Admiral Byrd was once Byfield's guest in the Pump Room. When the Admiral rose to dance with Mrs. Byfield, the host brought down the house warning him loudly, "Remember now, Admiral: no exploring!"

— Bennett Cerf, *Shake Well Before Using* (Simon & Schuster)

One of his customers once asked Byfield what made caviar so expensive. "Well, after all," said the host, "it's a year's work for a sturgeon."

— *Table Topics*

Shortly after Ernie Byfield's recent marriage, he asked his bride to pick her own place for the honeymoon. "Anywhere," he said. "Mexico, Paris, California, Hawaii — you name it."

The brand-new Mrs. Byfield purred gently: "Thank you dear. If it's all right with you — may I spend our honeymoon in Hattie Carnegie's?"

— Louis Sobol, King Features

Bride Ideas

In the Syracuse University paper an ad appeared offering the services of a group of fraternity boys as baby sitters. Shortly after, three of the boys were requested to come to a certain address — which they were amazed to find was a sorority house. But finally, they rang the bell and were assured this was the place. In the parlor three undated "babes" sedately awaited their tenders.

P. S. One of the couples was recently married. — Elizabeth J. Barick

She stood at the counter, an obviously new bride, while a clerk explained various household gadgets to her. He waxed enthusiastic about an electrically timed egg cooker, explaining that her husband's boiled eggs would be just right when timed by it.

"But I wouldn't need that," she said. "John likes his eggs the way I do them. I just look out the window at the traffic light, give them one red and two greens, and they're done." — John Powell

English society was agog when a duke married a blonde from the Music Hall chorus. It was even more agog when a Bond street art gallery exhibited a life-sized portrait of her in the altogether. The duke was furious. "I don't know what's biting you," said the wife. "Believe me, there's nothing wrong. He did it from memory."

— Bennett Cerf, *Laughing Stock* (Grosset & Dunlap)

One morning, a young man honeymooning in New York had a Wall Street appointment, and his pretty bride inspected him, admonishing, "Darling, you'd better get a shoeshine. I want you to look your best." A little later the bride boarded a Fifth Avenue bus to go shopping. Love and husband still very much in her mind, she happened to notice the shoes of the stranger sitting beside her which also needed shining. "Dearest," she said, tapping his knee, "you didn't get your shoes shined." She got off at the next corner. — *Rockefeller Center Magazine*

When my sister, a decided redhead — decided about everything — married a tall and taciturn ensign, everyone said he would soon be the world's most henpecked husband. Instead, she behaved from the start like a child the week before Christmas. I asked how it happened.

My sister blushed. "The first thing I saw after he carried me across the threshold was a pair of his trousers thrown over a chair. I started to put them away, but he stopped me. 'Put them on,' he said.

" 'But, darling, what for?' I protested. He just smiled. So, to find out what he had in mind, I put them on. They were about six sizes too big. 'Do they fit?' he asked. 'Oh, sweetheart, you know they don't,' I answered. He pulled me to his knees and said, his face perfectly dead-pan, 'Then never forget who wears the pants in this family!' "

— L. H. Bell

Just ahead of us in the supermarket an obviously new bride was confiding to an older friend the likes and dislikes of her wonderful Bill. Pausing before the shelves of canned fish, the bride picked up a can of tuna and gazed at it thoughtfully.

"You bought tuna yesterday," her companion remarked.

"I know," said the bride. "I've been giving him tuna every night for a week. And he *still* wants to go fishing!"

— Zephyr Shelton

Comic Relief

Walter Pidgeon's Aunt Nan — an old lady who lives in Canada — is one woman who is not impressed by the actor's charms. She always wanted Walter to become a lawyer, or at least something more respectable than an actor. So when she read in the papers that he had been ranked second to President Conant of Harvard among "The Ten Best-Dressed Men in America," she wrote:

"Dear Nephew: I am glad to see you finally associated with an intellectual. Kindly thank your tailor for me."

— This Week Magazine

A salesman rapped on the screen door at a house where, just inside and plainly visible, an eight-year-old was painfully practicing his piano lesson. "Sonny," he inquired pleasantly, "is your mother home?"

The boy gave the salesman a murderous look over his shoulder, then growled, "What do *you* think, mister?"

— Railroad Workers Journal

The father's tone of voice was severe. "Young man," he said, "do you think you should be taking my daughter to night clubs all the time?"

"Indeed not!" the boy answered, then added hopefully, "Let's try to reason with her."   — *The Lighthouse*

"Can you read the third line?" an oculist asked his patient.

"Sure," answered the man. "CWDK. I'm no good at pronouncing it, but I think he was left tackle at Notre Dame last year."

The meek little man approached a policeman on the street corner.

"Excuse me, officer," he said, "but I've been waiting here for my wife for over an hour. Would you be kind enough to order me to move on?"   — Jack Seaman

An architect was having a difficult time with a prospective home builder. "But can't you give *some* idea," he pleaded, "of the general type of house you want to build?"

"Well —" replied the man hesitantly, "all I know is it must go with an antique doorknob my wife bought in Vermont."

        — *Young America*

"And see this bear on the floor," said the garrulous explorer. "I shot it in Alaska. It was a case of me or him."

"Well," yawned the weary listener, "the bear certainly makes a better rug."   — *The Wingfoot Clan*

A man was consulting a psychiatrist. Among other questions, the doctor asked: "Are you troubled by improper thoughts?"

"Why, no," answered the patient. "To tell the truth, doctor, I rather enjoy them!"   — *Super Service Station*

At the time of the atomic bomb test in New Mexico, an Indian was smoke-signaling a love message to his girl friend. Suddenly a mushroom cloud covered the sky with smoke. The Indian stared in amazement, then muttered enviously, "Gee, I wish I'd said that."

        — John Garfield, quoted by Earl Wilson, Post-Hall Syndicate

A Century of Limericks

Condensed from The New York Times Magazine

H. I. Brock

Nineteen-Forty-Six was the centennial year of Edward Lear's *The Book of Nonsense*, which launched a literary diversion in England that continues to engage some of our best authors and countless wits of all nations. Lear was an artist and naturalist. His first published book was devoted to parrots, and bore the learned title, *The Family of the Psittacidae.*

Nobody seems to know for sure when or how the limerick got its name. Attempts to associate it with the Irish county of Limerick have lacked factual substance and got nowhere. In any case it was certainly Edward Lear who gave the skittish form its vogue.

Many popular limericks are by the acknowledged masters; but most of them go the rounds anonymously because even the authors have forgotten who wrote them.

Love

There was a young Lady of Lynn
Who was deep in original sin.
    When they said, "Do be good!"
    She said, "Would if I could."
And straightway went at it again.

There was a young fellow of Lyme
Who lived with three wives at a time.
    When they asked: "Why the third?"
    He replied: "One's absurd,
And bigamy, Sir, is a crime."

Human Foibles

There was an Old Person of Tring
Who, when somebody asked her to sing,

Replied, "Aren't it odd?
I can never tell 'God
Save the Weasel' from 'Pop Goes the King.' "

An epicure dining at Crewe,
Found quite a large mouse in his stew.
   Said the waiter, "Don't shout,
   And wave it about,
Or the rest will be wanting some, too."

Fun with Names

A silly young fellow named Hyde
In a funeral procession was spied;
   When asked, "Who is dead?"
   He giggled and said,
"I don't know; I just came for the ride."

A nice old lady named Tweedle
Went to church and sat down on a needle.
   Though deeply imbedded,
   'Twas luckily threaded,
And was deftly pulled out by the beadle.

There was a young fellow named Sydney,
Who drank till he ruined his kidney.
   It shriveled and shrank,
   As he sat there and drank,
But he'd a good time doin' it, didn't he?

Various Matters

There was a faith healer of Deal
Who said, "Although pain is not real,
   When I sit on a pin
   And it punctures my skin,
I dislike what I fancy I feel."

God's plan made a hopeful beginning,
But man spoiled his chances by sinning.
   We trust that the story
   Will end in God's glory,
But, at present, the other side's winning.

When Ladies Meet

Walter Pidgeon had just given a talk before a group of clubwomen. As he was leaving, a flustered matron waylaid him. "Oh, my dear Mr. Privilege!" she gushed. "This occasion has certainly been a pigeon!"

— Helen Davies

In New York the Women's Action Committee for Lasting Peace wrote to George Bernard Shaw in London asking him to autograph some books for a fund-raising auction. Shaw replied that he would not. He thought the cause of the United Nations was "too big for your little Women's Action Committee." He scoffed at some length.

The women went ahead with the auction anyhow. A popular autographed book brought only $70. But Shaw's grouchy letter sold for $170.

— New York *Herald Tribune*

Several women, members of a U. N. study group, sat near me in a restaurant. When the waitress asked one as to her preference for Russian or French salad dressing, the little lady spoke up excitedly. "Let's all have Russian dressing," she suggested. "It may help us to understand the Russians a little better."

— Chaplain Harold A. MacNeill

Charles W. Eliot, former President of Harvard, once confessed that the most unusual letter he had ever received came from a certain women's club. It read:

"Dear Sir: Our committee, having heard that you are the country's greatest thinker, would be greatly obliged if you would send us your seven greatest thoughts."

— *The Christian Science Monitor*

Lucian Cary, the author, tells about the time that the Secretary of the Ladies' Luncheon Club rose after coffee to present him as speaker of the day.

"Normally," she said with her brightest smile, "this honor would fall to our president, who has never missed hearing any of our speakers. But today she is down in Atlantic City — and how we all envy her!"

— Oscar Schisgall

When the noted French author André Maurois visited the United States some years ago, he gave a series of lectures in French before a woman's club. Maurois was delighted with the response to his talks, for the women attended regularly, hung on his every word and took reams of notes.

One morning, with their usual promptness and notebooks, the women arrived in the lecture hall, only to find Maurois was not present. After waiting an hour, they got in touch with the writer's secretary.

"Monsieur Maurois will not be there today," the surprised secretary said. "He announced that very clearly at last week's talk!"

— E. E. Edgar

Innocents Abroad

After sending a parcel to European relatives, we received a very grateful letter with this paragraph:

"If you can, please send us more pills. We didn't know what they were until Cousin Lempi came — she has studied English, you know — and read the name for us. Then we gave them all to Uncle Paul who has been suffering from rheumatism and he feels much better now. He says it is the best medicine he ever took. The pills are called *Life Savers*."

— Alice Murdock in *Pageant*

A Maine logger, fresh from the big woods, was watching a store clerk open a package of gaily colored men's pajamas.

"What's them?" he asked.

"Pajamas."

"Pajamas?" echoed the logger. "What are they for?"

"Why, you wear them nights," the clerk explained. "Want to buy a pair?"

"Nothing doing," said the logger. "I don't go nowhere nights except to bed."

— Royal Brown

My mother rented a room in our house to two boys whom she did not know. She was a little worried at first, but in a few days she stopped

fretting. "They must be nice boys," she explained. "They have towels from the YMCA."
— Floribel Flick

On their first visit to this country, the Albert Einsteins were given a dinner by the New York *Times*. A corsage for Mrs. Einstein ordered by the *Times* arrived late, after everyone was seated. So the two orchids were placed on her plate. Mrs. Einstein, who was nearsighted and always very anxious to conform to all foreign customs, showed no awkward surprise at this strange American hors d'oeuvre. She began delicately to eat it. A waiter relieved the situation: he tactfully removed the orchids.

But behind the scene there was great excitement. A hospital was called and asked whether eating an orchid was likely to hurt anyone. But the hospital had no recorded data on the effects of orchid eating. Until her death some years later, the wife of a German scientist knew more on that mysterious and unprobed subject than this great hospital.
— *Fortune*

When my friends arrived at the bungalow they had rented for the summer in a small New England town, they found just one flaw; there was no garbage collection. Inquiry revealed that the other summer residents bought a pig to consume the leftovers, so my friends found themselves the owner of a pig. The arrangement worked beautifully all summer.

When they were ready to return to their home in Washington, D. C., they let it be known that they had a pig for sale, and a prospective buyer inquired the price.

"Well," said the lady of the house, "we paid $12 for him — but we've used him all summer. Would $6 be too much?"
— Edgar V. Saugstad

The short-tempered golfer had spent a quarter of an hour unsuccessfully searching for a lost ball. Just as he was about to give up in disgust, an elderly lady seated on the links nearby called out to him: "Excuse me, sir, but will I be breaking the rules if I tell you where it is?"

All Aboard

One night William Howard Taft, then a young law reporter, finished studying a case in Somerville, Ohio, and discovered that he could not get back to his office that night unless he could stop a through express. He wired division headquarters: "Will you stop through express at Somerville to take on large party?" Promptly came back the reply: "Yes."

When the train arrived, the conductor said to Mr. Taft, "Where's the large party we were to take on?"

Mr. Taft regarded his own comfortable bulk ruefully and laughed. "I'm it," he said, stepping aboard the train.

— *The Christian Science Monitor*

A farmer boarding a city-bound train found himself next a man who was acting most strangely — glancing quickly out of the window, muttering to himself, glancing again. Curiosity overpowered him, and he asked the stranger if anything were the matter. "No, indeed," was the answer. "I'm a lightning calculator, you see. Just for fun I count the number of cars parked in the street as we pass towns, the number of people in the stations, the number of trees in a grove — I never make a mistake." "Wonderful," said the farmer. "In a few moments we're going to pass my pasture. I know the exact number of cows grazing there — would you care . . .?" The calculator was delighted to be put to the test. As the train flashed past he gave one glance at the cows and announced "157." "Amazing," exclaimed the farmer. "How did you do it?" "It's easy," replied the calculator. "All I did was to count the cows' teats and divide by four." — George T. Bye

Pullman passenger: "Porter, what about these shoes? One's black and one's tan!"

Porter: "Well, if it don't beat all! Dis is de second time dat's happened dis mawnin'!" — *Business Education World*

In a lounge car on the Denver Zephyr, I noticed a man across the aisle holding a magazine upside down. He seemed to be reading, for he turned the pages regularly. When I started back to my car I saw that though the cover was upside down the pages inside were rightside up. Curious, I asked for an explanation.

"Sit down," he said, "and I'll tell you. Whenever I travel, I buy a magazine, pull the staples out, and put the cover back on upside down. Then I come into the club car and start reading. Invariably someone spots me, thinks I'm faking, then sees the pages are rightside up and asks why. You'd be surprised how many interesting people I meet that way."   — Don Wharton

Jim Crowder, midwestern book magnate, finally got a seat in a railroad diner one day during the war. "Do you like split-pea soup?" asked the waiter. "No," said Jim. "Chicken croquettes?" "No." "Prune pie?" "No." The waiter took the napkin off the table. "Goodday," he said. "You is had your lunch."
                    — Bennett Cerf in *The Saturday Review of Literature*

Actor-producer Eddie Dowling tells this one:
With *Sally, Irene and Mary* I hit the Broadway footlights in 1917. I was anxious to have my parents visit me and share my glory. It was surely time they went somewhere. Mother was born on the family farm in Rhode Island and had never ventured more than ten miles away in her whole life. If Papa had covered more ground, it was his own secret.

Determined to make their first train ride an enjoyable one, I set out to get them a drawing room. It took plenty of pull and a little borrowed money to swing the deal. I sent the prize tickets and two new suitcases to the folks.

Mother was mad as a wet hen when she stepped off the train in New York. "We've never been so humiliated in our lives," she sputtered indignantly.

"What happened?" I cried.

Finally she calmed sufficiently to explain. "We got on the train where a lot of nice people were sitting — windows on both sides! Then some man in a shiny suit took one look at us and shut us up in a little closet!"   — Bart Hodges, *Life's Little Dramas* (Duell, Sloan and Pearce)

Going Around in Circas

An excerpt from the book "Acres and Pains"

S. J. Perelman

Is anybody looking for a bargain in an Early Pennsylvania washstand in mint condition, circa 1825? It's genuine pumpkin pine, with ball-and-claw feet, the original brasses, and a small smear of blood where I tripped over it last night in the dark. I'm holding it at $16, but not so tightly that I wouldn't let it go to the right party for circa ten cents.

I also have an authentic trestle table which collapses into a small space when you rest your elbows on it, and a patchwork quilt I bought from a very old lady who remembered seeing Lincoln. In fact I'm disposing of my entire collection of antiques to the lowest bidder, and if he doesn't want it I intend to set fire to it as soon as I am able to find an Early American match.

When we left a cozy New York flat to exile ourselves in a primitive farmhouse, back in the mid-'30's, we broke clean with the 20th century. We were ready to dip candles and card our own flax. We installed a spinning wheel in every room, in case anyone should need some quick homespun, and replaced our luxurious inner-spring bed with a period four-poster. (Our neighbor hesitated to relinquish it, as it had been

serving as a roost for his chickens, but finally exchanged it for five acres of prime bottom land.) We even discarded the electric stove and returned to cooking in the fireplace.

In spite of all our efforts, however, the house still seemed bourgeois and prosaic. The lamps gave off too much light and the bureau drawers worked too easily. We lusted for lamps made out of old seltzer bottles or apothecaries' jars, and Victorian dressers that nobody could open.

Then one day on a back-country road we stumbled into a web run by a spider named Jake Meserve. Outwardly Jake was a farmer. He had a long linen duster, steel-bowed spectacles, and a field of papier-mâché corn in front of his place as a blind. In his hayloft, however, he kept a few choice heirlooms you could persuade him to sell by dropping your hat. We immediately fell in love with a rare old cobbler's bench, as fine a piece as you would find outside the Metropolitan — that is the Metropolitan Shoe Repair Shop. After a brisk tussle Jake stowed away my $39 and hauled out a rickety sofa.

"You folks ever seen a real old-time Victorian courtin' chair?" he inquired, stroking the plush. "My Uncle Zeb proposed to Aunt Mildew in that chair. I wouldn't part with it if I was starvin'." Suddenly he choked back a sob and turned away. "Take it," he muttered brokenly. "Ninety-three dollars. It's like sellin' my own flesh and blood."

I whittled him down to $60, and drying his eyes he disgorged three more family mementos — a dough tray, a glass bell containing his mother's baby hair, and a little chest of drawers lettered, "Willimantic Spool & Thread Co." He stripped my wallet of everything but the social-security card, and we embarked. As I threw the car into

gear, he staggered up bearing a table.

"Just ran acrost this in my feed bin," he panted. "My grandpa bought it off Nancy Hanks. You can scrape off the paint with a stiff brush."

I threw him my watch and chain, and we whizzed away. I spent the next week hacking at the table with a blowtorch, steel wool, and sandpaper. It had six coats of paint, including one like porcelain that had been baked on. When I had finished, I overturned it accidently and discovered a sticker reading, "R. H. Macy & Co. Reduced to $3.98." And that, children, is how daddy met his first psychiatrist.

Heads and Tales

The New York *Daily News* goes in for impudent and brassily clever headlines. A story on meat prices and inflation was headed: "PRICES SOAR, BUYERS SORE, COW JUMPS OVER THE MOON."

When a strip teaser went on trial, the *News* headlined it: "3 JUDGES WEIGH HER FAN DANCE; FIND IT WANTON."

After Errol Flynn had kicked a New York cop in the leg, the New York *Star* headlined the story: "BARKING UP WRONG SHIN."

— Above items from *Time*

The New York *Journal-American* headlined a story about a thief who stole an electric clock: "STEALS CLOCK, FACES TIME."

When a Wallace, Idaho, policeman shot an elk that had been wandering around town for five hours, the New York *Herald Tribune* headed the story: "BAGS VISITING ELK."

— Above items from Kenilworth H. Mathus in *Pageant*

Headline in Oakland, Calif., *Tribune:* "TWO CONVICTS EVADE NOOSE; JURY HUNG!"
— Hy Gardner in *Parade*

Stork Quotations: Headline in Cleveland *Plain Dealer:* "GYPSY ROSE HAS A 5½-POUND STRIPLING" . . . The Boise, Idaho, *Statesman*, announcing birth of triplets: "THREE OF A KIND GIVES PAIR FULL HOUSE" . . . When two sets of triplets were born in Brooklyn, the *Daily Mirror* headlined the story: "COUPLE OF DADS IN DITHER AS THREES GROW IN BROOKLYN."

Marxmanship

Harpo Marx entered a railroad diner and was seated at a table for two. The little old lady who shared the table watched him devour a huge meal, carefully and silently. When the waiter brought the check, the lady stared at Harpo in horror and disbelief as he put salt and pepper on the check, and carefully and silently ate it.   — Leonard Lyons

Arthur Murray and Groucho Marx were discussing a certain actress. "She's her own worst enemy," Murray observed. "Not while I'm alive, she isn't," retorted Groucho icily.   — Andrew B. Hecht

As Chico Marx tackled a French menu, the headwaiter bowed and asked politely: "What's your pleasure?"

"Girls," said Chico. "What's yours?"   — Earl Wilson,
Post-Hall Syndicate

Groucho Marx was lunching with Arthur Murray. When the check came, they both grabbed, and Groucho won.

"Either you're losing your grip," said Groucho, "or I don't know my own strength!"   — Helen Huttner

Groucho Marx, after much evasion, finally succumbed to the blandishments of a realtor who wanted to show him a palatial ocean-front estate which was for sale. The salesman drove the comedian up the mile-long, beautifully landscaped approach, escorted him through the house, the stables, the gardens, the kennels, babbling of the wonders of this dream palace by the sea. Groucho patiently plodded after him, nodding gravely, apparently much impressed. Finally he was ushered out on the flagged terrace and the salesman waved proudly toward the broad expanse of the Pacific.

"Now what do you think?" he challenged.

"I don't care for it," replied Groucho thoughtfully, and he waved in turn at the view. "Take away the ocean and what have you got?"
— Peggy McEvoy

Post Masters

Directly above the letter slots in the Hastings, Neb., post office are placards with: "Have you mailed your wife's letter?"

— Beatrice Ford Parker

A woman was mailing the old family Bible to her brother in a distant city. The postal clerk examined the heavy package carefully and inquired if it contained anything breakable. "Nothing but the Ten Commandments," was the quick reply.

— Karl B. Rollins

A young air-force officer was waiting his turn at the parcel-post window. When he reached the head of the line, he stepped back a few feet and sent his package flying over the counter by means of a well-placed drop kick. Then he explained to the flabbergasted clerk, "I just wanted to see if the parcel could stand the type of handling it's going to receive."

— Ruby Lama

Just ahead of me in a long line before the window of a Los Angeles post office was a young mother with a husky baby in her arms. When her turn came, she held up the infant to the amazed postal clerk and said, "Will you weigh him, please?"

The clerk's face turned crimson, but he accepted the child, weighed him, and handed him back to his mother. "Seventeen pounds, ten ounces," he gulped.

"Thank you so much," said the girl, and sauntered out as if this were an everyday incident.

— Florence Bybee

A young woman buying stamps at the post office in Chicago dropped a paper. The slip fell directly in front of the gentleman standing next to her. He politely raised his hat. Then he kicked the paper over in front of her, making it easier for her to pick it up.

— June Provines in Chicago *Sun*

The Male Animal

To the young man at the perfume counter the clerk purred, "Now here's one called 'Perhaps.' It's $35 an ounce."

"Thirty-five dollars!" exclaimed the young man. "For $35 I don't want 'Perhaps.' I want 'Sure.'"

— H. Elmo Taylor

A submarine crewman, after a long siege at sea, met his commander on the way to their hotel one hibiscus-scented night in Hawaii. "Ain't it funny, sir," he remarked, "how far you can get behind on women and how quick you can catch up?"

— Fletcher Pratt in *Harper's*

than women and, meeting with stormy opposition, declared herself ready to substantiate her statement. Steering the conversation to men's fashions, she suddenly said in a loud voice:

"It's a pity that the most intelligent and learned men attach least importance to the way they dress. Why, right at this table the most cultivated man is wearing the most clumsily knotted tie!"

As if on a given signal, every man in the room immediately put his hand to his tie to straighten it.
— *L'Humeur*

When I was spending my vacation with a friend in Kentucky, he decided to take me up in the hills to see how the mountaineers lived. We came to a farm where a man was lying on the front porch, smoking a corncob pipe, and a woman was digging in a plot of land. I approached him and asked, "Isn't that hard work for your wife?"

He said, "Yep, but we work in shifts."

"Oh, I see, when she gets tired you take over."

"Naw," he said. "When she gets tired out in the garden she shifts to the house chores." — E. T. Silvestrini

At a large banquet Lady Astor once remarked that men were vainer

If a man makes a stupid mistake, men say: "What a fool that man is." If a woman makes a stupid mistake, men say: "What fools women are!"
— Quoted by H. C. L. Jackson in Detroit *News*

"Do you believe in clubs for women?" a friend asked W. C. Fields. "Yes," replied Fields, "if every other form of persuasion fails."
— *British Columbia Digest*

When a worried-looking man in a florist shop asked for potted geraniums, the clerk, out of geraniums, suggested chrysanthemums.

"No, they won't do," replied the man. "I promised my wife I'd water her geraniums while she was away."
— *Swanson Newsette*

Verdant Vernacular

Into town on his regular Saturday visit came a lanky Tennessee mountaineer and his young wife. In the crook of his right arm nestled a week-old baby.

The dry-goods merchant, who had not seen the couple in quite a long while, greeted them affably. "Come right in, folks, glad to see ye! Well, well, is that yore young 'un, Len?"

Len pondered thoughtfully for a moment, then replied, "Wall, yeah, I reckon it's mine. Leastaways, it wuz caught in my trap."

— Vadus Carmack

The cook, fresh from the Ozarks, was discussing her daughter's behavior: "I found out she ain't sick at all. It's just a case of the pokin' grits. That no-count man she wanted to marry left town with another woman, and my daughter's madder than mad, pokin' her chin out and grittin' her teeth. Ain't nothing the matter with her but the pokin' grits."

— Dr. Ruth Salmon

A mountaineer, forced to stand at close quarters with a young lady on a crowded Tennessee bus, leaned down and said: "I do hope I ain't clustering you too much."

— Rosanne Guess

When I asked one of the boys in my craft class if his father was handy with tools, he answered, "Of all the ain'ts my father ain't, that's his ain'test!"

— Mabel M. Osborne

When the circus came to town my cook, Odessa, confessed to me a longing to see the man shot from the cannon, so we took her to the circus with us. When we were all settled in our seats I noticed that Odessa was directly behind a very rotund matron who wore a huge picture hat. I leaned over and whispered, "Oh, Odessa, you won't be able to see a thing."

"Das all right," she replied. "Don't you worry. I'se goin' to set high rumpted."

— Mrs. C. H. Crutchfield

In a South Georgia town, a group of men discussing tobacco on a street corner were joined by a South Carolinian who owned one of the local warehouses.

"Abel," one of the men asked a farmer, "you know Bob Morgan, don't you?"

"Well," replied Abel extending a hand, "we've howdied but we ain't shook."

— Anna Pomeroy

A local fisherman, watching an overdressed summer visitor mincing down the street of a Maine resort town, observed to his friend, "Reckon the riggin's worth more than the hull."   — C. W. B.

A long-winded lecturer had been holding forth for over an hour, except for brief pauses from time to time to gulp a hasty drink of water. Finally, during one such "intermission," an old man in the audience leaned toward his neighbor and announced in a loud whisper: "First time I ever saw a windmill run by water!"

— Mrs. E. G. Covington

Speaking Out

The chairman replied in a few appropriated words (Cecil Hunt in *This Week Magazine*) . . . Franklin P. Adams: "Accustomed as I am to public speaking, I know the futility of it." . . . A speaker who does not strike oil in ten minutes should stop boring (Louis Nizer)

General Dwight D. Eisenhower, speaking at the National Press Club, told his audience that he regretted he was not more of an orator.

"It reminds me of my boyhood days on a Kansas farm," Ike related. "An old farmer had a cow that we wanted to buy. We went over to visit him and asked about the cow's pedigree. The old farmer didn't know what pedigree meant, so we asked him about the cow's butterfat production. He told us that he hadn't any idea what it was. Finally we asked him if he knew how many pounds of milk the cow produced each year.

"The farmer shook his head and said: 'I don't know. But she's an honest old cow and she'll give you all the milk she has!'"

"Well," The General concluded, "I'm like the cow; I'll give you everything I have."   — Gerry Robichaud in Pasadena *Independent*

In *Try and Stop Me* I told of the late E. Phillips Oppenheim's sure-fire formula for coping with dinner hosts who broke their promises and called on him for a speech. He would clear his throat with a series of garrumphs, and declare severely, "As King Solomon remarked to the Queen of Sheba, 'Madame, I did not come here to speak.' " J. B. Birmingham, of Nutley, now writes that he can improve on this story, and I think he proves his point. In *his* version, Cleopatra pouts to an over-loquacious Anthony, "Sire, I am not prone to argue."
                    — Bennett Cerf, *Shake Well Before Using* (Simon & Schuster)

In his own gentle, procrastinating way Dr. George Harris did much as president of Amherst College, but the unpleasant duties of such a post he neglected or ignored. He was not really opposed to work, but I never heard him say much in favor of it. One autumn he rose in chapel to address the students at the first assembly of the year, but after three or four sentences he got tired and, breaking into a happy smile, said:

"I intended to give you some advice, but now I remember how much is left over from last year unused."

With that he took his hat and walked out.
                    — John Erskine, *The Memory of Certain Persons* (Lippincott)

As President of Swarthmore College, Dr. Frank Aydelotte once invited Albert Einstein to be guest of honor at a dinner. When Einstein was called upon to speak he said: "Ladies and gentlemen, I'm sorry but I've nothing to say."

Then he sat down. When he heard the buzzing of the guests, he arose again and added: "In case I do have something to say, I'll come back."

Six months later he wired Dr. Aydelotte: "Now I have something to say." Aydelotte immediately gave another dinner, at which Einstein made his speech.   — Leonard Lyons

Once, when asked to make a speech in England, John G. Winant stood in agonized silence for four minutes, finally said, softly:

"The worst mistake I ever made was in getting up in the first place."

— Time

At a banquet given by a native king in Samoa for Dr. Victor C. Heiser, time came for the tribute to the guest of honor, but His Majesty still squatted at the feast, while a professional orator laid on the palaver for Dr. Heiser. When he ended, the doctor moved to rise but the King restrained him: "Don't get up; I have provided an orator for you. In Polynesia we don't believe public speaking should be engaged in by amateurs."

— The Commentator

The eighth Duke of Devonshire once told some friends: "The other night I dreamed that I was addressing the House of Lords. Then I woke up and, by God, I was!"

— Judge David Davies

During his campaign for governor of New Jersey in 1940, Charles Edison, son of the inventor, introduced himself by explaining: "People will inevitably associate me with my father, but I would not have anyone believe that I am trading on the name Edison. I would rather have you know me merely as the result of one of my father's earlier experiments."

— Carl John Bostelmann

Life with Father

Michael's first day of school arrived. I walked with him to the bus, which was waiting, fringed by a tight cluster of little boys eyeing each newcomer with suspicion. Michael's grasp tightened. I felt his apprehension.

"Michael," I said in a loud voice, "I want you to come straight home after school. Remember, you've got to be there to help me skin that elephant."

I pushed Michael toward the bus, and walked away. Silence. Then a babble of little boys' voices and the word "elephant" in shrill excitement. I glanced back. One little boy was holding Michael's books, another his lunchbox, a third boy was helping him on the bus. A great peace descended upon me. I had measured up to the responsibilities of fatherhood.   — Alonzo Hauser in *Coronet*

My brother put off telling his motherless daughter the facts of life as long as possible. But when she fell in love for the first time at 16, he realized that he had to talk to her. I overheard his concluding remark, "Jean, the best advice I can give you is written on the top of a mayonnaise jar."

That night, when I was mixing the salad for our dinner, these words on the mayonnaise jar leapt up at me: "KEEP COOL BUT DON'T FREEZE."
— Mrs. J. A. W.

King George V was noted for his frugality and thrift, qualities he tried to instill in his offspring. The then Prince of Wales, on the other hand, was pretty much of a spendthrift. While at school, he wrote his father pleading for some additional money. In return he received a stiff note of reproval urging him to change his ways and learn to be a businessman. In the next mail the king found a note from his son which said:

"I have taken your advice. Have just sold your letter to a collector for 25 pounds."   — Louis Sobol, King Features

A father and his small son were out walking one afternoon when the youngster asked how the electricity went through the lighting wires.

"Don't know," said the father. "Never knew much about electricity."

A few blocks farther on, the boy asked what caused lightning and thunder.

"To tell the truth," said the father, "I never exactly understood that myself."

"Say, Pop," began the lad after a while. "Oh, well, never mind."

"Go ahead," said the father. "Ask questions. Ask a lot of questions. How else are you going to learn?"   — Mrs. Steven M. Siesel

At the time of the Jim Corbett-John L. Sullivan bout, Steve Brodie of Brooklyn Bridge fame predicted loudly that the champion would knock out Corbett in the sixth round. When news of this reached Jim's father, he was highly indignant. Not long afterward, Corbett introduced him to Brodie. The old gentleman looked him over sourly, then said at last, "So you're the man who jumped over the Brooklyn Bridge."

"No, no," Brodie corrected him. "I didn't jump over it. I jumped off it."

Corbett senior snorted. "Oh," he said in thinly veiled contempt, "I thought you jumped over it. Any fool could jump off it."

         — Fred Stone, *Rolling Stone* (Whittlesey)

On a visit to Radio City Music Hall, I stopped to admire the life-size bronze statue of a girl. A young man was also admiring the statue, while his small son amused himself by climbing over its base. Suddenly the youngster looked up at the bronze figure, then turned to his father and asked, "What's that?"

"That's the figure of a woman, sonny."

After another inquiring look at the statue, the boy asked, "Daddy, is Mother a woman?"

Before Daddy could answer, Mother, a Mrs. Five-by-Five, waddled toward them. The father gulped, took one longing look at the statue, and then, as he turned toward his wife, said, "Fundamentally, sonny, fundamentally!"

         — Gertrude B. Linberg

Charles Coburn, the actor, tells this story:

As a boy, I fell in love with the theater and started seeing plays whenever possible. "One thing, son, you must never do," my father warned me. "Don't go to burlesque houses."

I, of course, asked why.

"Because you would see things you shouldn't," Father replied.

That settled it. The next time I managed to get the price of admission, I went straight to a burlesque house.

Father was right. I saw something I shouldn't have seen — my father.

         — Louis Azrael in Baltimore *News-Post*

Cartoon Quips

Small boy to father: "Here's my report card and one of yours I found in the attic."
— Hoff in *The Saturday Evening Post*

Radio announcer: "Tune in again next week — same station, same time, same jokes!"
— Mischa Richter, King Features

Woman at auction to friend: "I bid on every item last week, but I didn't get caught once!"
— J. Monahan in *This Week Magazine*

Girl on garden bench to youth beside her: "I feel a little chilly, Lester. Will you run inside and get me Jack Davis?"
— Bill King in
The Saturday Evening Post

Waiter, holding tray with change behind his back: "Your change is $2.66, sir. Want it?"
— Stan Hunt in
The Saturday Evening Post

One woman to another: "My husband is absolutely no good at fixing anything, so everything in our house works."
— George Hamilton Green in *Collier's*

Coming out of a movie theater, a couple discovers an enormous waiting line, and the astonished wife says: "We must have seen a good picture!"   — Reamer Keller in
The Saturday Evening Post

One girl to another: "Of course I wouldn't say anything about her

unless I could say something good. And, oh boy, is this good. . . ."
— Bill King in *Collier's*

On street corner, one man explains to another, as they watch a couple in a rapturous embrace: "It was love at first sight. I'm just waiting for a lull to introduce them."
— James Gibson, McNaught Syndicate

Hostess to guest on the beach: "When shall I wake you — rare, medium or well done?"
— Henry Boltinoff in
The Saturday Evening Post

Young girl at perfume counter, after looking at My Sin, Breathless, and the other lurid names: "Have you anything for a beginner?"
— Von Riegen in *Today's Woman*

Housewife to vacuum salesman: "You might try the people next door. We use theirs, and it's terrible!"   — d'Alessio, Publishers Syndicate

Bored wife to husband in noisy night club: "Why can't you be like other husbands and never take me any place?"
— William Von Riegen in *Collier's*

Miserable-looking woman riding horseback through the barren desert: "It is a wonderful vacation and I am enjoying it. It is a wonderful vacation and I am enjoying it. IT IS A WONDERFUL . . ."
— Corka in *Laughs from The Saturday Review of Literature* (Vanguard)

In Sickness and in Health

Condensed from "Mr. and Mrs. Cugat"

Isabel Scott Rorick

Mrs. Cugat turned in her bed and blinked lazily at the alarm clock. Half-past eight. Slices of yellow morning sun came through the Venetian blind: coffee flavored the air; she stretched placidly, then jerked upright. There in the other bed was Mr. Cugat — still there, at eight-thirty. "Hey!" she cried, "Look at the time!"

Mr. Cugat did not move, but his eyes opened slowly — clouded and apathetic. "I know," he said, and closed them again.

Alarm washed over her, and she regarded him wide-eyed while she groped for her slippers and robe. "You aren't going to the office?"

"No," he replied, eyes still closed, "I'm sick."

She bent to feel his head — it was hot. Mr. Cugat hunched deeper into the covers. Hurriedly closing the window she pattered distractedly into the hall. Mr. Cugat was never sick. It seemed appalling that, judging by the look of him, everything had given way at once. "Anna!" she called over the stair rail, "Mr. Cugat isn't feeling well. Will you bring breakfast upstairs?"

"It's Friday." Dark significance clothed this comment.

"I know, Anna, but you'll have to put off the cleaning until later. Mr. Cugat may be dangerously ill!"

"Saints!" said Anna, and vanished.

Mrs. Cugat returned to Mr. Cugat, who was gargling. "Shall I call Dr. Buell?" she asked anxiously.

"Maybe you'd better," he said, examining the contents of the medicine cabinet blankly.

She flew to the phone, colliding in the hall with Anna and an abundant tray. Compassionate eyes were bent on Mr. Cugat, who sat miserably on the window seat in everybody's way. Having left word for the doctor, Mrs. Cugat hastened back to Mr. Cugat's side, love and concern welling up within her. When she reached him she was smitten with unexpected shyness. Mr. Cugat, ill, was a complete stranger. She felt his head again timidly.

Mr. Cugat said he wasn't very hungry. It seemed advisable to start all over and try him with an egg. "Anna," she shouted, "Mr. Cugat thinks he might like a nice egg —" and, resignedly, the vacuum cleaner died away. By the time the egg arrived, however, Mr. Cugat had retired to the bathroom. Mrs. Cugat got dressed as best she could without her comb, powder or girdle, which were closeted with Mr. Cugat, and hastened down to cancel her hair appointment, get somebody to take her place at the Red Cross Rummage Sale, and phone her mother not to bring Cousin Melba from Cincinnati to tea. Between calls she ran to the window to see if she could see Doctor Buell. Suffocating pictures of life alone presented themselves. Mr. Cugat's last words — weak but brave. Mr. Cugat in his coffin, with his cutaway on. Mr. Cugat's pallbearers coming back to the house, the way Tommy Spencer's did, for one last sad drink. Her throat ached.

Mr. Cugat put an end to this by coming downstairs. He had put on a pair of gray flannel trousers over his pajamas and an old sweater used for duck hunting. Around his neck was his best white silk evening scarf, and over all his oldest bathrobe. His hair stuck up and he looked wistful.

"Do you think you ought to be downstairs?" she asked anxiously.

"I don't know; they're doing something to my bed," he said.

While she was looking into this the doctor came. Mr. Cugat had a cold. Nothing serious, but he'd better stay home for a day or so. Plenty of rest — stay out of drafts — lots of liquids — two pink tablets every hour — gargle with salt water. Mr. Cugat, consoled and interested, sat back and reviewed his symptoms. Vivacious with relief, Mrs. Cugat saw the doctor to the door. There was just time to get her hair appointment after all. On her way home she would pick up a detective story for Mr. Cugat. What fun having him

home! Darling Mr. Cugat, suddenly vulnerable and inadequate, with his hair sticking up — the Weaker Vessel.

"What about lunch?" Anna caught her at the garage door.

"Ask him what sounds good to him, Anna. I'll be back at one."

Laden with two books, three magazines, a pot of tulips and some white grapes, she came eagerly back up the walk at one to meet Belda, the laundress, emerging from the front door.

"Em goink by da A on P," she beamed in explanation.

"The A and P?" said Mrs. Cugat. "What for?"

"Eh nice stek."

"Oh — what else did Mr. Cugat order for lunch?"

"Franch frice — vechtible soup — shoclit keck — home med. Pore seeck men," her voice crooned, "hees hongreh!"

Mrs. Cugat steadied herself. "And what about the ironing?"

"Ha! Becawss da fuce — iss no ionink! Mist Cugat feexis lemps togedda — Zick! da fuce blos."

Mr. Cugat was discovered in the basement dispiritedly screwing and unscrewing things — apparently at random. He looked downhearted and was persuaded back upstairs. In the library she came upon the chain arrangement of lamps that had been designed to bring light to an obscure corner by the woodbox (out of drafts). His chair was there and two dismantled shotguns with cleaning equipment and a highball, and the white velvet chaise-longue cover from the guest room.

Lunch was disappointing. It was funny, he said, but nothing had any taste. Mrs. Cugat, to the best of her capacity, ate for two, but she was obliged to feed most of Mr. Cugat's chocolate cake to Lillian, the cat.

After lunch Mrs. Cugat came back to the library to find Mr. Cugat on a ladder shifting things around on the top bookshelf. "What's been done with my Law School Books?"

Law School books? She didn't think she'd ever seen them. Unconvinced, he remained disconsolately atop the ladder. "Doesn't anybody ever think to clean up here?" he asked. "It's positively filthy! Look —" A little cloud of dust rose to his righteous puff, but she wasn't looking. Her eyes were closed.

The doorbell pealed sharply. Mr. Cugat clambered down, took another pill, let himself carefully into his chair, and sighed.

"Funny," he said pensively, "I'm weak as a kitten."

Anna appeared. "Mr. Cartwright and Mr. Sturm are here."

"Mr. Cartwright! Good old Cory?" Mr. Cugat's face lit up with the touching eagerness and incredulous gratitude of a man who has spent the past ten years of his life on an island retreat of nuns. "Tell 'em to come in here, Anna," he said, removing the white velvet coverlet with a walloping kick.

"Well, well, how's the invalid? So they finally got you down, did they,

Georgie?" In came the Messrs. Cartwright and Sturm, looking fit, well-combed and ruddy. Mrs. Cugat's heart smote her. Mr. Cugat in his scarf and bathrobe, with his hair sticking up, seemed frail and touching.

Poor darling, she thought contritely. Perhaps she'd better have Doctor Buell drop in again tonight. She phoned the doctor and, suddenly weary, decided to go upstairs and take a bath.

As she floated in pine oil, there was a knock at the door. Anna's voice muted to a rasp came through. "Mr. Cugat's asked the gentlemen to dinner!"

"Oh," said Mrs. Cugat, and thought. "Is Belda still here? Send her to the A and P for another steak, and some lettuce and tomatoes, and some drugstore ice cream."

Dinner was very late, but after four Old Fashioneds nothing matters. Her throbbing head propped up by the chin, her eyes glazed, Mrs. Cugat listened to the wealth of detail embellishing what Cory had told the headwaiter at the Ambassador about wild turkey — and grouse — and terrapin. "Of course you were right, Cory," she heard her voice saying, far away.

The doorbell finally rang. Was it the doctor at last? It was. The Messrs. Cartwright and Sturm, taking a good deal of time over it, tactfully and jocosely withdrew. She waved them good-bye at the door and went back to the library. "Well," said Doctor Buell, folding up his instruments, "You're a pretty good nurse, young lady!"

"I am?"

"Yes, he'll be well enough to go to the office tomorrow. Now, if I might just have half a glass of water —"

"Hell, doc," said Mr. Cugat robustly, "I don't need any more medicine."

"No," said Doctor Buell gently, "but I think we'll just fix a little something for Mrs. Cugat."

Slips That Pass in the Type

In a letter renewing a subscription to the Geary, Okla., *Star:* "I personally enjoy your paper as much as my husband."

From the Niagara Falls, N. Y., *Gazette:* "Miss Rita Sugar, queen of the Niagara Falls, N. Y., centennial and Miss Lois Smith, chosen Miss Niagara Falls, Ont., met last night at the center of the bridge.

"The fireworks were visible for miles."

From the society column of the Clearwater, Fla., *Sun:* "Mr. and Mrs. Charles L. Thompson and Mr. and Mrs. Russell Hartwick of Tampa will entertain at open house Sunday, from three until tight."

Item in the Grand Rapids *Herald:* "Miss C—— H—— reported to police the loss of $20 today. She said the money was concealed in her stocking, and the loss was discovered soon after the departure of a vacuum-cleaner salesman who had been demonstrating his line."

From the Oklahoma City *Times:* "More than 5000 high school girls, most of whom are interested primarily in the homes they expect to ruin in the future, will gather here next week-end."

A sign in the Bronx says: "Piano lessons; special pains given to beginners."
— Earl Wilson,
Post-Hall Syndicate

From a Petersburg, Va., paper: "The doctor felt the patient's purse, and admitted that there was nothing he could do."

Situation Wanted ad in the New York *Times:* "Houseworker, plain crook, reliable."

From the Birmingham, Ala., *News:* "I have lived here for a long time. Besides this, my wife has man interests here."

From the Johnson City, Tenn., *Press-Chronicle:* "Fred V. Vance, deputy grand exhausted ruler of the Elks, will visit Johnson City on Thursday."

From the Warsaw, Va., *Northern Neck News:* "Mrs. Belfield is so sappy and jolly that it is really refreshing to be with her."

From a letter sent to a customer by a Sacramento, Calif., department store: "Although hundreds of letters and telephone calls come to us each day, we fake a personal interest in each one."   — M. Morris

A news item in the Omaha *Sunday World-Herald:* "Gene Autry is better after being kicked by a horse."

From the Mt. Carmel, Ill., *Republican-Register:* "The fifth grade chorus sang, 'Nobody Knows the Trouble I've Been.' "

From the Norwood, Ohio, *Enterprise:* "Marjorie Evans was slightly bruised Monday afternoon when a car struck her in front of the bank. George Baker, the driver, picked her up, and feeling her all over to make sure no bones were broken, insisted on taking her home where he could make a closer examination."

State of Superiority

A Texas preacher once prayed: "Oh, Lord, we thank Thee for the bounteous blessings bestowed upon Texas; and we beseech Thee to look with favor upon those places where Your feet have not yet trod."
                    — Paul Bolton in *Life*

A gentleman from New York, stranded for the night in a small West Texas town, sought to relieve his boredom. The hotel clerk suggested that he join some cattlemen who were playing cards and who would welcome a stranger — but, the clerk warned, the stakes were "pretty high."

The New Yorker called at the room designated and was invited to join the game. "Hear you fellows play for real money," he said. "Well, let me have chips for all of this." He tossed a hundred-dollar bill on the table, glancing about to catch the players' reaction.

Without even looking up, the dealer took the bill and slowly pushed one white chip toward the stranger.   — Richard M. Morehead

In the general post office at San Antonio there are three letter drops. One is labeled "Local," the second "Texas" and the third "Other States and Foreign Countries."
                    — George D. Stout in *Life*

A Bostonian visited San Antonio and asked a native, "What is that dilapidated-looking ruin over there?"

"That, suh, is the Alamo. In that building, suh, 136 immortal Texans held off an army of 15,000 of Santa Anna's regulars for four days."

"Um-m-m," said the Bostonian, "and who was that man on horseback on that hill over there?"

"That, suh, is a statue of a Texas ranger. He killed 46 Apaches in singlehanded combat and broke up 27 riots in his lifetime. . . . Where you from, stranger?"

"I'm from Boston. We have our heroes there, too. Paul Revere, for instance —"

"Paul Revere!" snorted the Texan. "You mean that man who had to ride for help?"

— Leonard Lyons

Some years ago when I was attending a convention in San Antonio a professor of economics from the University of Texas was one of the principal speakers. The audience included a large number of Oklahomans. When the speaker generously mentioned the neighboring state as an "outlying province of Texas" a husky Oklahoman jumped to his feet excitedly and shouted back:

"Brother, there ain't no state that can out-lie Texas!"   — E. C. Miller

Brush-Offs

One hot morning T. E. Lawrence, British hero of Arabia, was standing on the porch of his Cairo hotel. A woman anxious to be seen in his company approached him. "Imagine, Colonel Lawrence!" she cried, fanning herself vigorously. "Ninety-two already!"

"Indeed!" returned Lawrence. "Congratulations, Madam, and many happy returns of the day!"   — E. E. Edgar

When Cornelia Otis Skinner opened in a revival of Shaw's *Candida*, he cabled, "Excellent. Greatest." Miss Skinner, overwhelmed, cabled back, "Undeserving such praise." Shaw answered, "I meant the play." Miss Skinner bristled and replied, "So did I."

— Bennett Cerf in *The Saturday Review of Literature*

Slim and Johnny, Wyoming cowboys, were dismayed when they heard that Slim's eastern cousins (female) planned to pay them a long visit. However, they received them hospitably and had an excellent supper ready. Afterward the guests offered to wash the dishes.

"Naw, we never do dishes," said Slim. He sauntered to the door, whistled, and in rushed six hounds. Leaping onto the table they enthusiastically began polishing the nailed-down tin plates.

"Slim's cousins left the next morning," Johnny reported complacently. "It was hard work trainin' them hounds — and harder work breakin' 'em — but it sure was wuth it." — Louise M. Murray

A Hollywood gossip was telling Ilka Chase of the knock-down and drag-out affairs of a newly arrived couple next door. "Everyone is talking. Some are taking her part and some his," purred the informer.

"And," replied Ilka acidly, "I suppose a few eccentric individuals are minding their own business."

At a ball given at her home, a Boston hostess carried off without any loss of temper the difficult task of ridding her party of a girl who had arrived unbidden. She gave the girl just time enough to remove her coat. Then she moved quickly to the scene and, extending her hand, said in her most pleasant voice, "I hear you've been looking for me, my dear — to say good night."

— Cleveland Amory, *The Proper Bostonians* (Dutton)

Scottish playwright Sir James M. Barrie held probably the shortest interview on record. An enterprising newspaperman, gaining entrance somehow to the author's flat, began, "Sir James Barrie, I presume?"

"You do," replied Barrie, closing the door instantly. — E. E. Edgar

Ferenc Molnár, the playwright, has two ways of disposing of callers he does not wish to see. To people not really objectionable, Molnár's secretary says: "Sorry, but he's not in." But to callers against whom Molnár bears a deep dislike, the secretary says not only "Sorry, he's not in," but adds: "He left a moment ago, and if you rush down the street you'll catch him." — Leonard Lyons

A much-married Hollywood actor was confronted by a gay damsel. "Don't you remember me?" she greeted him. "Ten years ago you asked me to marry you!"

"Really?" yawned the actor. "And did you?" — Andrew B. Hecht

Matters of Tact

Perhaps the wittiest and most graceful tribute ever spoken by a man of his wife was said by Joseph H. Choate.

Someone asked him: "Mr. Choate, if you could not be yourself, who would you rather be?"

Instantly came the reply: "Mrs. Choate's second husband."

— William I. Jones

The Reverend C. P. Smith had just married a young couple, and the bridegroom asked him the price of the service.

"Oh, well," said the minister, "you can pay me whatever it is worth to you."

The young fellow looked long and silently at his bride. Then, slowly rolling the whites of his eyes, he said: "Lawd, suh, you has done ruined me for life; you has, for sure."

— A. C. Edgerton, *More Speeches and Stories for Every Occasion* (Noble)

Wilton Lackaye outshone tact itself when he walked into a bath occupied by a lady and calmly bowed himself out with: "I beg your pardon, sir."

— Carol H. Hanigan

At dinner one night, Chauncey M. Depew joined a small group of friends who were in the midst of an animated discussion.

"Oh, Mr. Depew!" exclaimed one of the ladies. "You are just in time to settle an argument. What is the most beautiful thing in the world?"

"A beautiful woman," replied the gallant Depew, without hesitation.

But his companion seemed shocked at his levity. "I contend," she said, seriously, "that sleep is the most beautiful."

"Well," said Depew, thoughtfully, "next to a beautiful woman, sleep is!"   — Alan Gray M. Campbell

Inscription on a cigarette lighter: "To My Matchless Wife."

— Painesville, Ohio, *Telegraph*

Burglar in the House

A policeman told us recently about a thug that they had brought into headquarters one night. He was a beetle-browed, hard-looking fellow who had been interrupted doing a job on a delicatessen store. During the routine questioning, his belongings, among which was a pair of brass knuckles, were inspected. "Be careful wid dem knuckles, sarge," the burglar requested a bit bashfully. "They mean something to me."

The knuckles were examined more closely and this inscription was found inside the little finger: "With truest love, from Mildred. August, 1926."   —PM

A young married couple who had just settled down in their new home got a pleasant surprise in their mail one morning — a couple of tickets to one of the best shows in town. But the donor had omitted to send his name, and for the rest of the day the question was: "Wonder who it was?"

They enjoyed the show; but when they reached home, they found that all their wedding presents had been taken. A note from the burglar said: "Now you know."   — *The Policy*

A committee appointed by *Redbook* to study the question of how best to hold a wife wrote a selected list of husbands. The only reply received was from a western penitentiary. It stated briefly: "I found the best way was around the neck, but it should not be overdone. Please note change of address."   — Edward Streeter in *Redbook Magazine*

Former Governor Christianson of Minnesota spoke one day before the convicts at Stillwater penitentiary. Forgetting his audience, he began, "Fellow citizens —." A murmur of delight sounded through the large room. Confused, the Governor started again. "Fellow convicts —," he stammered. The laughter grew louder. "Oh, you know what I mean," he exclaimed. "I am glad to see so many of you here." With that the laughter grew into an uproar and the Warden led the wilting Governor out into the open air.

A few years ago, when I was living in a town in the Deep South, the local chapter of the Ladies' Aid Society decided to bring a little sunshine into the state prison by writing cheery letters to the inmates. My landlady didn't quite know how to go about addressing a man she knew only by a string of numerals. But finally she achieved what she happily believed to be a measure of friendliness: "Dear 688395," she wrote. "May I call you 688?"   — Charles W. Creighton

International Correspondence Schools' most treasured letter is this one from the Federal Penitentiary in Atlanta: "I intend to resume my studies as soon as my personal liberty is restored. During the trial, my still was brought into court as evidence. The judge, the jury and the spectators were unanimous in the opinion that it was the finest piece of copper-smithing ever seen in Tennessee. I owe it all to the ICS sheet-metal course."

— Waldo C. Wright

The chief constable of my small home town is also the veterinary surgeon. One night the telephone rang and his wife answered.

"Is Mr. Thomas there?" asked an agitated voice.

"Do you want my husband as a veterinarian or as constable?"

"Both," came the breathless reply. "We can't get our bulldog to open his mouth, and there's a burglar in it!"

— Wesley A. Clark

For a Name's Sake

Some years ago the Brown Hotel in Louisville, Ky., adopted the custom of naming a room in the inn for each winner of the Kentucky Derby. There is a Zev Room, a Gallant Fox Room, a Whirlaway Room and so forth. But after the 1946 Derby the management decided to abandon the practice. The winner that year was Assault.

— Gordon Cobbledick in
Cleveland *Plain Dealer*

The delivery of the first of a series of lend-lease locomotives built in America for use in England was the occasion for a ceremony. Because the locomotive was stripped of all but essential parts the British, with typical reserve, named it the "*Austerity*." For the same reason the American workmen at Schenectady, where it was built, had called it the "*Gypsy Rose Lee*."

— H. Wilson Lloyd in *Life*

Dr. R. Seldin, a dentist, has a farm in Putnam County, New York, called "Tooth Acres."

— Walter Winchell

Students at Detroit's Redford High School have christened one of their drinking fountains "Old Faceful."

— *The Outpost*

A night club opening in New York chose the name "Chez When."

— Earl Wilson,
Post-Hall Syndicate

Ernest Pagano, Paramount script writer, christened his estate "El Rancho Costa Mucha."

A Methodist minister, retiring, happily named his first permanent home "Dunmovin."

Name of an Indianapolis antique shop: "Den of Antiquity."

— Carl Martz

Inmates of the Iowa State Penitentiary refer to it as "The Walled-Off Astoria."   — The Presidio

Alexander Woollcott once named his house "Wit's End"; Jerome Beatty has called his "Writer's Cramp."

A group of women searching for a name for their new club decided on "The Vicious Circle."

— Judy Thompson

A retired mathematics professor named his cottage at Carmel-by-the-Sea "After Math." — Chicago Tribune

So Well Remembered

In Cedar Grove, N. J., Private Dominic Donadio gave his newborn son a middle name: Furlough.   — Time

A Navy physician in the Pacific received from his fiancée a snapshot taken on a beach and showing two couples smiling contentedly while his girl sat alone at one side, forlorn and lonely. The accompanying letter explained that this was how she was fretting away the time until he returned. At first the physician was delighted, displaying it proudly to several fellow officers. That night, however, after studying it a long time in silence, he turned to his roommate. "John," he said, "I wonder who took that picture?"   — Robert J. Doyle

When London's Bank of England built an air-raid shelter underground to protect its staff, its ARP wardens sent a health questionnaire to employes to find out if they could withstand prolonged imprisonment in the narrow, crowded shelter. One question was: "Do you suffer from claustrophobia?"

To their amazement, 95 percent of the women employes answered, "Yes." Calling in the chief of the women's division, the ARP organizers asked her if she had explained to the girls exactly what "claustrophobia" meant. "Oh, yes," said she. "I told them it meant being afraid of confinement."   — Time

Gracie Fields told this air-raid story. The girl said, " 'Erbert, you really shouldn't 'ave kissed me like that, with all those people so close around us, even if it was in the dark."

"I didn't kiss you," said the boy, looking angrily around in the crowd. "I only wish I knew who it was — I'd teach 'im."

" 'Erbert," sighed the girl, "you couldn't teach 'im nothing."
— Boston *Daily Globe*

In an Army hospital, one nurse warned another: "These are the dangerous cases. They're almost well!"   — Lariar cartoon in *Liberty*

A sailor stationed on a far-flung U. S. outpost was noted for his loyalty to his fiancée. Then one day he received a callous letter telling him that she was going to marry a 4-F, and would he please return her picture.

He was so upset by this treachery that his buddies rallied to avenge their pal. A collection of photographs, snapshots and pin-up girls was made from every fellow on the base. They were packed into a huge crate and shipped to the fickle wench.

Upon opening the crate, she found a note reading: "Please pick out your picture and return the rest to me. This is a little embarrassing but I don't remember which one is yours."   — Shirley Loomis

An excited Army recruit asked his company commander for an immediate furlough — his wife was going to have a baby. Permission was granted, and when the furlough papers were drawn up and the soldier was leaving, the officer asked exactly when the baby was due. "About nine months after I get home, sir," replied the recruit casually.
— W. J. Furman

When a British sailor at the Hollywood Canteen complained about a sore throat, a solicitous hostess asked, "Have you ever tried gargling with salt water?"

"You're asking me — who's been torpedoed three times?"
— Hedda Hopper

On one of the Central Pacific islands, our Navy commanding officer decided that the native girls' habit of wearing only a grass skirt was definitely bad for military morale. Therefore, he presented each native woman with a "skivvy shirt," the Navy undershirt of heavy cotton with quarter-length sleeves. Overjoyed, the girls asked for two apiece.

Imagine the skipper's astonishment next day when he saw several girls proudly wearing their clean new shirts, each with two round holes cut in the most obvious and appropriate places! — W. Tim Welch

I was seeing my husband off on a Navy transport plane for duty in the Aleutians. Among the passengers was a little black cocker spaniel. Bemoaning my fate, I said to the officer in charge: "A fine thing — letting a dog have passage aboard the plane when wives must stay in the United States."

"After all, madam," replied the officer, "all the men can pat the dog."
— Shirley H. Crawshaw in *Coronet*

Private Jones, an inveterate and invariably successful bettor, was such a demoralizing influence in his unit that his lieutenant, after trying unsuccessfully to end his gambling, sent him before the captain. After the interview, the lieutenant was summoned.

"I've shown Private Jones he can lose a bet," the captain said. "I asked him why he couldn't stop betting, and he said: 'Sir, it's a habit I can't seem to lose. Why, I'll bet you $10 right now you have a mole on

your left shoulder.' Well, I knew darn well I didn't, so I took off my shirt and showed him. He admitted he had lost and paid the $10. I guess that'll hold him!"

The lieutenant was so noticeably silent that the captain asked: "What's the matter? Aren't you pleased?"

"No, sir," replied the lieutenant. "You see, on the way to your quarters Jones bet me $25 he'd have the shirt off your back in five minutes.
— Mrs. B. F. Etter

Ups and Downs

Alfred Hitchcock, director of movie mystery thrillers, stepped into a New York hotel elevator with a friend and immediately began talking as though continuing a conversation:

"So I turned on the light, and there was this girl in the middle of the floor. Her throat was slit and there was a great puddle of blood. Beside the body was a knife. I was in a spot. If I called the police, there'd be a nasty row, and if I didn't somebody would find me there. So I took out my handkerchief and carefully . . ."

At this point the elevator stopped at Hitchcock's floor and he quietly stepped off with his companion, leaving everybody in the car goggle-eyed. — Chicago *Tribune*

Want ad in a Pennsylvania paper: "Woman, 21, would like job running elevator in office building. Has no experience and would like to begin in low building."
— Fred Sparks in *Parade*

Two eminently successful psychoanalysts occupied offices in the same building. One was 40 years old, the other over 70. At the end of an unbearably hot, sticky day they rode down on the elevator together. The younger man was completely done in, and he noted with some resentment that his senior was fresh as a daisy. "I don't understand," he marveled, "how you can listen to drooling patients from morning to night on a day like this and still look so spry."

The old analyst shrugged his shoulders and said, "Who listens?"
— Bennett Cerf in *The Saturday Review of Literature*

The elevator girl in the Memphis, Tenn., Baptist Hospital waited pointedly for the man to call his floor. "What's yours?" she said at last.

He beamed. "It's a boy."

She let him off at the seventh floor, maternity. — AP

The elevator operators at the Capitol in Washington are given to brooding over the world's troubles. "How's business?" a passenger asked one of these up-and-down philosophers. The operator looked at him moodily. "I'm not a man," he said despondently. "I'm a yo-yo."
— Hal Boyle, AP

Girl elevator operator, alone in the car with a sailor, "Going up . . . going up . . . anybody else going up? Please, will somebody go up!" — Henry Boltinoff cartoon in *The Saturday Evening Post*

The elevator operator in a Birmingham hotel called each stop in the usual manner: "Eleventh floor." "Sixth floor." "Fourth floor." But at the lobby he threw open the elevator door with a flourish and proudly announced: "Birmingham!" — William E. Hudson

Impasse at the Elevator

Condensed from Pageant

Robert Benchley

It is all very well for writers on etiquette to tell us what to say when we are introduced ("Hi-ya!"), or when we take leave of our hostess ("Thanks a million, toots!"). But what do two strangers say to each other when they find themselves alone together?

You are in an apartment house or a hotel, and, for some reason, you are leaving. You may even have been asked to leave. You come down the hall to the elevator and find a stranger there waiting.

Now, presumably he has rung the bell already. He wouldn't be just hanging around watching the cars go up and down, unless he were the village idiot. But you march right up and ring the bell, too.

This distrust between strangers is instinctive. You have a feeling that he might not have pushed the bell hard enough. He might even have pushed the "up" bell. Anyway, you push the bell. Then you stand back and wait.

Naturally, this turns him against you. You have cast aspersions on his bell-pushing abilities. So he, too, steps back, giving you a dirty look. You each pretend that you are very busy with your gloves or your tie or your underdrawers, or something. It is the zero hour.

If you are representatives of two of the more prominent sexes, the strain is even greater. In fact, for a lady and a gentleman to be placid in this position is well-nigh intolerable, if the lift is a long time in coming — which it is.

The time for ice-breaking is right at the start, or not at all. After a 30 seconds' wait, the breach can never be healed.

Of course, in the case of two men, the obvious remark for the one who was there first is:

"I rang it once, you mugg!"

To which the equally obvious reply is: "How was I to know? I thought you were the floor clerk." (Or "the house detective.")

This exchange of courtesies, however, would not clear the situation up at all. Better to say nothing than to start snarling right off the bat.

The remark least calculated to end in bloodshed would be:

"Some service, eh?"

With the reply: "I'll say!"

Then what? You have established contact, and a reasonably friendly one, but where do you go from there? You can't talk about the weather, as neither one of you knows what the weather is at that moment, being on the way out into it. It is a pretty problem in etiquette, and, so far as I have been able to ascertain, one which has never been dealt with by the experts.

Of course, if Noel Coward or some other banterweight champion were there to banter his way through the situation, at least one party would come out beaming. A rather smart scene could be worked up between a Noel Coward character and a Dorothy Parker character meeting at an elevator. But, with the general run of everyday characters, it is anything but a smart scene. It is what people who speak French call an "impasse."

Now, since the etiquette experts know so much, why don't they tackle a problem like this? They always pick things like "How do you do?" (holding out the right hand with thumb up) or "So good of you to ask me" (with fingers crossed). I could think those up myself.

The answer to it all must be that, in the real crises in life, nobody knows what to say, which is why we all look so foolish.

Radio Quips

I've got a tooth that's driving me to extraction. — Charlie McCarthy

I was a Boy Scout until I was 16, then I became a girl scout.
— Bob Hawk

"What comes into your mind when you hear the word 'Tschaikowsky'?"
"*Gesundheit.*" — Fred Allen

The first thing I notice about a man is whether George is around.
— Gracie Allen

"Why did you leave your last position?"
"Illness. The boss got sick of me."
— Charlie McCarthy

I don't mind the loss of my watch, but in it I had a lock of my husband's late hair.
— Fibber McGee and Molly

Her face is her fortune — and it runs into a nice figure.
— Gay Nineties

In the spring a young man's fancy lightly turns to what a girl has been thinking about all winter.
— Eddie and Ralph

When a man brings his wife flowers for no reason — there's a reason.
— Molly McGee

Asked if he liked intellectual girls, he replied: "I like a girl with a good head on my shoulder."
— Blind Date

He hasn't an enemy in the world — but all his friends hate him.
— Eddie Cantor

"I saw you the other day at the corner of Hollywood and Vine winking at the girls."
"I wasn't winking. That's a windy corner. Something got in my eye."
"She got in your car too."
— Rudy Vallee Show

Very Much at Sea

A minister, a scientist, and a lawyer were adrift on a life raft in the tropics. At last they sighted land. But the wind died down while they were still a short way off the beach. The lawyer, the only one who could swim, volunteered to go ashore with a line and pull the raft to land. The minister knelt and prayed for his safety.

Then the lawyer dived in. His companions saw the black fin of a shark making straight for him. The shark disappeared, then came up on the other side, having passed under the swimmer. Shortly they saw an even bigger shark darting toward him, but this one also swerved just in time.

After the lawyer had reached shallow water, the minister said to the scientist: "There, you Doubting Thomas, there is proof of the power of prayer."

"Power of prayer, hell!" retorted the scientist. "That was just professional courtesy."

— Alex F. Osborn

When King George V was Prince George and a lieutenant in the Marines, he was undergoing his military formation tests one day, supervised by an Army man. The afterdeck of the battleship had been cleared for action, so there were no guardrails round the deck. As Prince George put his squad through several formations, his obvious unfamiliarity with things military caused the Army man to splutter under his breath. Finally the Prince got his squad into a double line marching hell-bent for the stern, and either lost his tongue or didn't know the command to bring them about. The Army man became purple in the face and, as the leaders of the squad came to within two

feet of the stern, he stormed across to the Prince and yelled: "Good God, man, can't you at least say 'Good-bye' to them?"
— Harry Price in *Review of Reviews*

In June each year, First and Third classmen at Annapolis make a ten-week cruise to Europe. Schooled to the technique of returning social courtesies, they were posed a stiff problem when invited to the Vatican for an audience with the Pope. After His Holiness had made his ceremonial entrance into the hushed hall, had solemnly addressed his young guests in Latin, and was about to withdraw, his appreciative guests wanted to do something. But what? Well, there was something they could give His Holiness — something peculiarly their own. With a sudden leap the cheerleaders signaled for the treasured "4-N" yell, and the midshipmen responded with a roar that echoed through corridors unprofaned by such sounds through the centuries:

NAVY!   NAVY!   NAVY!

N-N-N-N — A-A-A-A — V-V-V-V — Y-Y-Y-Y

NAVY!

POPE!   POPE!   POPE!

His Holiness appeared vastly amused and entirely delighted.
— Kendall Banning, *Annapolis Today* (Funk & Wagnalls)

The shipwrecked sailor had spent nearly three years on a desert island, and one morning was overjoyed to see a ship in the bay and a boat putting off for the shore. As the boat grounded on the beach an officer threw the sailor a bundle of newspapers.

"The Captain's compliments," said the officer, "and will you please read through these and then let him know whether you still wish to be rescued."
— *Tit-Bits*

Women are wonderful, especially if you haven't seen one for a year. Our LST had been in the New Guinea area for about that long when we learned there were three Red Cross girls on the beach at Hollandia. Our skipper invited them aboard for dinner and sent a young ensign ashore to bring them out. When the ensign returned, he rushed over to where I was standing with the supply officer, and said breathlessly,

"One of those girls slipped while she was getting out of the boat and I caught her! I had her right in my arms!"

The supply officer nodded. "I touched one once," he said, his eyes fogged with memory. "Soft, ain't they?"
— Charles E. Parker, Jr., in *The Saturday Evening Post*

The captain of a ship once wrote in his log, "Mate was drunk today." When the mate became normal, he was terribly chagrined and angry, he pleaded with the captain to strike out the record; he declared that he had never been drunk before, that he would never drink again. But the captain said, "In this log we write the exact truth."

The next week the mate kept the log, and in it he wrote, "Captain was sober today." — William Lyon Phelps, *Adventures and Confessions* (Scribners)

The Fourth Estate

The Springfield *Republican*, edited by Samuel Bowles, rarely made a mistake, but once it reported the death of a citizen who was very much alive. He came into the editor's office later in the day to protest.

"I'm sorry, but if the *Republican* says you're dead, then you are dead," insisted Bowles. The only compromise he would make, after long discussion, was to print the man's name in the birth notices the next morning.   — Frank Ellis

The journalism professor was passing out a few hints on writing. "A good introduction," he explained, "is highly important. Always remember the young man who, desiring to marry Angus MacPherson's comely daughter, opened his interview with, 'Sir, I'd like to show you how I can save you some money.'"
— *The Christian Science Monitor*

When James Gordon Bennett, Jr., was guiding the destinies of the New York *Herald*, he issued an edict that under no circumstances should the name "Herald" appear except in italics.

One printer really showed his unflinching obedience to the order when, during the holiday season, he set up a Christmas program announcement with the following item: "Hark the *Herald* Angels Sing." — *The Christian Science Monitor*

A copyreader on an Illinois newspaper couldn't believe it when he read a reporter's story about the theft of 2025 pigs. "That's a lot of pigs," he growled, and called the farmer to check the copy. "Is it true that you lost 2025 pigs?" he asked.

"Yeth," lisped the farmer.

"Thanks," said the wise copyreader and corrected the copy to read "two sows and 25 pigs." — INS

Some years ago a Chicago Gold Coast millionaire was sued for divorce, and a reputedly beautiful young woman of dubious background named corespondent. When no picture of the lady appeared in the earliest possible edition of the *American*, Editor Foster Coates expressed polite astonishment.

"Our best man is trying," was the answer. "He can't get anywhere."

"Send some more men," said Mr. Coates. The day wore on, and still no pictures. Mr. Coates kept prodding. "Have they tried the servants?"

"We've offered them plenty."

"How about the photographers?"

"If she's ever had her picture taken in Chicago, no photographer will admit it, not for $100."

"Hmm," said Coates. "Well, one more try. Who's that very young man who just came in?"

"Him? Oh, he's a kid we just hired. Just breaking him in."

Foster Coates beckoned to the youngster. "Will you please try to get a photograph of Mrs. Maysie de Smythe? She lives at this address."

Within an hour the cub was back with an excellent picture, a little bewildered by the excitement it produced. Coates assembled the whole staff. "Now, Mr. Jones, will you please tell these gentlemen how you got the photograph?"

"Why," said the astonished cub, "I went to the house, rang the doorbell and asked the lady for it, and she gave it to me." — Marc A. Rose

A British fledgling reporter had been reprimanded for his overlong accounts and told to be brief. His next story was turned in as follows:

"A shocking incident occurred last night. Sir Reggy Blank, a guest at Lady Briny's ball, complained of feeling ill, took his hat, his coat, his departure, no notice of his friends, a taxi, a pistol from his pocket and, finally, his life. Nice chap. Regrets and all that."

— John Canning, Jr.

When Bret Harte was editing a little paper in a mining settlement in California the wife of the leading citizen died and it became his duty to write an editorial obituary. He concluded with the remark, "She was distinguished for charity above all the other ladies of this town."

"I dropped into the office later," said Bret Harte, "to look at the proofs. I found that the intelligent compositor had made me say, 'She was distinguished for chastity above all the other ladies of this town.' I crossed out the insulting s, put a big query mark in the margin and went home. To my horror in the morning I read, 'She was distinguished for chastity (?) above all the other ladies of this town.'"

— E. P. Mitchell, *Memories of an Editor* (Scribners)

Banner Boners

Headline in a New York newspaper: "FATHER OF TEN SHOT — MISTAKEN FOR RABBIT."   — Quoted in Jonesboro, Ark., *Evening Sun*

The Chico, Calif., *Enterprise* announced: "MRS. ROBERTSON IS HEAD OF COMMITTEE FOR CHEST DISPLAY."

Headline in Minneapolis *Tribune:* "WEEK-END GUESTS DUE: MRS. KNOBLAUCH TO GO WEST."

Headline from Redondo Beach, Calif., *South Bay Daily Breeze:* "MANY ANTIQUES AT D.A.R. MEETING."

Headline in Springfield, Mo., *Leader-Press:* "NEW ORLEANS POLICE WARM STRIP-TEASERS."

The Key West, Fla., *Citizen* announced: "PRE-NATAL PARTIES FOR BRIDE-ELECT."

Headline in Hollywood, Calif., *Citizen-News:* "EGG-LAYING CONTEST WON BY LOCAL MAN."

The Spokane *Chronicle* announced: "GRILL SUSPECT OVER BIG BLAZE."

The Halifax, Canada, *Herald* reported: "JUNE BABIES FLOOD OTTAWA HOSPITAL."

A story about efforts to solve budget matters in the Parkersburg, Pa., *Post* was headed: "BOROUGH FATHEDS HAVE BUDGET TROUBLE."
— Quoted in *Editor & Publisher*

The Madison, Wis., *Capital Times* printed these two headlines side by side:
"55 ROOSTERS STOLEN AT TOWN OF OREGON FARM."
"SOCIALIST CLUB TO HOLD CHICKEN SUPPER."

Case of the Empty-Handed Musicians

THE MUSICIANS sketched here are working under one bad handicap — they haven't got their usual instruments. Nevertheless, you ought to be able to tell from the positions they're in what instrument each plays. The gent clawing the air in Picture Number 1 obviously is a piano player without his piano; maybe it's better that way. What do the others play? You should be able to equip six out of nine.

— B. F. Caslon and Bill Bailey in
The Saturday Evening Post

Answers

2. Flute
3. Violin
4. Harmonica
5. Harp
6. Bassoon
7. Trombone
8. Cymbals
9. Bass Viol
10. Cello

The Children's Hour

A civil servant who had been stationed in Egypt and was about to return to England had a small son who showed a touching attachment to a statue of General Gordon mounted on a camel. The boy begged for a farewell visit. "Good-bye, Gordon," he sobbed. The father was moved by such patriotic sensibility. Then, as they turned away, the youngster asked suddenly, "Daddy, who's that man on Gordon?"

— *The British Weekly*

Mother had just finished a stern lecture on the subject of Barbara's wayward little playmates. "Now tell me, dear," she concluded in a kinder tone, "where do bad little girls go?"

Barbara smiled winsomely: "Everywhere."   — *Vr-1 Wing Tips*

Announcing her dancing class's recital, the child said, "We are going to have real people there — not just mothers and fathers."

A few days ago I overheard my small grandson doing his arithmetic homework. "Three plus one, the son of a bitch is four," he was saying. "Three plus two, the son of a bitch is five. Three plus three, the son of a bitch is six." And so on. Horrified, I asked him where on earth he had picked up that language. "Oh, that's the way they teach us at school," he replied. The following day I went to see his teacher and asked her about it. At first she was equally horrified, then her face broke into a grin. "I get it!" she cried. "We teach the children to say 'Three plus one, the sum of which is four. Three plus two, the sum of which is five.' "   —F. H.

A little girl's thank-you note: "Thank you for your nice present. I always wanted a pin cushion, although not very much."

— *The Wall Street Journal*

The teacher wrote on the blackboard: "I ain't had no fun all summer." Then she asked a youngster in the front row: "Harry, what should I do to correct that?"

"Mebbe — get a boy friend?" he suggested helpfully.

The English writer Francis Toye tells of a schoolmaster he had at Winchester who enjoyed a reputation for short reports to parents. On one occasion he wrote of a certain boy, "Trying," which delighted the boy's parents until the next report came in. This one read, "Very trying."

— Bennett Cerf in *The Saturday Review of Literature*

The modern child quizzed her mother as to her origin, and was given the traditional answer: "God sent you." "And how did you get here, Mother? Did God send you, too?" "Yes, dear." "And grandma?" "Yes, dear." "And great-grandma?" "Yes, dear." "Do you mean to say, Mother, that there have been no sex relations in this family for over 200 years?"

— Mary Ware Dennett

When the librarian questioned the little boy's book choice, *Advice to Young Mothers*, he explained, "I'm collecting moths."

Remarkable Explanations

In Tyler, Texas, an understanding judge accepted Mrs. Harriett Wood's excuse for parking overtime outside a women's shop: unavoidably detained in a girdle. — *Time*

One morning Mose came to work with a black eye, a swollen lip, and other troubles. "Mose," asked his boss, "what in the world happened to you?"

"Well, boss, I was a-talkin' when I shoulda been a-listenin'."

— Edison Marshall

A man got off a train one day, green in the face. A friend who met him asked him what was wrong. "Train sickness," said the traveler. "I'm always deathly sick when I ride backwards on a train."

"Why didn't you ask the man sitting opposite you to change with you?" asked the friend.

"I thought of that," said the traveler, "but there wasn't anybody there." — *Esquire*

Small boy explaining broken window to policeman: "I was cleaning my slingshot and it went off."

— Gene Carr cartoon in *The Saturday Evening Post*

In a trim bungalow near Manhattan lived a rising young novelist and his wife, presided over by a Scandinavian servant whom everyone described as a gem and who reminded the men, at least, of Ingrid Bergman. This paragon one day approached her mistress in tears and announced: "I must leave on the first of the month."

"But why?" demanded the housewife. "I thought you were perfectly happy here." It wasn't that, sobbed the maid; she had met a handsome soldier a few months before, and now — and now — "Don't do anything until I've consulted my husband," said the wife. She was back from his study in a trice. "We have decided that you must stay," she announced. "We will adopt your baby."

In due course, a son appeared upon the scene, the author adopted him legally, and all was serene for another year, when the maid again announced she was leaving. This time she had met a sailor. The author and his wife went into another huddle, and the maid was told, "It is unfair to bring up a child alone. We will adopt your second baby."

The second baby was a darling little girl, and the bungalow resounded with happy laughter. Then the blow fell. The maid resigned again. "Don't tell me," gasped the wife, "that this time you met a Marine."

"It's not that at all, ma'am," said the servant with dignity. "I'm resigning because I simply cannot work for such a big family."
— Bennett Cerf in *The Saturday Review of Literature*

Drunken driver's alibi: "I didn't know I was loaded."   — *As-U-Go*

A lady in our town who may be best described as a perpetual talker was asked by one of her long-suffering neighbors if she ever thought about what she was going to say before saying it. "Why, no," said the lady solemnly. "How on earth could I know what I think about a thing until I've heard what I have to say on the subject?"
— Murl Corbett

High Ways

As I stood by the curb in Selma, N. C., I observed a young man mopping his brow and peering nervously up the street. At that moment an old Ford convertible came slowly around the corner, a girl of about 20 gripping the steering wheel and gazing fixedly ahead. As she approached us, the young man gestured frantically and yelled. "Keep more to the right! Shift into high. Don't forget the clutch or you'll strip your gears!"

The car passed out of sight and he relaxed momentarily, then began peering up the street again. Soon the Ford rounded the corner once more, sputtering and jerking even worse than before. "Choke 'er!" he shouted.

The car leaped forward. "Brake down and shift to second at the corner," he called as the car passed.

Turning to me he explained, "It's my wife learning to drive."

"But couldn't you teach her better if you were in the car?"

"Maybe," he replied. "But the car's insured, and my life ain't!"
— W. Howard Rambeau

Driving back from Washington one rainy week-end, we stopped behind a little Crosley whose further progress was blocked by a pool of water across the road so deep that it would have flooded its engine. At that moment a large truck drove up alongside the tiny car and the driver called down to the Crosley: "Hop in, Elizabeth! Here's my cloak."

Pulling up in front of it, he let down the apron of the truck. The little car chugged up it and was decanted safe and sound on the other side of the water.   — Pearl Delson

A somewhat tipsy gentleman boarded a two-story bus in Chicago and sat down near the driver. He talked and talked until the driver tactfully suggested that he go up to the top deck to enjoy the fresh air. The drunk amiably clambered upstairs. In a few minutes he was back.

"What's the matter?" asked the driver. "Didn't you like it up there?"

"Yep, nice view, nice air," answered the drunk. "But it ain't safe — no driver!"   — University of Washington *Columns*

Actor Dick Erdman had this motto lettered on his car: "Some of the world's bravest women pass through these doors."
— Andrew B. Hecht

Duke, Frank Delappe's prize pointer, always rode in the trunk of the car whenever his master took him on a hunting trip. He would leap in the moment Frank lifted the lid. Recently Delappe brought home a new car — a Studebaker — and opened the hood to check the carburetor. Duke bounded across the lawn and jumped in, sprawling clumsily across the engine. Delappe hauled the confused dog out.

Later, his master came back and found him circling the new car curiously, carefully studying each end.   —UP

Du Bose Heyward, distinguished playwright and poet, had delivered a lecture in Detroit. Following it, a group of eager ladies gathered around him and refused to go without hearing his precise opinion of "our own poet, Eddie Guest."

Finally an embarrassed Mr. Heyward confessed that he did not consider Mr. Guest's output to be poetry.

"Mr. Heyward," then said one old lady, piercing him with a steely eye, "what make of car do you drive?"

Mr. Heyward suggested that poets do not usually have the wherewithal to own motorcars.

"Mr. Guest," said the lady triumphantly, "drives a Packard."
                                                             — *Golden Book*

Society Notes

A friend of ours is renowned in our little town for her malapropisms. At a tea recently, one of the guests complimented her on the new shoes she was wearing: "They're very handsome, and they look comfortable, too."

"Yes," she agreed pleasantly, "I like their comfort — they make streetwalking *so* easy."   — Fels Hecht

A Hollywood writer with a reputation as a Lothario tried to refuse when a witty hostess invited him to a charity affair, pleading that he was working on something important.

"Oh, in that case just bring your work with you," the lady suggested. "We'd love to have her, too."   — Robert Arthur

There was no avoiding it: the hostess was going to sing. The new guest said to his host in surprise, "I didn't know your wife sang."

The host settled himself deeper into his chair for the ordeal.

"Never heard her before?" he grunted. "Then you've got a great deal to look backward to."   — Norman Stanley Bortner

Lynn Bari, describing a glamour girl's gown at a Hollywood party, said: "It was one of those black numbers that pick up everything — including men."

— Erskine Johnson in *Photoplay*

My husband, a lawyer, often refuses to accompany me to parties because so many people spoil his evening by asking him for advice. I asked a doctor if this happened to him. "All the time!" he said.

"Then how do you get rid of these people?"

"I have a wonderful remedy," the doctor grinned. "When someone begins telling me his ailments, I stop him with one word, 'Undress!'"

— Betty Ross

It was one of those Hollywood parties. The usual bore was there — you know, the guy who calls everyone by his first name after two minutes. This particular clunk fastened himself on Ethel Barrymore. He kept Etheling her to temporary insanity. Knowing the explosive temper of the stage's First Lady — the other folks just sat back and waited for the detonation. Finally, Eth reached the berling pernt. Giving the heel a thump on the back, she cried: "Ethel, hell! Don't be so formal. Call me Cuddles!"

— Walter Winchell

At a dinner party in New York, a South American visitor was telling about his country and himself. He concluded, "And I have a most charming and sympathetic wife but, alas, no children." Then, as his companions seemed to expect further enlightenment, he continued haltingly, "You see, my wife is unbearable." This was greeted with puzzled glances, so he sought to clear the matter up: "I mean, my wife is inconceivable." Seeing that this, too, was not understood, and floundering deeper in the intricacies of English, he finally explained triumphantly: "That is, my wife, she is impregnable!"

Against her will, the wife of a famous author attended a reception. All went well until the very moment of departure, when she seized the hand of her hostess, and assured her warmly, "It was so nice of us to come!"

— Bennett Cerf in *The Saturday Review of Literature*

Out of My Mind

From the book by Katharine Brush

There are moments when we all make blithering idiots of ourselves. Among my own embarrassing moments I confess the following: There was my parting tribute to a very distinguished guest of honor at a reception — I assured him fervently that I was terribly sorry to have met him; and this misstatement so flurried me that when he smiled forgivingly, and tried to introduce me to a lady standing with him ("Mrs. Smith, this is Miss Brush"), I responded with redoubled earnestness by saying, "How do you do, Miss Brush?" — thereby confusing Mrs. Smith and myself no little.

There was also the time I tried to dance with a headwaiter (it was in a crowded night club, and he had stood behind my chair and murmured something, and I had risen automatically, thinking he was one of the men of our party and continuing so to think until I'd practically propelled him into motion). And there was the day I stepped out of the door of a shop at Madison Avenue and walked up the street, serenely unconscious of the fact that the six policemen I saw ahead of me were part of a platoon, and that there were 12 more policemen behind me — all marching two-by-two in a column, with me in the middle of it. I must indeed have looked like dangerous jail-fodder to the passers-by.

And then there was the time somebody told me that black mustache-wax made a wonderful mascara for the eyelashes, and I tried it out. It seemed to work, and I went to a party all really quite starry-eyed with mustache-wax. The trouble came later in the evening when a man I was talking to said to me, "I beg your pardon, but you have a black smooch on your cheek."

"Oh, dear," I said to him, "that's my mustache-wax." And — busy getting it off — I never did have a chance to explain. By the time I remembered to, the man, looking shaken, had moved off.

— Published by Doubleday

Spiced Tongue

Children grow by leaps and bounds — especially in the apartment overhead (George Allen)

Child reciting the Golden Rule: "Do unto others before they do unto you."

Just about the time you think you can make both ends meet, somebody moves the ends (Pansy Penner)

Road maps tell a motorist everything he wants to know except how to fold them up again . . . Among other things that don't turn out quite as you expect are people who drive cars.

Deft definitions: Psychologist — a man who, when a good-looking girl enters a room, watches everybody else (*Punch*) . . . Confirmed bachelor — one who thinks that the only thoroughly justified marriage was the one that produced him (Harlan Miller) . . . Press agent — a man who hitches his braggin' to a star (Hedda Hopper) . . . Parking space — an unoccupied area along the curb on the other side of the street (Cedric Adams) . . . Raisin — a worried grape (Milton Berle) . . . Egotism — usually just a case of mistaken nonentity (Barbara Stanwyck)

The Browns arrived home, brag and baggage (Marcia C. Power)

After her first horseback ride, a young lady was heard to make this comment: "I never imagined any thing filled with hay could ride so hard!" (Jean Tennyson)

Many a woman who can't add can certainly distract . . . Some women take the diaper as others take the veil (E. Arnot Robertson) . . . She has not only the seal of his approval, but the mink also (George Ryan) . . . She's the sort of bridge partner who calls a spade two spades (Russel Crouse in New York *Post*)

Gardening — man's effort to improve his lot (Ted Taylor and Leonard L. Levinson) . . . Give dandelions an inch and they'll take a yard (Edith A. Van Sant) . . . I'm so disgusted with my garden that I'm ready to throw in the trowel (Leo, Bob Burns show) . . . FOR SALE CHEAP, wife-sized lawn mower (Parkersburg, W. Va., *Sentinel*)

High heels, according to Christopher Morley, were invented by a woman who had been kissed on the forehead.

Speeches are like babies — easy to conceive, but hard to deliver (Pat O'Malley)

One hospital refers to accident cases as its bumper crop (*L & N Employes' Magazine*)

Bob Hope on transportation, "To give you an idea of how fast we traveled: We left Spokane with two rabbits and when we got to Topeka, we still had only two."

Local Color

My friend from the Maine woods was paying his first visit to Florida. He delighted at first in our sunny, mild weather, but after weeks of flawless sunshine he looked out the window one morning and muttered, "Oh, hell, another damned beautiful day."   — Walter A. Pearce

All the time-honored harbingers of spring — such as the first robin or crocus — take second place with me after an incident I witnessed one spring at my father's farm. I was sitting on a fallen tree at the edge of a wood, watching the "hired man" plow a field. At the end of each furrow the old fellow would take out a large blue bandanna and mop his brow. Finally, after a particularly prolonged application of the handkerchief, he stalked off into the woods.

Ten minutes later he reappeared carrying a bundle which he placed on the ground a few yards in front of the horse. Returning to the plow, he held a course which turned the earth directly over the object and, after a satisfying backward glance, continued across the field.

Spring was definitely here: Old Joe had just plowed under his long winter red-flannels!   — Damon C. Lamance

"Doc," said the old mountaineer, leading a gangling youth into the presence of the village medico, "I want you should fix up my son-in-law. I shot him in the leg yesterday and lamed him up a mite."

"Shame on you, shooting your own son-in-law!" scolded the doctor.

"Wal, doc," rejoined the mountaineer, "he warn't my son-in-law when I shot him."   — *The Wall Street Journal*

I learned that our elderly Cape Cod neighbor had been seriously ill from eating clam chowder, and in the afternoon I called to see how she was. "Come in and see for yourself," said her daughter.

"Oh, don't disturb her," I began — and then I saw the old lady. There she sat at the table, a napkin tied under her chin, eating clam chowder.

"But," I exclaimed in surprise, "I thought it was clam chowder that made her sick!"

The old lady looked me in the eye. "It did! But I don't aim to have my stomach dictatin' to *me* what I can eat!" — Nora A. Brophy

A New Yorker, pointing to a hillside field, complimented the New Englander on his corn.

"How do you plow that field? It looks pretty steep."

"Don't plow it; when the spring thaws come, the rocks rolling down hill tear it up."

"That so? How do you plant it?"

"Don't plant it really. Just stand in my back door and shoot the seed in with a shotgun."

"Is that the truth?" asked the New Yorker.

"Hell, no. That's conversation."

Visiting us at the ranch last summer was a bit of feminine attractiveness from the East whose sentiments toward Frank, one of the cowboys, were a mixture of romantic design and hero worship. At one Saturday night dance in town she made a particular effort — every curve and curl and eyelash was calculated to awaken his interest — but Frank confined his conversation to beef cattle, and before long retired to the bar. Soon she appeared beside him. "That cowhand over there made passes at me," she said indignantly, "and I've never even been introduced to him!"

Frank knew a gentleman's duty. Walking manfully over to the cowpuncher, who outweighed him by 50 pounds, he asked his name. Then he politely introduced him to the girl, and returned to his drink. — Lawrence Cardwell

Uncle Horace's aversion to tractors is well known in Riley County, Kansas, where he farms his 260 acres entirely with horses. However, an enterprising tractor salesman persuaded Uncle Horace to let him put on a demonstration.

"Mighty fine, mighty fine," admitted Uncle Horace afterward. "And when you can get those 200 horses' power in that there engine to produce fertilizer, I'll buy one." — Wayne Bloomberg

Sam Russell, justice of the peace in Crawfordsville, Iowa, was a reticent man. One day a saleslady breezed into his residence and inquired if his wife was at home.

"No, she ain't home," the justice said.

"Do you mind if I wait?" the visitor asked.

"Nope, have a chair."

After a full hour of waiting, the woman asked, "Where is your wife?"

"She went out to the cemetery."

"How long do you think she'll be gone?"

"Well, I don't know," said the justice deliberately, "but she's been out there 11 years now."   — Ralph E. Shannon in *The Rotarian*

The Business Whirl

A Boston surgeon visited a little inn in the tranquil village of Wellfleet, on Cape Cod. Old Captain Curran was in charge. The Cape was feeling the pinch of depression; summer folks were scarce and trade was at low ebb.

"Hello, Captain," sang out the surgeon. "And how is the hotel business?"

"Waal," drawled Captain Curran, "I ain't never yit made enough to quit, an' I ain't never yit lost enough to quit. I hope to the Lord I do one or the other this season."   — Dr. Robert M. Bartlett

"You ought to feel highly honored, young man," said the big businessman to the life insurance agent. "Do you know that today I have refused to see seven insurance men?"

"I know," replied the agent. "I'm them."

— Neal O'Hara, McNaught Syndicate

The cashier of the Louisville *Courier-Journal* in the days of the famous editor, Henry Watterson, was in a perpetual dither, for he faced the daily problem of a shortage in his cash drawer. Whenever the editor felt the need, he would fill his pocket from the till and be off without consulting anyone.

One day, with the cashier in tow, the business manager appeared before Mr. Watterson's desk. "It isn't that we object to your taking the money," the manager explained. "But it would help keep the record straight if you would note the amount taken on a slip of paper, initial it and leave it in the drawer." The editor grudgingly agreed.

That afternoon Watterson entered the cashier's cage, busied himself at the till, scribbled a notation on a piece of paper, placed it in the drawer and hurried out. Hardly had he quit the cage before the cashier and business manager were at the till. In the drawer emptied of cash lay a note. It said: "I took it all. H. W."   — Frank C. McLearn

The personnel manager asked the youthful ex-lieutenant what business experience he had. "None," was the reply. "I just got out of college when the war started."

"Well, what kind of job do you think you could handle?"

"Oh," breezed the applicant, "something executive. A vice-presidency, for instance."

The partner looked thoughtful. "I guess that lets us out," he answered. "You see, we have 12 vice-presidents already."

The ex-louie waved a hand nonchalantly. "Oh, that's all right," he said. "I'm not superstitious."   — John Straley in *Investment Dealers' Digest*

Needing a new secretary, the firm's president decided to have applicants judged by a psychologist. Three girls were interviewed together.

"What do two and two make?" the psychologist asked the first.

"Four," was the prompt answer. To the same question the second girl replied: "It might be 22." The third girl answered: "It might be 22 and it might be four."

When the girls had left the room, the psychologist turned triumphantly to the president. "There," he said, "that's what psychology does. The first girl said the obvious thing. The second smelled a rat. The third was going to have it both ways. Now, which girl will you have?"

The president did not hesitate. "I'll have the blonde with the blue eyes," he said.   — *The Canteen*

"Honest, Claude, I don't see how you make a living on this farm," I once remarked to a Vermont Yankee. "Look at the rocks everywhere!"

"I ain't so poor as y' think I be," retorted the farmer. "I don't own this durn farm!"

— Donald Wilhelm

To let his employer know what he thought about his alleged salary, a young New Yorker carefully wrote above his signature, when he cashed his check, "Any resemblance between this and a living wage is purely coincidental."

— _Rockefeller Center Magazine_

McTavish was the proud owner of a new cash register. One day when an old friend came into the shop and bought a sixpenny cigar, the customer noted that McTavish pocketed the money instead of putting it into the drawer.

"Why not ring it up?" he asked. "You'll be forgetting it."

"Oh, I'll no forget it," replied the Scot. "Ye ken I keep track in my head until I get a dollar, an' then I ring it up. It saves the wear-r and tear-r on the machine."

— Montreal _Star_

The man at the bar finished his second glass of beer and turned to ask the manager of the place, "How many kegs of beer do you sell here in a week?"

"Thirty-five," the manager answered with pride.

"Well, I've just thought of a way you can sell 70."

The manager was startled. "How?"

"It's simple. Fill up the glasses."

— Oscar Schisgall

In Washington, an attractive young Government worker made a practice of coming in about one minute late every day. Repeated warnings by her supervisor had no effect. Finally in exasperation he announced, "Miss Brown, I am tired of talking about your tardiness. I am, therefore, suspending you for one day without pay. When would you like to take the day?"

"Well, if it's all right with you," she replied instantly, "I'd like to use it up being late."

— Celia L. Carpenter

A youth from our town got a job as a radio announcer in a neighboring city. Everyone thought he'd be a great success, but soon rumors began circulating that things weren't going well. George was too fond of rearranging prepared scripts to agree with his own ideas. In a short time he was back in town. "I'm not going back there until they take back what they said," he told me.

"Why, what did they say?" I asked innocently.

"They said I was fired," came the answer.   — Robert F. Higgins

Good Clean Fun

A housewife sent her best colored luncheon cloth and two of the matching napkins to the laundry. They came back miserably faded. She stormed into the laundry and got into line at the complaint desk. When her turn arrived, the clerk informed her seriously, "If you'll bring in the remaining napkins, madam, we'll be glad to fade them to match the rest of your set."   — Marcia Winn in Chicago *Tribune*

A young bride from the West moved to a small Vermont village, and months went by with little sign of friendliness from her neighbors. At last she spoke about it to the woman who cleaned for her.

"I don't see what else you can expect," responded the Vermonter crisply, "considering what the people here are saying about you."

"Saying about me!" gasped the bewildered bride, whose life was above reproach.

"Yes, about your washing. I don't know how you do things in California, but here we do not hang our pink panties out for everyone to see. We pin them up on the line *inside* of pillow cases."
          — Lois Hanscom

In Phoenix, Ariz., Mao McElhinney got his shirt back from the laundry, plus the address book he had left in his pocket — plus 12 new girls' names, addresses, phone numbers.   — *Time*

The old Negro laundress came one day with a tale of woe. "Cheer up, Mandy," said her mistress consolingly. "There's no use worrying."

"How come dere's no use in worrying?" she demanded. "When de good Lawd send me tribulation He 'spect me to tribulate, ain't He?"
— *Public Speaker's Treasure Chest*, edited by
Herbert V. Prochnow (Harper)

A man who had neglected his account with his laundress for months, finally found this note among his clean clothes:

"Dear Sir: You have owed me six dollars for four months. If you do not pay the whole by next week, I will put too much starch in your collars. Cordially, Mrs. Smith."

Recently I have been having trouble with public laundries shrinking my unmentionables, so I found a large railroad spike and tied a tag to it with the inscription: "Try and shrink this!"

When my laundry was returned the next week, I opened it and found a small carpet tack with a tag attached. On it was inscribed: "We did!"
— C. G. Babcock

Anything for a Laugh

One of the assistant editors on a national magazine wore a new hat to the office one day. While he was in conference with his boss, a writer on the staff inspected the hat, then went down to the store it came from and bought an exact duplicate, complete even to the monogrammed initials on the sweatband. There was only one difference — it was three sizes larger than the original. Back at the office, he switched the hats. At the end of the day when the editor put on his hat, it fell over his ears. Thoroughly mystified, he took it off and examined it. There were his initials — it must be his hat.

The next day, he was again wearing the hat, which now seemed to fit pretty well. As soon as he went out of the room, the writer inspected the hat. He found the sweatband was stuffed with tissue paper; so he took the paper out, stuffed it in the original hat, and put that on the rack. At the end of the day, when the editor put on his hat, it just sat on the top of his head. Again he looked inside — and immediately went off to Bellevue Hospital for an examination.
— Robert Markewich

William Sydney Thayer, later a professor at Johns Hopkins, and his Harvard friends were delighted during their student days when the danseuse, Loie Fuller, arrived in Boston. In her finale, Loie would suddenly whiz down the stage and end seated with legs and arms stretched apart as if she were about to split. Returning a second night armed with a number of highly starched collars, Thayer and Company secured seats in the front row. At the moment that Loie seemed about to split they tore the collars, making an unearthly rending screech. The audience went wild; even Loie seemed to think she was actually splitting. — Edith Gittings Reid, *The Life and Convictions of William Sydney Thayer* (Oxford University Press)

One afternoon Smith heard a call for help from his neighbor Jones. Rushing over, he found Jones in the front yard, struggling with a horse. "Lend a hand," said Jones, "I want to get him up on the porch." Smith was a kindly man, and full of curiosity, so he lent a hand.

When the horse was safely on the porch, Jones said: "Hold the door for me; I want to get him into the house." When the horse was in the hall Jones ordered, "You push while I pull. I want to get him up the stairs." They heaved and hauled and the horse whinnied and stumbled, but they got him up.

"My!" panted Jones. "I didn't think we'd make it." Then he led

the horse into the bathroom, and pointed to the bathtub. "In he goes."
With toil and infinite ingenuity they got the horse into the tub.

"And now," asked Smith, "will you please tell me what it's all about?"

"Well, you see," answered Jones, "I have a brother-in-law who
thinks he knows everything. He knows all the answers. And it makes
me tired. So when he comes here tonight he'll go to the bathroom and
see the horse in the bathtub and come rushing out and yell, 'Great
guns, Bill, there's a horse in the bathtub!' and I'll just say, 'Well,
what of it!' and let him worry."

                                                        — Lowell Thomas

When Philip Guedalla was president of the debating society at
Oxford, he begged a friend to ask him two special questions — there
are always questions before the debate starts — to which he had
carefully prepared answers. The friend agreed and put the first question. Mr. Guedalla's witty reply sent a ripple of laughter through
the assembly. His brilliant retort to the second question brought down
the house. The friend now felt it was his turn and, rising gravely from
his seat once more, inquired: "What was the third question you
wished me to ask you?"   — Hesketh Pearson, *Ventilations* (Lippincott)
                                              Copyright 1930 by Hesketh Pearson

Don Marquis used to tell of a time in Hollywood when he was taken
ill with a heart attack. It was urgent for him to be got to a hospital
at once; all the ambulances were in service, so a hearse was sent to
fetch him. In this somber, glass-paned vehicle he was laid on a stretcher
and rolled off toward the clinic. On the way, halted in a traffic jam,
the hearse pulled up next to a smart little open roadster in which
two frolicsome young women were gaily chattering. In the middle
of their mirth, noticing the transparent chariot alongside, they piously
withheld palaver, and glanced reverently through the glass panel
where Don's burly figure lay decently composed under a blanket.
At that moment he caught their gaze and in spite of heartburn and
syncope appalled them with a slow and magnificent wink. He had the
large and lustered eye, the heavy reef of eyebrow, which could make
a wink seem as physically massive as a shrug. The damsels fell into a

hysteric seizure, and as his carriage rolled away he saw them crash into another car and attempt, with screams, to explain to a disbelieving policeman. "I'll bet," he used to add, "they led better lives after that." — Christopher Morley in *The Saturday Review of Literature*

Robert Bridges, one-time editor of *Scribner's Magazine*, often told the story of a Princeton classmate, who on a trip to Egypt had for several days a French-speaking native guide and courier. Near the end of the trip, the guide said, "Sire, teach me some words of your language, that I may attract your countrymen." The Princetonian complied. A year or so later, returning to Egypt, he looked up his guide and presently asked, "How did you get along with the English I taught you?" "Sire," the guide replied, "some smiled and came with me. Others were angry and turned away."

The phrase the courier had learned was "To hell with Yale."

The late Douglas Fairbanks couldn't resist keeping up his reputation as a practical joker even after death. Four close friends who had been led to believe they would be remembered in his will were surprised when it made no mention of them. However, an envelope to be opened 60 days later was placed in the custody of Douglas, Jr. When the friends had given up any thought of an inheritance, Douglas had his joke. The envelope contained a supplementary will leaving them $60,000 apiece. — Peggy McEvoy

A friend of mine in the island of Guernsey one day settled down in a small, deserted bay to read, hidden behind a sand dune. Presently two young girls came along and seeing no one, undressed and stretched out to sun-bathe. Soon a parson appeared carrying a camera, and believing himself alone, left his clothes on the beach and swam around the neighboring headland.

Out from behind their sand dune stole the two girls to where the parson's clothes lay, picked up his camera and each snapped a picture of the other. After which they replaced the camera containing these candid portraits and returned to their hiding place.

— Viscountess Rhondda, *Notes on the Way* (Macmillan)

McEvoy in Nurseryland—1

By J. P. McEvoy

When I was young and charming I had a small son who refused to practice the piano, so I told him sternly: "No practice, no lessons," which seemed eminently fair, logical and satisfactory to him. So he grew up without piano and has lived to regret it. Me, too.

Now I have a little daughter age seven who also refuses to practice her piano lessons. But this time I know better than to give her the choice — and the out. For I had read a zillion books and articles on child psychology, and I was particularly sold on one expert who held that children always learn by example, not precept. "Expose the darlings to outstanding exponents of success and you'll be surprised what those sensitive little photographic plates will develop." It says here.

Well, my friend Yehudi Menuhin was coming to give a concert in Havana where we live and I said to my wife, "Let's ask him to come out to stay with us and bring his fiddle. It may be the turning point in the life of our little Pat. Peggy, too, for that matter, because she doesn't practice, either." I asked Menuhin and he said sure and he hoped I wouldn't mind if he practiced before the concert instead of having dinner, and I told him fire away, trying to make it sound casual, although I was all of a flutter. So we moved him into the guest room next to the nursery where we herded the children and mounted guard on them so they couldn't get away and Yehudi shut himself in, and sawed away on a Brahms concerto all through dinner hour. I looked up to see the children standing outside his door on the patio balcony listening with their four little ears sticking out like clam shells.

All puffed up with pride over the success of my strategy I went up to clinch matters. "How do you like it?" I asked them.

Seven-year-old Pat looked at me gravely and asked, "Who's that in there?" I told her that was Yehudi Menuhin, one of the world's greatest violinists, who was giving a concert that evening in the biggest theater in Havana. "What's he doing in there?" asked Peggy, age six.

"He is practicing the pieces he is going to play tonight," I said, not too smugly I hoped. Pat was incredulous. "You mean he doesn't know them yet?"

"Of course he knows them." I was a trifle irritated. "But a great artist believes one should never be satisfied with less than perfection. That is why he is still practicing."

"I see," said Pat thoughtfully. The next day I waited with superb confidence. No practice. Slightly shaken I said nothing, but waited until the following day. No practice. "It's developing slowly," I said hopefully. "Their little brains are just like photographic plates. That's what the man said. Tomorrow she'll start practicing."

After a week I confronted her. "Pat," I said grimly, "I haven't heard the piano around here for days. Why?"

"Maybe because I haven't practiced," said Pat.

"Exactly, and why haven't you practiced? Why? Why?" I'm afraid I sounded a bit shrill but there are limits to a father's patience. "Well, Daddy," she said, "I've been thinking about Mister Meenooning and I said to myself that if Mister Meenooning has to practice after all these years what's the use. So I've quit."

What do I do now?
Any suggestions?

McEvoy in Nurseryland—II

My wife claims all little children dawdle over their food, and all parents have trouble getting children to eat, and this is the nature of children, and our children are no different — and nothing can be done about it. And I claim this is all nonsense and pure defeatism. The children claim nothing. They just do as they please. Some days they are still eating breakfast when it's naptime. Other days they gulp everything down like a couple of small boa constrictors.

Recently I decided that the well-meaning but ineffectual fumbling which women call their intuition was getting nowhere, and it was time for me to step in with my calm, dispassionate and logical mind. "Children are just little animals," I said, "and all animals eat when they're hungry."

"Animals also eat the wrong things," said my wife, "and they overeat and get sick. Did you ever hear of a horse foundering?" And I said, "Did you ever hear of a child foundering?" My wife replied triumphantly, "That's different. Or are you trying to say Pat and Peggy are not as bright as an old horse?"

"Let's go out and come in again," I said. "Children are just little animals, and if I had my way I'd put their food on the table and yell: 'Come and get it!' And if they came, all right; and if they didn't, I'd just leave it there until they did. But, of course, you wouldn't subscribe to anything so logical as that."

"Logical!" sniffed my wife. "What kind of children do you think we would have? They'd eat like animals."

"Exactly," I said, "and their eyes would glow, their hair would glisten, their teeth would gleam, and they'd grow up as healthy as bear cubs and sleek as pussycats."

"Perhaps you'd like to go out and come in again," said my wife.

"Very well," I replied stiffly. "For your information, I have been reading up on parental authority and filial obedience, and the experts say children are little primitives. They can be trained, like savages, to accept authority when it is transferred to an inanimate object like a totem pole, or a fetish, or a stone idol. In this case you merely transfer your authority to something which the children cannot argue with."

"Like what?" said my wife.

And then I came up with my great idea: "The alarm clock! It rings. So does the school bell — and the school bell spells authority. Set the alarm to ring at the time you want the children to finish their breakfast. Tell them the clock will warn them when breakfast is over, and when the bell rings the plates will be whisked away to the kitchen."

"It won't work," said my wife.

"You'll see," I told her.

Next morning I set the alarm clock. The two little girls sat fascinated over their breakfast, watching the minute hand creep around to the fatal spot. On previous mornings they ate something, at least. But this morning they were so hypnotized, watching the clock and waiting for the bell to ring, they wouldn't eat anything. When the alarm sounded I was ruthless. I whisked the plates away. The children whisked right after me with howls of rage. I was calm but firm. Result: the children had such hysterics they couldn't go to school.

Naturally, my wife was inordinately pleased with the collapse of my theory, but I pointed out to her that this was not a fair, scientific test. After all, the electric light, telephone and radio were not all perfected with just one experiment. "We'll try again tomorrow."

And we did. And just as I predicted, the result was different. Again the children were fascinated, watching the hand go round, but also they remembered that when the bell rang their food disappeared. So just as the bell started to ring they began gulping everything down as fast as they could. I tried to take the plates away from them, but I wasn't strong enough. They wolfed everything down in one minute flat. Result: they had such violent indigestion they couldn't go to school that day, either.

"I hope you're satisfied now," said my wife, and her triumph was something majestic. "For the innocent habit of dawdling over their food you have substituted two vicious habits which will probably stay with the poor little dears all their lives, blasting their health, happiness, and careers as wives and mothers: (a) you have turned them into clock-watchers; (b) you've started them down the road to dyspepsia and stomach ulcers."

I still think there's a place in this cockeyed world of intuitive mothers and unpredictable children for the calm, logical, masculine mind.

But I can't find it.

To the Point

A visitor to West Point noticed that all the names engraved on a famous battle monument were those of men in the Union Army, killed in action during the Civil War. "Say," he called to a passing cadet, "what is this?"

"A tribute to the marksmanship of the Confederacy, suh!" drawled the cadet. —Lt. Christy Munch

Commencing a discussion having to do with the atomic theory, the instructor of a West Point physics class wrote an equation on the board and stated that a certain number of electrons were involved. From this he developed an entire board full of equations, winding up at the bottom with, "So you see we have five less electrons than at the start. What has become of them?"

Not a sound from the class. Imperiously the instructor asked again, "Gentlemen, where are those electrons?" It was time for action, and from a rear seat came a voice in gruff command: "Don't nobody leave dis room!" — *The Pointer*

West Point's drawing department is intended to teach young officers-to-be engineering drawing, map reading, and photo reading, but every so often some cadet attempts to express a sprightly artistic originality. On one occasion a cadet, required to make a drawing of a bridge over a rural stream, playfully sketched in a couple of children sitting on the bridge rail. Naturally this did not meet with the approval of his instructor who sharply directed him to "take those children off the bridge."

The next time the instructor made his rounds, he found that his orders had been obeyed to the letter — the children had been transferred to the riverbank. "No, no!" he protested. "Get rid of them!"

On the third trip the instructor found that the children had indeed been done away with. In their place stood two pathetic little tombstones. — Kendall Banning, *West Point Today* (Funk & Wagnalls)

This Way Out

The iron-clad rule that there must never be an off-color situation, an indecent word or suggestion in *The Saturday Evening Post* was broken when Katharine Brush's *Red-Headed Woman* began its serial run. The end of the first installment found the secretary-heroine having a drink with her boss at his home, the boss's wife away and night drawing on. To the profound shock of numerous readers, the second installment began with the two having breakfast. Editor George Horace Lorimer prepared a form letter to answer the indignant mail. "The *Post*," he said "cannot be responsible for what the characters in its serials do between installments."

— John Tebbel, *George Horace Lorimer and The Saturday Evening Post* (Doubleday)

At a large dinner party a financier was placed next to a lady whose name he didn't catch. During the first course he noticed at the left of the host a man who had bested him in a business transaction. "Do you see that man?" he muttered ferociously to his dinner partner. "If there's one man on earth I hate he's it."

"Why," exclaimed the lady, "that's my husband!"

"Yes, I know," said the financier glibly. "That's why I hate him."

— Thomas L. Mason, *Listen to These* (Doubleday)

In preparation for a banquet at Radcliffe College, the chairs had been given a new coat of varnish. The evening was hot and humid, and as the after-dinner speaker started to rise, he found himself stuck to the seat. However, he was unabashed. "Ladies and gentlemen," he said, "I had expected to bring you a plain and unvarnished tale, but circumstances make it impossible."

— *Modern Humor for Effective Speaking*, edited by Edward Frank Allen (Citadel)

An anecdote of the late Cardinal Gibbons offers a good example of how to avoid futile argument on doctrinal themes. A lady with more naïveté than good sense approached the prelate and said:

"Now, your Eminence, with all your ability and brilliance, surely you can't believe in the infallibility of the Pope!"

"Well," said the Cardinal soberly, "the last time I was in Rome he called me Jibbons."   — *Collier's*

H. L. Mencken invented a happy formula for answering all controversial letters. It is final, courteous, and can be employed without reading the letter to which it replies. He merely says:

"Dear Sir (or Madam): You may be right."
                              — Alexander Woollcott, *Letters* (Viking)

A few years ago a man operating a soft-drink stand was called before a magistrate for selling adulterated syrups and instructed to tell the truth about the ingredients. Later, when an agent checked up on the man, he was found to be complying with the law and his business was booming. In front of the stand was a new sign reading: "All of our soft drinks are guaranteed to be highly adulterated."
                              — Better Business Bureau of Long Beach, Calif.

In a swank photography studio a society matron was looking at a new picture she'd had taken. "Why that picture's an outrage!" she stormed. "Now I ask you, does it look like me?"

The suave photographer was flustered for a moment, but quickly regained his composure. "Madam," he said, bowing slightly, "the answer is in the negative."   — Grace Perkins Oursler

"What kind of sport has our distinguished guest had?" Lord Minto, one-time viceroy of India, asked the servant who had attended an American guest.

"Oh," replied the Hindu, "the young Sahib shot divinely, but Providence was merciful to the birds."   — *Capper's Weekly*

Native Wit

A District Officer in India was transferred to a lonely post in Bihar where many of the tribes are thieves by heredity, caste and tradition. Several days after his arrival, a native came to him. "It is the custom," said he, "for the Sahib to hire one of us as watchman. In that way you will be sure of protection and none of your things will be stolen."

"I don't need your protection," said the officer shortly. "I have my own servants."

The next morning he awakened to an extraordinary sight. He had been sleeping under a tree in the garden because of the heat. In a circle around his bed stood his piano, dining table, writing desk. In a second circle stood all the chairs. Within reach of his hand lay his money, neatly spread out, none of it missing. As a crowning touch, the leaves of a low hanging branch beside him were pasted thick with his postage stamps!

Later in the day the tribesman reappeared, "Well, Sahib?"

He got the job.   — Mrs. Vivian Bose

A tourist in Nome, Alaska, seeing his first Eskimos, noticed a native mother with a blond, blue-eyed baby slung to her back and asked, "Is your child a full-blooded Eskimo?"

"Half," was the native's reply.

"Half Irish? Half Scotch? Half what?" the tourist asked.

"Half Coast Guard," the mother replied.   — Robert C. Byers

Lowell Thomas tells about an explorer who brought an Indian maharajah some gifts which were unobtainable in Asia. The grateful potentate wanted to reciprocate, and after much pleading he finally got the explorer to suggest: "Oh, well, if in your travels around England you happen to find any golf clubs, buy a few for me."

Later the maharajah reported: "I've bought two golf clubs for you. Both have 18 holes, and one even has a swimming pool. But I have a disappointment for you. St. Andrews refuses to sell." — Leonard Lyons

The odd things the Japs do with the English language have been a source of continual amusement to the American occupation forces. Recently, however, they ceased to amuse several Red Cross girls who have a private house in Yokohama with a Japanese butler named George. Having served as a steward on passenger liners before the war, he insisted on calling all visitors "passengers." The doorbell would ring, George would answer it, climb the stairs, and announce: "Miss So-and-So, you have three passengers."

Finally, one girl spent a half-hour coaching him over and over: "Not passengers, George. Callers, or visitors, or company." That evening the doorbell rang, and George trotted upstairs to announce two male guests. Proud of his newly acquired knowledge, and anxious to show off before company, he poised at the top of the stairs and bellowed: "Miss Smith, you have two customers."　　*— Newsweek*

Air Breaks

Selected by Earl Sparling

An announcer on KNX was trying to plug a baker's slogan: "The Best in Bread." What he actually advised his listeners to get was "The Brest in Bed."　　— Contributed by Announcer Arthur Van Horn

The announcer neglected to appear at a little southern station and the engineer had to give the time signal. Unused to the job, he could not keep up with the racing second hand. "The correct time," he announced, "is now twenty . . . uh fif . . . uh ten . . . Oh, hell, it's pretty near seven o'clock."　　— Contributed by Announcer Bob Shepard

Fred Hooey, WNAC: "Good afternoon, Fred Hooey, this is ladies and gentlemen."　　— Contributed by Announcer George Hogan

John Gambling: "I always delve into these products before I tell you about them. This morning I'm going to discuss bloomers."　　— WOR

Keyes Perrin: "The Duck and Doochess of Windsor."　　— WMAS

Tro Harper: "The RAF dropped two and four ton blondes on Berlin."　　— WOR

Frank Knight: "The weather report — tomorrow rowdy, followed by clain."　　— WOR

Announcer Bob Denton was introducing Helen Heiett, back from two years in Spain. He gave her to the radio audience as "NBC's only woman commentator in pain."　　— NBC

Star-Spangled Banter

Jack Haley tells about visiting the small birthplace of a famous Hollywood star. "Does he ever come back here?" Haley asked.

"Yep," responded an old villager, "he's been back here five times."

"Did he ever bring his wife?"

"Yep," was the answer, "each time, and five prettier girls you never saw!"   — Erskine Johnson, NEA

At a birthday party for a producer's young son, one of the guests expertly climbed a tall tree. The other youngsters watched him in awe. When he came down, one of the boys asked him: "Who is your tree-climbing tutor?"

— Leonard Lyons

A New York show girl decided to try for a Hollywood career. She had been told that the key to success in Hollywood was to create a grand impression. So she traveled with a maid.

At the hotel she registered: "Mary Doe and made."   — Andrew B. Hecht

A producer was objecting to a line that script-writer Walter Bullock had put in a character's mouth. "That's terrible," said the producer. "That's old-fashioned."

"But that's the kind of fellow he is," Bullock tried to explain. "The kind who talks in platitudes."

"Okay, okay," said the producer, "but at least let's get some fresh platitudes!"   — Sidney Skolsky,
United Feature Syndicate

It was the Hollywood première of *The Broadway Melody* at Grauman's Chinese Theater. Thousands were straining against police lines to watch the celebrities when the fabulous Wilson Mizner, accompanied by a beautiful damsel, pulled in to the curb in a woebegone, dilapidated jalopy. He alighted casually, assisted the lady to the sidewalk, and proceeded toward the lobby with a shocked usher at his heels.

"Do you," asked the usher, "want your — er, car — parked, sir?"

"Don't bother," Mizner replied haughtily. "Keep it."

The broken-down contraption stalled traffic and made a shambles out of the opening, until the furious Grauman finally located Mizner inside the theater and had him arrested for disorderly conduct.

— Dorothy Kilgallen, King Features

A screen writer just back from a trip to New York ducked into a booth and called his girl friend. In a few minutes he came out looking very bewildered. "She's gonna get married," he said to a friend.

"Aw, forget it," advised the friend. "There are lots of girls."

"Yes," replied the writer, "but she's gonna marry me!"

— Andrew B. Hecht

Young in Heart

One day when I was assisting my physician husband at his office, a charming little old lady in her 70's came in for consultation. She expounded all her ailments, real and imaginary, but seemed most concerned about a recurring dream in which she was diligently pursued by a personable young man whose intentions seemed dishonorable. The doctor was properly sympathetic and advised her how she might sleep more soundly. In a few days she returned, still woeful. "Don't tell me you aren't sleeping better nowadays," teased the doctor.

"Oh, I'm sleeping just fine," the patient replied. "But to tell the truth, Doctor, I certainly miss that young man." — C. Y. Schriber

A traveling salesman, caught in a torrential rainstorm, stopped overnight at a farmhouse. In the morning, he looked out on a flood coursing through the front yard. He watched pieces of fence, chicken coops, branches, and an old straw hat floating past with the current. Then he saw the straw hat come back, upstream past the house! Then he saw it go down again. Pretty soon it came back upstream — and by now the salesman wondered if he had gone crazy.

Finally he called the farmer's daughter. "Oh," she said, after a glance out the window, "that must be Grandpa. He said yesterday that in spite of hell or high water he was going to mow the yard today."

— Marguerite Coyle

An elderly gentleman — wealthy and very deaf — came into our shop to purchase a much improved hearing aid. Two weeks later he returned to report that he could hear conversations quite easily, even in the next room.

"Your friends and relatives must be very happy that you can hear so much better," I said.

"Oh, I haven't told them," he chuckled. "I've been sitting around listening — and do you know what? I've changed my will twice!"

— Katheryn Lyons

Lander, Wyo., is noted for its colorful rodeo and pageant every 3rd, 4th and 5th of July. People for miles around come to town for a rip-snorting celebration. One well-known pioneer, who was in town for this annual spree, was asked at which hotel he was staying. Startled, the old-timer exclaimed, "Hotel! Why man, I'm only going to be here three days!"

— Mrs. M. C. Henrich

Three old men were passing the time of day discussing the ideal way of leaving this world. The first, aged 75, remarked he'd like to go quickly, and suggested a crash in a speeding car. The second, aged 85, agreed on a speedy end, but thought he'd prefer a jet-propelled plane.

"I've got a better idea," mused the third, aged 95. "I'd rather be shot by a jealous husband."

— Variety

Charles W. Eliot, president of Harvard University for 40 years, grew steadily younger in the eyes of the undergraduates. Shortly before his retirement, Eliot said: "When I was elected president, I was only 35. Of course I was very dignified, and I suppose a little frightening. As I walked about the campus, students would point at me and say: 'There goes old Eliot.'

"But now that I am 75," he continued, "they look at me and say: 'There goes Charlie.'"

— E. E. Edgar

At 90, the Baroness Burdett-Coutts was asked, "When does a woman stop hoping for romance?" She answered, "Goodness, I don't know yet!"

— Channing Pollock

Pen Portraits

At a concert in Detroit, quarters were decidedly cramped and Madame Ernestine Schumann-Heink, the soloist, had to make her entrances from the rear, down through the orchestra with its maze of music stands. All went well till her familiarly large proportions began knocking over the music racks.

"Go sideways, Madame," hissed Conductor Gabrilowitsch in an excited stage whisper.

Ernestine wrinkled her brow, gave a puzzled look from right to left, and called back to the conductor in a hoarse whisper, "Mein Gott, I have no sideways!" — E. R. Brite

Introducing Thomas Alva Edison at a dinner, the toastmaster mentioned his many inventions, dwelling at length on the talking machine. The aged inventor then rose to his feet, smiled and said gently: "I thank the gentleman for his kind remarks but I must insist upon a correction. God invented the talking machine. I only invented the first one that can be shut off." — Louis Sobol, King Features

After retaining his heavyweight crown by knocking out challenger Joe Walcott, Joe Louis was taken to see movies of the fight. Asked how he liked the picture, Louis commented laconically, "It had a real nice ending." — Hy Gardner in *Parade*

Bernard Shaw one day received an invitation from a celebrity hunter: "Lady X will be at home Thursday between four and six."

The author returned the card; underneath he had written: "Mr. Bernard Shaw likewise." — *Neues Wiener Tagblatt*

Clifton Webb started taking liver shots some time ago and ever since has been busily selling the idea to all his friends. Helen Hayes was one who succumbed in the face of his enthusiasm. "Do they really make you feel better?" I asked her.

"Oh, they're wonderful!" she said. "I feel full of vigor and vim." Her voice dropped a little. "Except once in a while when I forget I've taken them — then I feel terrible." — Dorothy Kilgallen, King Features

Cordell Hull is an extremely cautious speaker, striving always for scientific accuracy. One day, on a train, a friend pointed to a fine flock of sheep grazing in a field. "Look. Those sheep have just been sheared," he said.

Hull studied the flock. "Sheared on this side, anyway," he admitted.

— *The American Magazine*

Golfing one day, director Mike Curtiz stepped up to the tee, took one swing at the ball and made a hole-in-one. He turned to the caddie and inquired earnestly, "What did I do that was right?"

— Jimmy Starr in Los Angeles *Herald and Express*

Attending a church bazaar, Abraham Lincoln tendered a $20 bill to pay for a bunch of violets. The lady at the booth, making no attempt to return any change, gushed, "Oh thank you, Mr. President."

Lincoln reached down from his great height, and gently touched the lady on the wrist, saying, "And what do you call this?"

"Why, Mr. President, that is my wrist. What did you think it was?"

"Well," drawled Lincoln, "I thought it might be your ankle. Everything is so high around here."   — Ethwell Eddy Hanson

Bing Crosby and Damon Runyon sat for four hours at New York's Stork Club, discussing horses and fighters. Runyon recited the life history of every horse and fighter Crosby mentioned. "Damon," said Bing admiringly, "you must listen to everything you hear!"

— Leonard Lyons

One afternoon John Barrymore strolled into a haberdashery on Hollywood Boulevard and asked to be shown some hats. After looking over several he selected one. "I'll take that," he said. "Just charge it."

"Yes, sir," the clerk said eagerly, "and to whom shall I charge it?"

One famous eyebrow went up. "Barrymore," The Great Profile said icily.

"Yes, sir," said the clerk, "and what's the first name, please?"

This was too much for the actor. "Ethel!" he barked, and stormed out of the store.   — Amasa B. Windham in Birmingham *News*

Zoo's Who

Mama Skunk was worried because she could never keep track of her two children. They were named In and Out, and whenever In was in, Out was out; and if Out was in, In was out. One day she called Out in to her and told him to go out and bring In in. So Out went out and in no time at all he brought In in.

"Wonderful!" said Mama Skunk. "How, in all that great forest, could you find him in so short a time?"

"It was easy," said Out. "In stinct."

— *This Week Magazine*

Noah, after the flood subsided, opened the doors of the Ark and released the animals. All living things rushed to freedom, except two snakes who lingered in a corner. "Why don't you go forth and multiply?" asked Noah in a stern voice.

"We can't," moaned one. "We're adders!"   — Grace Perkins Oursler

The turtle lives 'twixt plated decks
Which practically conceal its sex.
I think it clever of the turtle
In such a fix to be so fertile.
— Ogden Nash, *Hard Lines* (Simon & Schuster)

Two ants were running along at a great rate across a cracker box when one asked, "Why are we going so fast?" "Don't you see?" said the other. "It says 'tear along dotted line.'"   — Myrtle Reed

"Well, bless my wool," said the ram as he plunged over the cliff, "I didn't see that ewe turn."

Once upon a time two large turtles and a little one went to a bar to quench their thirst with a mug of sarsaparilla. As they began to drink it, one of the large turtles commented that it was raining. After a lively discussion, it was decided that the little turtle should go home for their umbrella. The little turtle demurred, afraid that if he went the big turtles would drink his sarsaparilla. But they convinced the little fellow they would leave his sarsaparilla alone, and he started after the umbrella.

Three weeks passed, and finally one of the big turtles said: "Let's drink the little guy's sarsaparilla."

"I've been thinking the same thing," said the other, "so let's do it."

From down at the end of the bar near the door, a shrill voice cried: "If you do, I won't go after that umbrella."   — Capper's Weekly

Eat, Drink and Be Merry

A drunk shambled into a bar and bet the barman that he could tell the ingredients in any drink the barman cared to mix. The barman stooped behind the bar and emptied into one glass the remains of several drinks — a Martini, a Scotch and soda, brandy, a rum punch, etc. The drunk sipped the drink, and, one after the other, correctly named the contents. He offered to do it again, and this time the barman filled a glass with water.

The drunk tasted it, thought reflectively for a moment, tasted it again and then announced: "I don't know what it is, but it won't sell!"
          — Allan Michie

When somebody phoned Mike Romanoff's restaurant in Hollywood and asked, "How much is dinner?" Joe, the maître d'hôtel, replied with sympathy in his voice: "If you have to ask, believe me, you can't afford it."
          — Andrew B. Hecht, *Hollywood
          Merry-go-round* (Grosset & Dunlap)

A meek little man in a restaurant timidly touched the arm of a man putting on a coat. "Excuse me," he said, "but do you happen to be Mr. Smith of Newcastle?"

"No, I'm not!" the man answered impatiently.

"Oh — er — well," stammered the first man, "you see, I am, and that's his overcoat you're putting on."   — *Irish News*

The slightly over-rouged young lady summoned the headwaiter. "That's Clark Gable at the bar, sn't it?" she asked. He assured her that it was. "He's annoying me," he said. "Annoying you?" The headwaiter raised an eyebrow. "Why he hasn't even looked at you!" "That," said the young lady, "is what's annoying me."

— Bennett Cerf, *Laughing Stock* (Grosset & Dunlap)

At the breakfast hour a waitress in a busy Chicago drugstore served coffee and toast to a patron: ten minutes later she breezed in with his orange juice. The customer complained of the cockeyed sequence. "Are you married?" asked the waitress.

"Yes," said the customer. "What's that got to do with it?"

"Well," said the girl, "why don't you have breakfast at home?"

— *Quote*

A thirsty gentleman wandered into a corner saloon and ordered a dry Martini. He drank it with relish, and allowed as how it was the best darn Martini he ever tasted. The barkeeper whipped up another, and the customer declared it was even better than the first.

"Such genius deserves a reward," he said. He reached into his pocket and produced a live lobster. "Here! Take this with my compliments," he said.

The barkeeper held the live crustacean gingerly at arm's length. "Thanks," he said dubiously. "I suppose I can take it home for dinner."

"No, no," objected the customer. "He's already had his dinner. Take him to a movie."

— Bennett Cerf, *Anything for a Laugh* (Grosset & Dunlap)

A Hollywood actress was shredding a reputation at a night club. She stopped backbiting long enough to order a chicken sandwich and a glass of milk.

"Wouldn't you," asked a friend of the victim, "prefer the milk in a saucer?" — Walter Winchell

Bill Bowers, a writer at Universal-International, went to dinner one night with a bad case of sniffles. "What's the matter, Mr. Bowers," asked a sympathetic waiter, "you fighting a cold?"

"Yeah," said Bill.

The waiter shook his head. "Too bad you don't have pneumonia," he said. "The doctors know what to do for that."

— Harrison Carroll, King Features

A man obviously in bad condition from the night before stepped up to a bar and sputtered through trembling lips, "Give — give me something for a hangover."

"What do you want?" asked the bartender.

The sufferer could only manage to blurt out: "Tall — cold — and full of gin."

"Sir," snapped a drunk who was standing next to him, "you are referring to the woman I love!"

— Frazier Hunt

Foot-in-Mouth Disease

The screen "discovery" was disconsolate. "Did you see how that critic panned me?" he wailed to the producer.

"Forget it!" replied the latter expansively. "That guy's nothing more than a parrot. He only repeats what everybody else is saying!"

— Jack Seaman

The haughty dowager called at the hospital to see her injured chauffeur. "He's a very sick man," said the nurse. "Are you his wife?"

"Certainly not — I'm his mistress," the good woman blurted.

— Public Service

In a small New England city the community-fund campaign had just gone over the top. The secretary of the campaign, a prim, gray-haired little lady, was called upon to say a few words about the chairman, a Mr. Smith, at a victory dinner. "Ladies and gentlemen," she said, "in China there is an ancient custom that parents must kiss their offspring on that part of their anatomy through which they hope the children will become famous. If they want their child to be a philosopher, they kiss him on the forehead. If they want him to be an orator, they kiss him on his mouth. If they hope he'll be a singer, they kiss him on the throat. Now, I don't know on what part of his anatomy Mr. Smith's parents kissed him —" she paused an instant for effect — "but he certainly makes a wonderful chairman." — William A. H. Birnie

A discharged Wac telephoned the veterans' center in Cambridge, Mass., to inquire whether the GI Bill of Rights covered hospitalization for maternity. "That depends," replied the clerk absent-mindedly. "Is this a service-incurred disability?"

— UP

A county agent, after addressing a group of poultry farmers in a small town, was prevailed upon by one lady to inspect her pen of White Rocks. In with her flock of White Rock chickens was a New Hampshire Red cock.

"But my dear lady," he exclaimed aghast, "if you wish to keep these White Rocks pure, you must get that Red rooster out of here!"

"Oh, I've taken care of that," she replied quickly, "by removing him every night."

— George S. Ham

My husband likes to tell of a baptism he attended many years ago in Sioux Falls, S. D. One couple were having some difficulty quieting their infant son. In an effort to put the parents at ease, the pastor beamed at the congregation as he happily remarked, "And the baptism of this little baby gives me great pleasure — it was such a *very* short time ago I married this couple."

— Mrs. Carroll M. Dewey

Ad-Ventures

A theater manager in San Francisco took the public into his confidence, put up on the marquee:

SAME OLD STUFF 2 FEATURES
ONE PIPEROO ONE STINKEROO

— *Time*

FOUND — Lady's purse left in my car while parked. Owner can have same by describing property and paying for this ad. If owner can explain satisfactorily to my wife how purse got into car, will pay for ad myself.

A YOUNG GENTLEMAN on the point of being married is desirous of meeting a man of experience who will dissuade him from such a step.

— Above ads collected by Lockwood Barr

From the Bridgeport, Conn., *Post-Telegram:* "I will do anything your husband won't. Minor house repairs, grass cutting, painting, cleaning, etc."

From a Wellesley, Mass., newspaper: "Puppies, six Who-Done-Its. Cute as can be and cheap."

Notice in a rural weekly: "Anyone found near my chicken house at night will be found there next morning."

— *The Highway Traveler*

Three successive notices from the classified column of a small Connecticut paper tell their own story:

March 22nd: "For sale. Slightly used farm wench in good condition. Very handy. Phone 366-R-2. A. Cartright."

March 29th: "Correction. Due to an unfortunate error, Mr. Cartright's ad last week was not clear. He has an excellent winch for sale. We trust this will put an end to jokesters who have called Mr. Cartright and greatly bothered his housekeeper, Mrs. Hargreaves, who loves with him."

April 5th: "Notice! My W-I-N-C-H is not for sale. I put a sledgehammer to it. Don't bother calling 366-R-2. I had the phone taken out. I am NOT carrying on with Mrs. Hargreaves. She merely L-I-V-E-S here. A. Cartright."

— Jim Greene

Classroom Classics

After several synonyms had been given for the word "jubilant" in the sixth-grade spelling hour, one little boy added: "Oh, I know what you mean now — it's like jubilant delinquency!"
— Florence Wade

William R. Webb, famous Tennessee schoolmaster, was invited to speak at a conference at Pomona College on "The Place of Humanities in Education." The man who preceded him didn't think much of the humanities and emphasized the importance of practical education. "What I want my son to know how to do, for example, is to milk a cow."

"That is a very good idea," said Webb when his turn came. "A very good idea. I want *my* son able to milk a cow, but I'd also like him able to do some things that a calf can't do better!"
— Dr. Remsen D. Bird

A kindergarten teacher smiled pleasantly at the gentleman opposite on the trolley car. He did not respond. Realizing her error, she said aloud, "Oh, please excuse me. I mistook you for the father of two of my children."

She got out at the next corner.
— *The Wall Street Journal*

For a number of years, I taught in the Blue Ridge Mountain schools of Virginia. Trying always to impress the virtue of honesty upon my students, I required them to give a pledge that they had neither given nor received help on their examinations. One young girl handed in her paper with this pledge on it: "I haven't received no help on this exam, and God knows I couldn't give any."
— S. E. L. Warwick

A teacher, making a trip with a group of children, stopped for lunch at a restaurant where one youngster noticed a slot machine and asked what it was. The teacher launched into a lecture on the evils of gambling. To emphasize the futility of trying to get something for nothing, she said she'd show them what she meant. She marched up to the machine, put in a nickel, pulled the handle, and hit the jackpot.
— Herman M. Patton

One of the prettiest of our young teachers had just announced her engagement. Fellow teachers and pupils heaped good wishes upon her, but she was hardly prepared for a note from one eight-year-old, which read:

Dear Miss Smith,

I hope you have a happy and sexfull married life.

Your friend, Mary
— Margaret Kirkpatrick

A sixth grade English class was rehearsing its own radio program. One child, acting as announcer, asked for the imitation of a cat, then a dog, and so on until he came to Tommy, a quiet, shy youngster. "Tommy," said the announcer, "let's hear your imitation of a wolf."

Gravely, young Tommy gave a low meaningful whistle.
— Marie Rheinfrank

It was one of those blistering Alabama days. I had called on a student to read aloud a brief paragraph from an essay. This he did, laboriously. When he finished, I asked him to comment on the significance of the passage which he had just read. His earnest reply brought even the sleepiest student to an hilarious awakening. For he said, "I am sorry, sir, but I wasn't listening."
— John Newton Baker

In Wilmington, Del., the local Power Squadron class was taking an oral quiz and the instructor asked a female student, "What signal would you give if you were coming out of your slip slowly stern first?"

The class recessed without delay.
— Ellen Crosman in
Wilmington *Sunday Star*

A chemistry professor asked his class what they considered the most outstanding contribution chemistry had made to the world. The first student to answer shouted: "Blondes."
— Chub DeWolfe in Toledo *Blade*

Caught in Passing

At a party several young couples were discussing the difficulties of family budgets.

"I really don't want an awful lot of money," said one young matron. "I just wish we could afford to live the way we are living now."
— Kenneth L. Booth

The perfect answer to the question, "What's wrong with the movies?" came from a little man sitting in a Los Angeles theater. After the trailer was over, he sighed and whispered to his wife: "Always is coming next week a good picture."
— Leonard L. Levinson in *Variety*

Wife to husband, "You'd better get up and go see why the baby's not crying."

First woman: "Helen and Paul are going together again."

Second woman: "It's one of the most mixed-up things I ever heard."

First: "It's just one of those post-war divorces that didn't pan out." — *PM*

A woman on a Milwaukee trolley was discussing washday with her companion. "I ain't gonna wash Monday until Tuesday," she said, "and then if something else has gotta be done Tuesday I ain't gonna wash this week till next week."

— Milwaukee *Journal*

One woman to another: "Why, no, I didn't tell anyone — I didn't know it was a secret."

A woman in the midst of divorce proceedings was complaining to a friend about the boring conference she had to endure with lawyers. "Oh," said her friend, "don't talk to me about them! I've had so much trouble over my property that sometimes I wish my husband hadn't died." — Walter Winchell

Young thing: "Not only has he broken my heart and wrecked my life, but he's messed up my entire evening!" — *Onward*

A man gazing incredulously at a huge mounted fish said: "The man who caught that fish is a liar!"

A new note on sight-seeing in New York was struck in an animated conversation between two ladies riding on a Fifth Avenue bus. With a happy sigh one remarked to the other: "You know, it's wonderful how I've been able to get around town and see things, now that we're on strike."

— New York *Times Magazine*

Along the Avenue

Waiting at the bus stop, I idly watched a janitor mopping down the marble steps of a large Seattle store. As my bus approached, he dashed to the curb and thrust his mop in front of the nearest wheel. Then, with the mop thoroughly wrung out, he went sedately back. He had licked one nasty job. — Mrs. Guy Bowden

Walking on New York's 42nd Street during the noon hour, I felt the elastic in my panties pop. Down they slithered to my knees — my feet. In horror I looked up and met the sympathetic yet amused eyes of a young Air Force captain. Without a word, he turned and hurried to the curb, yelling excitedly, "Look! Look!" and pointing upward. My growing audience rushed to his side. Taking advantage of the diversion, I gathered up my private apparel, stuffed it into my coat, and melted into the crowd. Observing my escape, the captain pushed his way through the crowd and went off grinning happily.

At a busy intersection in Oklahoma City, as a traffic signal turned red, a four-door sedan rolled to a stop, completely blocking the pedestrian crosswalk. Instead of following a flow of pedestrians around the front and rear of the car, a middle-aged man walked straight ahead, opened the rear door, climbed through the car and stepped out the other door, leaving both doors wide open, while amid the honking of horns the driver stared bewildered after his retreating form.

— Oscar E. Gram

On New York's lower East Side, an urchin always stopped on his way to and from school to gaze in a jewelry-store window at a cheap gaudy brooch. His greatest desire was to present it to his "girl friend," and each day he'd ask the jeweler if it had been reduced. One day while his nose was pressed against the windowpane he was horrified to see the jeweler take it from the display.

Then the jeweler came out with a neatly wrapped package. "Here, kid," he said, "give this to your girl friend. And now please stop pressing your nose on the windowpane. It costs me much more than 98 cents to have my window cleaned!"

— Mrs. Vincent Percoco

A cowboy in town with a rodeo was walking down Fort Worth's "Canyon of the Winds" when a gust of wind carried his Stetson to the third floor ledge of an office building. Unperturbed, the cowboy went to his hotel, got his lariat, lassoed the hat and went on his way.

— Fort Worth *Star-Telegram*

The Los Angeles street was teeming with people. A man, evidently late for work, ran past me, dodging swiftly through the throng. Just then the crowd ahead divided as if it had come upon some obstacle; and there was a woman, weighing at least 180 pounds, leaning over tying her shoelace.

Unable to stop, the sprinter had no alternative. He put his hands upon her hips, leapfrogged over and with an extra spurt disappeared into the crowd again.

— Bernice E. Hagen

Having lived among self-contained Easterners most of my life, I am constantly delighted by Los Angeles, that city of rugged individualists where I manage a small stationery shop. Last February, to call attention to our valentine display, I put a large red heart bearing the words I LOVE YOU in the show window.

It hadn't been up long when a well-groomed, mild-appearing gentleman walking past paused briefly, then stuck his head inside the door and directed a cordial smile at all within. "I love *you*, too," he announced, and sauntered on down the street.

— Jo Maylard

Strolling along a residential street in New York one afternoon, I saw a group of people hovering around a baby carriage. Noticing that each person turned away with a chuckle or an outright laugh, I peered into the carriage, too. There was a sleeping baby, with a note pinned to the blanket:

"Please leave this baby *completely alone*. I know she is here and she is probably crying. *Do not rock her*. The Mother."

— Margaret A. Rasmussen

Terse Verse

Career girls, when they're badly harried,
Think perhaps they should have married.
Married girls, reduced to tears,
Regretfully regard careers.
　　　　　— Rod Maclean in *Collier's*

A husband is the kind of man
Who drives me to a rage:
He can't recall my birthday
But always knows my age.
　　　　　— Mrs. Vashti Balker in
　　　　　　Capper's Weekly

Don't tell your friends about your Indigestion:
"How are you!" is a Greeting, not a Question.
　　　　　— Arthur Guiterman,
　　　　　　A Poet's Proverbs (Dutton)

Children aren't happy with nothing to ignore
And that's what parents were created for.　— Ogden Nash

Here is a definite feminine trait
Clearly worth the knowing:
When a woman says, "It's time to go,"
It doesn't mean she's going.
　　　　　— Philip Lazarus in *Liberty*

Bookplate

They borrow books, they will not buy,
They have no ethics nor religions.
I wish some kind Burbankian guy
Would cross my books with homing pigeons.　— Carolyn Wells

Patter

Old saws sharpened: One good turn gets most of the blanket (*Radio Daily*) . . . Mother is the necessity for convention . . . Money can be lost in more ways than won (Sayre, Pa., *Times*) . . . As ye smoke, so shall ye reek . . . Where there's a will there's a lawsuit.

Dinner check of gastronomical proportions (Robert Lamy) . . . Tip — hover charge (*Mexican-American Review*) . . . He ordered as one to the menu born (O. Henry)

Road signs: Sign on left rear of truck, "Passing Side," on the right, "Suicide" . . . Along a highway in Tennessee, "Take notice, when this sign is under water this road is impassable" . . . At Lynbrook, Long Island, where the congestion of traffic is most annoying, a sign tauntingly says, "If you lived here you'd be home now!" (New York *Mirror*) . . . The harassed driver approaching a narrow pass on a tortuous Rocky Mountain road is confronted by the reassuring sign, "Oh, yes, you can. Millions have!" (Gwen Johnson)

She's been on more laps than a napkin (Walter Winchell) . . . When they kiss and make up, she gets the kiss and he gets the make-up (George Storm)

Hospital patient: "I've been on pills and needles all week" . . . I'm in the punk of condition (Norma B. Carder)

Seasickness — traveling across the ocean by rail (*Hudson Newsletter*)

Being an old maid is like death by drowning — a really delightful sensation after one ceases struggling (Edna Ferber)

The season when gentlemen be-fur blondes (Win Elliot) . . . The only difference between April and March is that you expect it in March (Elizabeth Pearson) . . . It's a sure sign of summer if the chair gets up when you do (Luke McLuke, quoted by Walter Winchell)

He married again — took a new leash on life . . . Bachelor: "She was another one of my near Mrs." . . . "My wife and I had words — but I never got to use mine" (Fibber McGee)

Fashion notes: Nothing can turn a woman's head faster than a mink coat going by on another woman (D.M.K. in New York *World-Telegram*) . . . There'll be little change in men's pockets this year (*The Wall Street Journal*) . . . A dress that held on tight going around the curves (*Eagle Magazine*) . . . A hat with delirium trimmins (Roy M. Cloutier, Jr.) . . . I was worried about the woman in the strapless evening gown; I kept wondering if her gown would get up to go when she did (Bob Burns) . . . A question to women who wear slacks: "Does your end justify your jeans?" (Earl Wilson)

Vice—or Versa?

Bruce Hutchison in Winnipeg Free Press

I have always had a deep sympathy for those afflicted with the tobacco habit. That is, I've always had it during the last nine days since I gave up the filthy weed myself. And with my head cleared of fumes and my blood of nicotine poison, I've been able to give some lucid thought to this problem.

I've calculated that the average cigarette smoker spends $127.50 a year on his vice — enough to buy some 45 good books, or a couple of suits, or a comfortable chair, or a nice holiday. All of these go up in smoke. Calculating still further with my new clarity of mind, I discover that in 30 years the average smoker spends $3810. In other words, if I had sworn off 30 years ago I would now have the price of a high-class automobile, or a trip abroad, or the first payment on a house.

I have heard the economic problems of our time explained in many different ways, but their real cause has been totally overlooked. If there were no tobacco, the average family (since both men and women are slaves to the weed) would have something over $20 a month more to spend on groceries, rent or furniture. Our whole living standard would improve.

In short, after nine days of reformation I can see that our civilization is not dying of poverty or war but of tobacco. It is smoking itself to death. How can we possibly see the solution of our larger problems when our eyes are blinded with smoke?

As I say, it is nine days since I first grasped these truths. Apart from the fact that I have felt sick the whole time, have been unable to work, have been unfit to live with, have lost the affections of my family, insulted my friends and hoped on rising every morning that I would die before night — apart from that, these have been the happiest days of my life. I am free at last, and as I swore off for one month, I still have 21 days of freedom left before I am plunged back into slavery again. I am counting those days.

Political Science

In Washington a group of Democrats were discussing the problem of disassociating themselves from some of the organizations with which they have become linked. "They cost us lots of votes in the campaign," said one. "We've got to break off our connections."

"You can't," said Leon Henderson. "It's like the young college boy who came home from school and told his father: 'I need your help. I've got to get something off my chest.'

" 'I'll listen,' his father said. 'Tell me.'

"The boy said: 'I'm going to marry Anne, but I've got to get this off my chest.' He bared his chest, on which was indelibly tattooed: 'I love Mary.' "

— Leonard Lyons

A delegation from Kansas, calling upon Theodore Roosevelt at Oyster Bay, was met by the President with coat and collar off. "Ah, gentlemen," he said, mopping his brow, "I'm delighted to see you, but I'm very busy putting in my hay just now. Come down to the barn and we'll talk things over while I work."

When they reached the barn, there was no hay waiting to be thrown into the mow. "James!" shouted the President to his hired man in the loft. "Where's that hay?"

"I'm sorry, sir," admitted James, "but I just ain't had time to throw it back since you forked it up for yesterday's delegation."

— *The Christian Science Monitor*

Last summer my uncle in Mississippi was campaigning for sheriff. One night a stranger knocked at his door.

"Need a little help," he said. "My car went dead while I was getting some water outa the spring. How about helpin' me shove off?"

"Sure," said Uncle Bob. We followed the man to his car and he got in. But before we could begin to shove he stepped on the starter and the motor roared. Leaning out, the driver said, "Jist wanted to know if you was the right kind of man to vote fer."

— Thomas Hal Phillips

When Bill O'Dwyer was running for District Attorney in Brooklyn, he would appear on the platform with a piece of paper in his hand, ostensibly covered with notes. Looking around the audience, he would say "Hello, Joe," "Hello, Harry," and remark that he hadn't known there'd be so many friends there tonight. "I don't need notes to talk to *you* people," he would say. "To you I can speak from my heart." And then he'd throw away his piece of paper.

A reporter who had seen O'Dwyer do this in every Brooklyn neighborhood mounted the platform one night and picked up the discarded paper. It was an old laundry bill. — *PM*

A candidate for county sheriff was soliciting votes in a small town in Oklahoma. After giving an attentive Negro a fervent campaign speech, he asked for his support.

"Well, Mister Lee, I tell you, you are my second choice."

The would-be sheriff pondered a moment. Then, concluding that he could easily eliminate the Negro's first choice by maligning the man, he asked cheerfully, "And who's your first choice?"

"Well, sir, just anybody." — Ruby A. Meek

A western Congressman, defeated in his fight for re-election, inserted this ad in his local newspaper: "I wish to thank all those who voted for me, and my wife wishes to thank all those who didn't." — Bennett Cerf, *Laughing Stock* (Grosset & Dunlap)

The Marry-Go-Round

A multimillionaire, being interviewed about his self-made fortune, commented: "I never hesitate to give full credit to my wife for her assistance."

"In what way did she help?" the reporter asked.

"Well, if you want the whole truth," replied the man, "I was curious to find out if there was any income she couldn't live beyond." — Joe Harrington in Boston *Post*

The gentleman was gazing rapturously at "Spring," a large oil painting of a shapely girl dressed only in a few strategically arranged leaves. Suddenly the voice of his wife snapped, "Well, what are you waiting for — autumn?" — Neal O'Hara, McNaught Syndicate

As we munched cheese and crackers in the general store of a Vermont hamlet, we watched a group of men sitting around a big pot-bellied stove in the middle of the room. Now and again one of the men shifted in his chair or relighted his pipe. No one spoke.

Finally, a white-whiskered old fellow untangled his legs, stood up and reached for his coat. Another broke the silence: "Goin', Jeff?"

"Yep," Jeff replied. "Goin' home."

"A mite early, ain't ye?"

"Yep. Goin' early a-purpose. If supper ain't ready, I'm a-goin' t' raise hell. And if 'tis, I ain't a-gonna eat it."

And he stalked from the store.
— Don Wayne

A friend of the George Bernard Shaws tells of an evening he spent with them. While G.B.S. told stories, Mrs. Shaw busied herself knitting. "What are you knitting?" asked the guest in an aside.

"Oh, nothing, nothing at all," whispered Mrs. Shaw. "It's just that I've heard these stories of his 2000 times, and if I didn't do something with my hands, I'd choke him." — Leonard Lyons

As my friend and I were driving downtown, we were hailed by a traffic cop. "Hey, you!" he shouted. "Pull over."

We did. The next day the judge fined my friend $25 for speeding. She was anxious to keep her husband from learning of the incident. And so, since he regularly examined her checkbook, she marked the stub: "One pull-over — $25."
— Stella E. Pape

Heading the list of the people who try us
Are husbands who blissfully sleep on the bias.
— Wilma Dennis in *Post Scripts: A Collection of Humor from The Saturday Evening Post* (Whittlesey)

On exhibition at the Missouri Historical Society in St. Louis is a Mark Twain (Samuel L. Clemens) collection, and among the papers is an envelope addressed to the author's wife and marked: "Opened by mistake to see what was inside — S.L.C." — *American Legion Monthly*

Mom Williams ran a little tourist camp in the mountains west of Denver. She was married to a man of few words and even fewer deeds. Day after day, he sat behind his newspaper, never bothering to speak to anyone who came in. Mom worked all the time, cheerfully looking after the tourist cabins.

One day I met her in the grocery. "Pa didn't eat his cereal this morning," she said. "I always try to change before he gets tired of anything. It makes it kind of hard," she added. "Pa just ain't any hand to tell you what he likes."

"He certainly doesn't talk much, does he?" I said sympathetically.

"No, Pa don't talk much," Mom answered. "But," she added fondly, "he's something alive around the house." — Evelyn Mullenax

In a reminiscent moment Mother was telling me about the first time she drove a car. "Your father was along," she said, "and we had a frightful time. I stalled the engine right in the middle of some railroad tracks, with a train coming. . . ."

"There wasn't any train coming," Father demurred mildly.

"There was a train coming sometime," said my mother — and went right on with her story.

— Katharine Brush

After a tiring day at the studio, a star changed into a strapless evening gown and was ready to leave the house to attend a party. "I am so exhausted that I really don't feel like going," she told her husband.

"Okay," said the coöperative husband, "put on something and let's go to bed."

— Andrew B. Hecht

Having been married 20 years, a couple decided to celebrate by taking a little trip. While talking over their plans one evening, the husband now and then glanced into the next room where a little old lady sat knitting. "The only thing," he finally said in a hushed voice, "is that for just this once I'd like to be by ourselves. I'd like to take this trip without your mother."

"*My* mother!" exclaimed the wife. "I thought she was your mother!"

— Bernardine Kielty in
Book-of-the-Month Club News

With her hand on the light switch, the woman paused in her interminable chatter to inquire: "Is everything shut up for the night, dear?"

Out of the darkness came her husband's patient reply: "Everything else, dear."

— The Wall Street Journal

Woman trying on mink coat, to salesgirl: "If my husband doesn't like it will you promise to refuse to take it back?" (Gregory d'Alessio cartoon, Publishers Syndicate) . . . Smiling wife reading to disgruntled husband from his wartime letters: "And here's one from January, '45 . . . 'food awful . . . been raining for three weeks . . . if I ever get home I'll never complain about anything' . . . Want me to read more?" (Charles Pearson cartoon in *Collier's*) . . . Wife to husband when asked how she was feeling, "As well as can be, expecting."

Highly Specialized

During a discussion of movies one evening, I asked a young doctor if all those many pots of boiling water that country doctors on the screen invariably ask for are really necessary in delivering a baby at home.

"I wondered about that myself, because the only boiling water you really need is a very small panful for your hypo," the physician replied. "But one of my medical school professors, who had been a country doctor for many years, gave a good explanation. 'If you ever deliver a baby at home, the thing that will give you the most trouble will be the expectant father,' he warned us in a lecture. 'He'll be so nervous that he'll continually pester you and be underfoot unless you give him something to do. Tell him you'll need lots of hot water. Most farm-

houses have coal or wood stoves, and keeping the fire hot and the water boiling will get the father out of your way. After it's all over and you tell him the glad tidings, why you and he have the makings for some steaming hot coffee!'" — Mrs. T. R. Weiss

A hypochondriac told his doctor in great alarm that he had a fatal liver disease. "Nonsense!" protested the doctor. "You wouldn't know whether you had that or not. With that disease there's no discomfort of any kind."

"I know," gasped the patient. "My symptoms exactly."

Samuel F. B. Morse, who was an eminent painter before he invented telegraphy, once asked a physician friend to look at his painting of a man in death agony. "Well," Morse inquired after the doctor had scrutinized it carefully, "what is your opinion?"

"Malaria," said the doctor.

To illustrate the importance of making prescriptions clear to patients, Dr. William Osler used to tell his students this story:

A doctor once told a foreign patient, "The thing for you to do is to drink hot water an hour before breakfast every morning."

After a week the man returned to the doctor's office. "How are you feeling?" asked the physician.

"I feel worse if anything."

"Did you follow my directions and drink hot water an hour before breakfast every morning?" asked the doctor.

"I tried my best," replied the patient, "but I couldn't keep it up for more than 15 minutes at a time."   — Mrs. H. L. Harrell

A Yankee doctor practicing in the heart of Virginia begged his Virginia-born colleague at the hospital to see one of his new patients.

"I'm terribly busy," protested the Virginian. "What's the matter with her?"

"It's such a rare case that I think you must see her," said the Yankee. "She's a Virginian with an inferiority complex!"
                                        — Louise Gaston McCasland

"If a mother is disquieted," wrote Robert Burton in *The Anatomy of Melancholy*, in 1621, "or if by any casualty she be affrighted by some fearful object, she endangers her child."

In his book *Ourselves Unborn*, the embryologist, George Washington Corner, laughed off Burton's catalogue of prenatal horrors with one of his own: "As an honest man of science, I have to admit that I myself know of a remarkable case. A woman of my acquaintance had a craving to read *David Copperfield* while she was expecting and, upon my word, her child was full of the Dickens."   — *Newsweek*

Grandma: "Yes, I feel much better now, and I don't think there is anything wrong with my appendix. But it was nice of the minister to call and see about it."

Daughter: "But, Mother, that wasn't the new minister, that was a specialist from the city who examined you."

Grandma: "Oh, he was a doctor, was he? I thought he was a little familiar for a minister."   — *National Farm Journal*

"My family thinks there's something wrong with me," a woman complained to the psychoanalyst, "simply because I like buckwheat cakes."

"But there's nothing wrong about liking buckwheat cakes," the doctor murmured, puzzled. "I like them myself."

"Oh, do you?" The woman was delighted. "You must come up some day. I have seven trunks full."   — Oscar Schisgall

Tales with a Twist

Hoping to inspire his workers with promptness and energy, a New York executive hung a number of signs reading "DO IT NOW" around his factory and office. When he was asked some weeks later how his staff had reacted, he shook his head sadly. "I don't even like to talk about it," he said. "The cashier skipped with $4000, the head book-keeper eloped with the best secretary I ever had, three typists asked for an increase, the factory workers voted to go out on strike, and the office boy joined the Navy."   — Sid Ascher in *Caravan*

A Broadway playboy had a closer shave than he bargained for in a local barbershop. His manicure girl was very beautiful and he suggested dinner and a show that evening. "I don't think I ought to," said the girl demurely. "I'm married."

"Ask your husband," suggested the playboy. "I'm sure he wouldn't mind."

"Ask him yourself," said the girl. "He's shaving you."
— Bennett Cerf, *Laughing Stock* (Grosset & Dunlap)

It was a pretty shoddy-looking shirt, but the best he could find during the wartime shortage, so Jenkins bought it. Inside he found a slip of paper bearing a girl's name and address and the message: "Please write and send me your photograph."

On a romantic impulse, Jenkins wrote to the girl and sent her his picture. In a little while an answer came. With great excitement, he opened it and read: "Thanks for the photograph. I have been making these crumby-looking shirts for a long time, and I just had to see what kind of fellow would wear one of them."   — *Los Angeles School Journal*

On my first evening back from overseas, my girl's understanding parents left us alone in the living room. Naturally we didn't talk all the time, and in the midst of a kiss I noticed her little sister in her nightgown watching us from the doorway. "If you'll be a good girl and go to bed," I said, "I'll give you a quarter."

Without taking the bribe or saying a word she ran off, but soon was back again. "Here's half a dollar," she said. "Let me watch."

— Henry Schenker

One night Mrs. Amos Pinchot dreamed that she had written a poem so beautiful, so wise, so close to the ultimate truth of life that she was immediately acclaimed by all peoples of the earth as the greatest poet and philosopher of the ages. As the dream ended, she stumbled out of bed, still half asleep, and scribbled the poem down, realizing she must take no risk of forgetting such deathless lines.

She awoke in the morning with the feeling that something wonderful was about to happen . . . oh, yes! her Poem! Tense with excitement, she read what she had written:

Hogamus Higamus
Men are Polygamous
Higamus Hogamus
Women Monogamous.

— Claire MacMurray in Cleveland *Plain Dealer*

Irwin Edman, professor of philosophy at Columbia University, spent an evening with a colleague and his wife, and the conversation was spirited until about two o'clock in the morning. After several elaborate yawns had been ignored, the colleague said, "Irwin, I hate to put you out, but I have a nine o'clock class in the morning."

"Good lord," said Irwin, blushing violently. "I thought *you* were at *my* house!"

— Bennett Cerf, *Try and Stop Me* (Simon & Schuster)

A businessman in love with a night-club entertainer employed a detective agency to check up on her. He received the following report: "The young lady has an excellent reputation. Her past is without a blemish. She has many friends of good social standing. The only scandal associated with her is that she has often been seen lately with a businessman of questionable character."

— *Phoenix Flame*

On location for *Red Stallion* the entire company was amazed at the unfailing weather predictions made by an old Indian. He was consulted daily and his forecasts proved reliable. Then one day he refused to predict the weather. "Is anything wrong?" inquired Robert Paige.

"Yes," said the Indian, "radio broke."

— Andrew B. Hecht

Wise Guys and Gals

Sue: "I wonder if Jack loves me?"

Mabel: "Of course he does, dear. Why should he make you an exception?"

— *The Kellogg News*

"I'm Mr. Brown's wife," said a brunette, introducing herself to a blonde at a party.

"I'm his secretary," said the blonde.

"Oh," said the brunette, arching her eyebrows slightly, "were you?"

— Vancouver *Daily Province*

A soldier called at the chaplain's office. "I just came to ask you," he said, "whether you think it's right for any person to profit by the mistakes of others?"

"Most certainly not."

The soldier brightened and held out his hand. "Then perhaps you'll return the dollar I gave you last June for marrying me."

— *The Communiqué*

Angry boss: "You should have been here at nine!"

Tardy stenographer: "Why? What happened?"

— *Rotary Letter*

"Daughter," said the mother, "didn't I tell you not to let strange men come to your apartment? You know things like that worry me."

"Don't be ridiculous, Mother!" laughed the girl. "I went to his apartment. Now, let *his* mother worry!" — *Super Service Station Magazine*

"How long was your last cook with you?"

"She was never with us. She was against us from the start."

— Henry Swicegood in *Young America*

Pvt: "What's the best way to teach a girl to swim?"

Pfc: First you put your left arm around her waist, then you gently take her left hand and —"

Pvt: "She's my sister."

Pfc: "Oh — push her off the dock."

— Belvoir *Castle*

"Why haven't you mended the holes in these socks?" he demanded.

"You didn't buy that fur coat I wanted," replied his wife. "So I figured if you didn't give a wrap, I didn't give a darn." — *Pyramid Bulletin*

Long After Audubon

Condensed from "Dithers and Jitters"
Cornelia Otis Skinner

I am the victim of intermittent but passing attacks of ambition to patch up a faulty education. The latest spell was brought about by a friend who, sitting on my porch, suddenly exclaimed, "Why, I never realized you had pitpits!"

For an uncomfortable moment I thought she referred to some infirmity. Then when she said, "Hear him? He's in that bush," I realized that it was all about a bird.

"Oh, yes," I said complacently. If she was going to show off I could too. "We have flocks of them."

"But they don't go in flocks!"

"They do here," I countered, lamely.

Although my friend departed in haste she succeeded in sowing in me the birdseeds of discontent. A book on ornithology seemed imperative, and my bookseller assured me he had just what I needed. It turned out to be a bird guide the size of the Greater New York telephone book. As it has the weight of an anvil, the only way to look up a bird is to go out and stare at it until your eyes get out of focus, then rush indoors and try to find something in the book that remotely resembles it. The chances are that after you think you've made your find and are feeling pretty smug about it the thing listed in the book turns out to be an inhabitant of Manitoba.

In looking up birds, you have to memorize them in a flash, and if you think memorizing a restless bird is easy you'd better consult a psychiatrist. Then you have to guess what category he belongs in — whether he's a warbler, a flycatcher, a marsh-dweller or a totipalmated swimmer and if you can do that you probably know what the bird is anyway. How is the novice to tell? Warblers aren't always warbling, flycatchers are seldom catching flies, marsh-dwellers may be a long way from home, and as for those other things I don't even let myself think what they might be up to.

There is an exasperating little creature I've been trying for weeks to place. All I can determine is that he (or possibly she . . . God knows I'm not that far!) is smallish and of a color you call olive only because it isn't any color at all. It flits about in thick foliage and its note resembles the squeak of a shoe. The chances are it's either a red-eyed vireo, a pine siskin (immature), or a Spizella Passerina Passerina (the double name as in Corona Corona doubtless indicates a superior variety). The detailed descriptions don't get you anywhere. One of the above, for instance, is distinguished by a marking "dull whitish on the lower eyelids." But what bird will stay still long enough to let you investigate its lower eyelid?

One means of identification is by description of the song. This is pretty bewildering. We are told, for instance, that one little codger is easily discovered by his cheery "tra-ree-rah, ree-rah-ree" while another says "chink" while flying and "chunk" when feeding. The sort that go in for catchwords like "Eat, Potter, eat" or "Sow wheat, Peverly, Peverly" I find difficult, due either to my lack of perception or the bird's faulty diction. Anyway, even the best authorities disagree. In the case of the olive-sided flycatcher, Thoreau thinks it says "till, till, till," while someone else describes it as "hip-pui-shee."

I learned that the song of the white-throated sparrow can best be approximated if "played with a very executed effect on the E string of a fine violin," but I don't know Heifetz well enough to ask him to play this for me. One amazing outburst of gladness is the happy voice of the yellow-breasted chat which goes (cross my heart, I'm not making this up) "crr-rwhrr-that's it, chee, quack, cluck-yit, yit-now, hit it, tr-r-rwhen, caw, caw-cut, tea-boy, who-who-mew-mew." The book doesn't state whether or not at the end of all this the bird falls in a faint.

A further handicap is, as in the case of an encyclopedia, the number of fascinating distractions that lure you far afield from the bird you're looking up. Start searching for some ordinary local variety of sparrow and on the way you'll come across such fabulous creatures as the *tufted puffin*, an ancient murrelet, and something that apparently doesn't get a break, being known as a *least auklet*. These congregate in the Bering Straits where "they are very playful and chase each other in great good will," and feed on seafleas. Well, well!

One thing ardently to be wished is that the people who write about birds were not so blessed with the "keep smiling" spirit. Somehow, to learn that the nuthatch is the "small boy of the feathered world" or that the chipping sparrow is a "contented, modest little bird who tries hard to believe in the goodness of human nature even though he meets with but little encouragement" puts one off ornithology.

Cartoon Quips

One young modern to another: "It was so strange the way we met — we were introduced."
— Melisse in *The Saturday Evening Post*

Child specialist giving advice to mother: "You'll have to handle this child carefully; remember you're dealing with a sensitive, high-strung little stinker."
— Jeff Keate in *The Saturday Evening Post*

Woman to husband as she arrives in auto with smashed front: "And the policeman was so nice about it. He asked if I'd like for the city to remove all the telephone poles."
— Mort Walker in *The Saturday Evening Post*

One stenographer to another: "You'll like it here — lots of opportunity for advances."
— Hank Ketcham in *True*

Clerk selling customer pair of skis: "This little pamphlet goes with them — it tells how to convert them into a pair of splints!"
— Dick Turner, NEA

Barfly to neighbor at bar: "My wife is the most wonderful woman in the world, and that's not just my opinion — it's hers."
— Kirk in *The Saturday Evening Post*

Woman, clad in a suit jacket and slip, to man at department-store Lost and Found: "Did anyone return a blue skirt with four children from three to seven clinging to it?"
— Gregory d'Alessio, Publishers Syndicate

Weatherman on telephone: "My corns hurt too, madam, but we still say it will be clear and sunny."
— Reamer Keller in *Redbook*

Schoolboy in geography class: "The principal export of the United States is money!"
— Ben Roth in *Collier's*

Girl to escort: "Let's have a cocktail first — I never eat on an empty stomach." — Al Ross in *Collier's*

Housewife to plumber: "It must have been the family living here before that sent for you, but they moved out over a year ago."
— Bill King, Chicago Tribune-New York News Syndicate

Wife to irate husband: "Normally I wouldn't dream of opening a letter addressed to you, but this one was marked 'private.'"
— Leslie Stark in *Collier's*

Sun-tanned businessman to envious colleague: "It ought to be a wonderful tan. I figure it cost me $173.78 per square inch."
— Herb Williams in *Collier's*

Girl answering telephone: "Marie isn't in just now. This is her 111-pound, five-foot-three, blonde, blue-eyed sister." — Kirk Stiles in *Collier's*

Pert and Pertinent

The Department of Internal Revenue received a typed income-tax return from a bachelor who listed one dependent son. The examiner returned the blank with a penciled notation: "This must be a stenographic error."

The blank came back promptly with the notation: "You're telling me!" — *Gould Battery News*

An admirer encountered Vicki Baum for the first time. "Why, Miss Baum," she gushed, "it's nice to find you so blonde and young. I had imagined you were much older and a brunette!"

"My dear," replied the author, "I am!"
— Lucius Beebe in New York *Herald Tribune*

A Hollywood writer, present for a conference, patiently listened while a producer ranted into the telephone. As he slammed down the receiver, the writer remarked, "If you're not careful, you'll get ulcers."

"I don't get them. I give them," the producer snapped back.
— Tom Jenks, quoted by Sidney Skolsky, United Feature Syndicate

"I'm thinking of writing the story of our life together," Alexander Woollcott once said to Neysa McMein, with whom he was more or less in love for many years; then added, "The title is already settled."

"What is it?" she asked.

"Under Separate Cover." — Samuel Hopkins Adams, *A. Woollcott: His Life and His World* (Reynal & Hitchcock)

Poet Edwin Arlington Robinson was asked by an aspiring young poet: "What is the most important qualification for a beginner in poetry?"

Robinson, speaking from experience, replied: "A small appetite."
— E. E. Edgar

An attractive young woman once asked a leading New York dermatologist what to do for her prematurely graying hair.

"Admire it!" he advised. — Jerome W. Ephraim, *Take Care of Yourself*
(Simon & Schuster)

A Boston brokerage house advertised for "a young Harvard graduate or the equivalent." Among the answers was one from a Yale man: "When you speak of an equivalent," he wrote, "do you mean two Princeton men or a Yale man half-time?"   — *This Week Magazine*

Shaw's romance with the actress Ellen Terry has been the subject of infinite anecdotes and conjectures. When she requested permission to publish some of the voluminous correspondence he had addressed to her in the course of a lifetime, he refused indignantly, saying, "I will not play the horse to your Lady Godiva."

— Bennett Cerf in *The Saturday Review of Literature*

"Your friend Rogers is a good fellow," someone said to Mark Twain of H. H. Rogers of Standard Oil fame. "It's a pity his money is tainted."

"It's twice tainted," drawled Mark. "'Tain't yours and 'tain't mine."

— *Francis Wilson's Life of Himself* (Houghton)

The Writing Public

During the man-power shortage a man of ambition but sketchy education was promoted to a pen-and-paper job. Shortly thereafter, his home office received the following communication: "Dear Sirs: I need a dick I need a dix. Please send me a book that tells how to spell words and what they mean. Thanks. Joe."   — Mary Bowles

In a school in one of Chicago's poorer districts, a questionnaire was sent home with a new pupil, requesting information regarding the home environment, number of brothers and sisters, father's occupation, etc. The next day she returned with a scrap of paper on which was the following: "We have 18 children. My husband can also do plumbing and carpentry work."   — Eileen S. Oswald

To Congressman L. C. Battle: I know I can only vote for one candidate but how many can I vote against? Irma D——

— Juliet Lowell, *Dear Mr. Congressman* (Duell, Sloane & Pearce)

The editor of a Vermont weekly sent to one Hiram Sparks a notice that his subscription had expired. The notice came back with the laconic scrawl: "So's Hiram." — Theodore Rubin

Editors of *Collier's* received a letter from an aspiring contributor: "I am enclosing another of my masterpieces which I have been sending you since 1930. You never paid me for any of them though I know you took ideas from all of them, even from the ones I never mailed to you. Please attend to this matter as soon as possible." — W. D. in *Collier's*

While in New York, Gene Fowler had his wallet stolen in the subway. The following morning he received a letter reading: "Sir, I stoal youre munny. Remauss is noring me, so I send sum of it back to you. Wen it nors again I will send sum more." — Irving Hoffman, King Features

A farmer who sent for a book on *How to Grow Tomatoes* wrote the publisher: "The man who writ the ad shoulda writ the book." — *The Mining Journal*

A Seattle firm, having difficulty in making a collection, finally wrote: "Dear Mr. Jones: What would your neighbors think if we came to your town and repossessed your car?"
A week later they received their letter back. Scrawled on it was: "Sir: I took the above matter up with my neighbors and they think it would be a lousy trick. Sincerely, Lester Jones." — Fred R. Fritch

A man wrote Congressman Gore that he'd like to be an inventor but didn't want to waste his time on things already invented. "Will you please go down to the patent office," his letter read, "and get me a list of things that haven't been invented. Get me the answers by return mail as I'm anxious to get to work." — Washington *Post*

Letter to a Boston paper: "Dear Sir: When I subscribed a year ago you stated that if I was not satisfied at the end of the year I could have my money back. Well, I would like to have it back.
"On second thought, to save you trouble, you may apply it on my next year's subscription."

Strange Logic

In Newark, N. J., Mrs. Belle Bearison lost a purse containing $25, got it back with only $17, plus a note from the anonymous finder explaining that she herself had once lost a purse with $8 in it. —*Time*

Producer Jerry Wald tells the story of the executive assistant who went to the studio chief and asked for an extra two-weeks vacation. "You know how hard I have been working and how I concentrate on my work," he told the chief.

"That's exactly why you don't need an extra vacation," the chief replied. "With your ability to concentrate, you should be able to cram more recreation into two weeks than other people get into four weeks."

— Andrew B. Hecht

An Englishwoman who kept two cows for her household's use found that while her children were off at school she had more milk than she needed. Knowing it was illegal to sell the surplus, she gave it away to deserving people in the village. Soon an official arrived to say that even giving it away was illegal, unless the recipients were in her employ.

"You surely don't want me to pour it down the drain," said the woman.

"Of course not," replied the official. "My Ministry is against waste of any sort. You must only draw off as much as you require!"

— London *Evening Standard*

The fat man and his wife were returning to their seats in the theater after the intermission.

"Did I tread on your toes as I went out?" he asked a man at the end of the row.

"You did," replied the other grimly, expecting an apology.

The fat man turned to his wife. "All right, Mary," he said, "this is our row." — *The Highway Traveler*

The gravediggers of Memphis, Tenn., have organized, taking out cards with the CIO Canners' and Packers' Union.

— St. Louis *Globe-Democrat*

A Raleigh newspaperman separated two men whom he found exchanging blows. "What's this all about?" he asked.

"I called him a liar," growled one.

"Suppose I *am* a liar!" roared the other. "I've got a right to be sensitive about it, haven't I?" — John Harden in Greensboro, N. C., *Daily News*

Lana Turner was exclaiming over the fact that pressure cookers will cook spinach in two minutes. "So what?" retorted George Sidney. "You just have to eat the stuff 14 minutes sooner."

— D.D.T. in *Daily Variety*

Harry D. Arrast tells about Charlie Chaplin's battle with a fly that kept buzzing around him during a picture conference. After slapping at it several times Charlie became exasperated and called for a swatter. As the discussion continued, he sat with the swatter poised and a menacing eye on the elusive fly. Three times he swung at it; three times he missed. At last the fly settled on a table directly in front of him, and Charlie tensed for the kill. Slowly, cautiously, he raised the swatter. But just as he was ready to deliver the deathblow, he deliberately lowered his weapon and allowed the fly to escape.

"For heaven's sake!" someone blurted out. "Why on earth didn't you swat it?"

Charlie shrugged. "It wasn't the same fly."

— M. M. Musselman, *It Took Nine Tailors* (Whittlesey House)

In Hollywood, a Hays Office censor phoned a studio official about some stills showing a girl in a rather revealing costume. "They're okay if that's an evening gown," said the censor, "but if it's a nightgown, the picture's out!" — Walter Winchell

Caustic Comment

An ermine-bedecked show girl entered a New York night club. When someone commented upon her wrap, she replied, "Oh, this, I got it for a song."

To which Joan Davis cracked:

"It looks more like an overture to me." — Mitch Woodbury in Toledo *Blade*

Oscar Wilde's greatest rival for conversational honors was the painter Whistler. On one occasion, while discussing a work of art, Whistler made a witty comment. "I wish I had said that," exclaimed Wilde.

"You will, Oscar, you will!" Whistler retorted.

— *Art of Conversation*

A five-star general was asked if he knew General MacArthur personally. "Know him!" he replied. "I studied dramatics under him for four years."

— Bennett Cerf in *The Saturday Review of Literature*

Tallulah Bankhead and Peggy Joyce were chatting at the Stork Club. "I met the most marvelous man," said Tallulah. "He'd be wonderful for you."

"Is he my type?" queried Peggy.

"Sure," quickly responded Tallulah. "He's alive and breathing."

— Irving Hoffman in *The Hollywood Reporter*

A young actress had redecorated her New York apartment in ultra-modern style. She was showing it one day to Ethel Barrymore. "Do tell me how you like it," she said proudly.

"How wonderful," the great actress exclaimed, "to be young enough to have the stamina to live with it!" — Mona Gardner

A woman with a fuzzy poodle under her arm swished into a cocktail lounge. Then, ignoring the waiter who came up, she fussed over her fidgeting animal, cooing baby talk: "There, there. Nobody's going to hurt mamma's itsy-bitsy baby." Finally the dog settled down and the woman turned to the waiter. Without batting an eye he asked courteously — if somewhat coldly — "Your first dog, madam?"

Visiting a newly rich friend in the country, Wolcott Gibbs refused to be impressed by tennis courts, swimming pools, stables, and other forms of luxury. Finally, returning to the house, the owner pointed to a magnificent elm growing just outside the library window and boasted: "That tree stood for 50 years on top of the hill. I had it moved down here so on pleasant mornings I can do my work in its shade." Said Gibbs: "That just goes to show what God could do if he had money."

— Frank Case, *Do Not Disturb* (Lippincott)

At a party in Paris, the American bullfighter, Sidney Franklin, was cornered by an American dowager who took him severely to task for the alleged cruelty of his art. She would have none of his careful explanations, but pattered on endlessly about the "poor helpless bulls." After ten minutes of this, Franklin came to the limit of his patience.

"Madam," he said, "I can't agree with you. I have killed many bulls, but I have always spared them the ultimate cruelty — not one did I ever bore to death!" — Ken W. Purdy

A chorus girl was telling the other girls in the dressing room about her birthday party the night before. "You should have seen the cake!" she exclaimed excitedly. "There were 17 candles."

"Seventeen candles?" queried one of the chorines. "What did you do, burn them at both ends?"

— *Catholic Mirror*

"I'm a smash hit," boasted a conceited actor to his dinner host, Oliver Herford. "Why, yesterday during the last act, I had the audience glued in their seats!"

"Wonderful! Wonderful!" exclaimed Herford. "Clever of you to think of it!"

— E. E. Edgar

Wedding Receptions

At a fashionable wedding, the groom noticed that one of the guests looked rather glum. "Have you kissed the bride?" he asked by way of cheering the gloomy one up.

"Not lately," replied the guest with a faraway look in his eyes.

— Edmund and Williams' *Toaster's Handbook* (H. W. Wilson)

During the war a nurse in New Guinea fell in love with an officer patient, and they planned to wed the day he was released from the hospital. Not wishing to be married in her khaki uniform, she got permission to wear a wedding gown. After the ceremony the overwhelmed groom announced to all: "Isn't she lovely? This is the first time I've ever seen her with a dress on!"

"Isn't he handsome?" the excited bride exclaimed. "It's the first time I've ever seen him when he wasn't in pajamas!"

— Will Oursler, quoted by Walter Winchell

At a wedding reception in Charlotte, N. C., a friend of the groom decided to find out whether anyone in the receiving line knew what the hundreds of people filing past were saying. As he moved along, he purred, "My grandmother just died today."

"How nice!" "Thank you so much!" "How sweet of you to say so!" — were the responses to his announcement. No one had the slightest idea what he said, least of all the groom, who exclaimed jovially, "It's about time you took the same step, old man!" — Una Taylor

Bride's father to groom: "My boy, you're the second happiest man in the world."

— Pete Simer

A film star who has had a series of unhappy marriages told Marc Connelly, "I'm being married next week."

Connelly asked, "Against whom?"   — Leonard Lyons

When Roderick Peattie was married in Chicago, a column-long story of the wedding appeared in the society section. On the train afterward, the newlyweds wanted to conceal their new status, so the young man was very nonchalant when he handed their long tickets to the conductor. The official read and read. Finally, he raised his voice so the entire car could hear and said, "My friend, this is a very interesting account of your wedding, but where are your tickets?"   — *The Woman*

A U. S. Weather Bureau forecaster at the Washington National Airport reported that a woman called up one day in March to ask what the exact weather would be on June 18. She was planning a bang-up outdoor wedding for her daughter.

"We can't look that far ahead," the weatherman told her.

"What's the matter with you people?" she snapped. "Haven't you got an almanac?"   — Frank Carey, AP

An old gentleman asked a splendidly attired Negro at a wedding, "Pardon me, suh, is you de groom?"

"No, suh," replied the young man gloomily. "Ah was eliminated in the semifinals."   — *The Franklin News*

At the Providence, R. I., railroad station a flustered young bridegroom starting on his honeymoon absent-mindedly asked for one ticket. But when his wife said, "Why, Tom, you've bought only one ticket," he answered without a moment's hesitation:

"By thunder, you're right, dear! I'd forgotten myself completely."   — David Gordon

Quick Recoveries

In a secluded corner of their club, a film actor was being berated by his shrewish wife. "You mean skunk," she announced. "Of all low-down reptiles I think you're the worst!"

The actor, noticing that a group of friends had taken a table within earshot, quickly broke in, "Quite right, dear. And what else did you say to him?"   — Montreal *Star*

During the war the English told a story about a reluctant conscript asked by the army oculist to read a chart. "What chart?" asked the draftee. "Just sit down in that chair and I'll show you." "What chair?" asked the man. Deferred because of bad eyesight, the draftee went to a nearby movie. When the lights came on, he was horrified to discover the oculist in the next seat. "Excuse me," said the conscript as calmly as he could, "does this bus go to Shipley?"   — *Newsweek*

Opie Read, the humorist, was playing golf in a foursome when his ball landed in a sand trap. Hidden from view he hacked away at the ball. When he finally drove it out, his friends asked: "How many strokes, Opie?"

"Three."

"But we heard six!"

"Three," said Opie, "were echoes."   — James Martin in *Your Personality*

An old Negro was watching his boys trying to break a mule. As fast as the youngsters climbed aboard, the critter tossed them off. Finally he could stand it no longer. "Bring dat mule here, Rastus! You-all don't know nuthin' 'bout ridin' a mule! LemME show you!"

The old man hopped astraddle with confidence. As Lizy began to buck, he talked to her: "Lizy, you ain't foolin' with the boys now — you's got de ole man on yo' back, so you might as well quiet down."

Just then Lizy managed to toss the old man about six feet out onto the ground. He picked himself up, turned to the boys and said: "Now, boys, dat's de way to do — when you-all see she's gwine to fling ye, *jump off!*"   — J. W. Cunningham

Wilson Mizner once wrote a play which was backed by an aging dowager. During a rehearsal Mizner, without thinking, asked her how old she was. "Why do you wish to know?" was her icy query.

"Dear lady," Wilson covered quickly, "I merely wanted to know at what age a woman is most fascinating."   — Walter Winchell

What Is a Man?

Condensed from Glamour

Elizabeth Dunn

By the time I was ten I knew that men are strong, self-controlled, logical, realistic, accurate about facts and almost invariably right. Since this has been my basic belief ever since, it is understandable that life, for me, is never dull.

However, it isn't only a case of believing that men are strong, realistic and logical: I can prove it. Just take the matter of strength.

My husband is a charming but sedentary fellow who likes to translate the Odes of Horace into English verse. Nonetheless, with an effortless twist of the wrist, he can put the top on a thermos bottle so securely that it has to be sent all the way back to the factory to be opened again.

And take the classic example of Mr. A., who came into his own dark living room after a late party and stumbled over a mahogany footstool. As a mark of disapproval he kicked the stool the length of the room, breaking two of his toes, the leg of a piecrust table, and most of the things on the table. No woman could possibly have done such a thing. Even supposing her courageous enough to have kicked a footstool in the first place, she could never have sent it 15 feet into a piecrust table.

In cases like this the muddleheaded and the prejudiced confuse the issues with idle talk of impulsiveness and short temper. But I contend that Mr. A.'s action arose solely from an excess of masculine strength. It had nothing whatever to do with a lack of self-control, as some people have insisted. Self-control — in the male — is something quite different.

To illustrate: Let us consider Man and Suffering. Men simply do not have the various little ailments that women are constantly nursing: a migraine headache, a touch of laryngitis, a slight conjunctivitis. Men suffer only on a large, I might even say a majestic, scale, and what is more they are not in the least ashamed of it.

Mr. R., a man of rugged constitution, was felled by the common cold. Mrs. R., after a long day spent in nursing him, dropped in to have a cup of tea with me. My telephone promptly rang. Over it, Mr. R. announced in a thick tenor that all the buttons had fallen off his pajamas, his teeth were jangling and would Mrs. R. please come home at once. Under similar circumstances a woman might have sulked, rebelled, or wept in self-pity. Mr. R. showed no such lack of self-control; he simply sent for his wife.

No one, surely, will question male superiority in matters of logic. Occasionally something does occur in masculine thinking which I am not quite able to follow, but I put this down to weakness of intellect on my part. I ask myself, isn't the mind that is capable of grasping bills of lading, the rules of poker, or why gold is buried in Kentucky above

criticism? The answer is invariably Yes.

Another friend of mine, Mrs. L., is married to a man of outstanding mental attainments. He can describe stocks and bonds so that you can really understand them, sometimes for days afterward.

During the war, his wife said to him one evening: "When we go to England again, darling, let's go on the *Queen Mary*, but this time let's not go Tourist — let's go First Class. Shall we?"

Mr. L. looked up from his book. It took him a moment to think, but when he spoke it was mildly and reasonably. "But if we go Tourist, dear," he said, "we'll get there in five days."

Mrs. L., having brooded over this conversation ever since 1943, is left with the disturbing mental picture of the First Class section of the *Queen Mary* being hauled into Southampton a day or two after the stern has arrived.

However, a man said it, so Mrs. L. feels that it must mean *something*.

Now about realism. Everyone knows that women are romantic dreamers; perhaps the best example is in their sentimental attitude toward servants.

We once had a valuable but highly temperamental German cook-housekeeper. For five years my behavior toward her was that of gingerly respect; my husband treated her with the sort of carefree abandon that marked the attitude of Simon Legree toward the slaves. If I ventured a criticism to Greta, a cold front advanced upon the household. And yet my husband . . .

Well, one hot August night, with thunderstorms growling nervously, he asked Greta to bring him a whisky and soda. Just as she reached the living room bearing a loaded tray, the first thunder cracked directly overhead. Simultaneously something terribly complicated ensued, involving Greta's feet and the hooked rug and resulting in her rising into the air, tray and all, and landing at the master's feet on her face. Since she was not a small woman, the crash was deafening; the house shook, the clocks all struck, and the living room, as far as the eye could reach, was awash with whisky, soda, ice and broken glass.

I sat paralyzed. Greta's dignity — Greta's sensibilities — the possibility of splinters of glass in Greta's person . . .

The clocks ceased, the thunder died away, and my husband looked upon our handmaiden with astonished distaste.

"I don't know what you think you're doing," he roared, "but whatever it is, for God's sake be quiet about it!"

Greta got to her hands and knees and crawled away through the whisky and soda. Then she cleaned it up and started over — humble, apologetic and anxious to please. If I had spoken a word she would have given notice on the spot. My husband acted like a brute and she loved it.

In view of these things I maintain that Man is strong, self-controlled, realistic, logical, accurate about facts and almost invariably right.

The Pay-Off

Two Hollywood writers rented a house for a year and got a promise from the landlord to redecorate the place. When it became obvious that he wouldn't keep his promise, the writers had their attorney draw up a paper giving them permission to decorate the house at their own expense. The landlord was happy to sign.

Two days before they moved out, they had the whole place painted black.

— Andrew B. Hecht

Not so many years ago, George Bernard Shaw, poking fun at all things American, came out with some unusually caustic comments. A number of newspapers rose to the bait and howled in protest, but one editor held his fire until Mr. Shaw paid his much-publicized visit to Miami. This editor's paper published a lengthy report of the arrival of Mrs. George Bernard Shaw. Mrs. Shaw went to this dinner, Mrs. Shaw attended that function. Mrs. Shaw said this, and Mrs. Shaw did that. Then at the bottom of the long article was this casual after-thought:

"Mrs. Shaw was accompanied by her husband, George Bernard Shaw, a writer."   — *The Christian Science Monitor*

An enthusiastic amateur gardener spent all his spare time puttering around the yard in his oldest clothes. One Saturday when his wife was giving a very formal tea, she gave him strict orders not to garden, saying he was just too disreputable-looking. He took it very meekly, so she was completely bewildered when her guests looked out the window and began shrieking with laughter. There on the front lawn, pushing the lawn mower in precise lines, turning square corners with a click of his heels, was the head of the family — immaculately clad in white tie and tails.   — Louis Burno

Frequently, Ferenc Molnár, the Hungarian dramatist, has invited cronies to his home for lengthy card-playing sessions. Molnár's first wife was not particularly keen about these get-togethers. When, during a noisy game lasting into the wee hours of the morning, Molnár asked his wife to fix some refreshments, she soon came into the room bearing a tray. Triumphantly she placed before each man a dish of cards — well fried in butter!   — E. E. Edgar

A Georgia gentleman who is still fighting the Civil War was highly indignant when his daughter, Mary, insisted on going up North to college. There she fell in love with a boy from Boston. Her letters to her mother spoke more and more glowingly of Bill, and finally Mary wrote that he had asked her to marry him. The mother dreaded her husband's reaction to this news, but she screwed up her courage and asked, "What would you think if Mary married a damyankee?"

"Well," he said with vehemence, "that's one way to pay 'em back."
— Alex F. Osborn

Tourists at Large

"Major" Brooks, an ardently loyal Southerner, had become landlord of a small-town hotel in Montana. One night the usual crowd around the stove in the lobby was joined by an uncompromising Yankee who harshly criticized most everything south of Mason and Dixon's line. The Major, though hard pressed, managed to maintain his usual courtesy.

When the guest was ready to retire, the landlord showed him the way. Preceding the stranger into his room, the Major started to take a large framed photograph of General Robert E. Lee from the wall.

"Oh, you needn't remove the picture," the guest hastened to assure him. "I shan't be offended by its being there."

The Major unhooked the picture, put it carefully under his arm and proceeded to the door. There he paused a moment, and with a stately bow to his guest, said, "It's the General I'm thinking of, suh."
— Helen Spain Parkins

Upon their return from Europe, a movie producer and his wife were telling about a painting of Adam and Eve and the serpent they saw in the Louvre. "You see," gushed the lady, "we found it especially interesting because we knew the anecdote!"
— Irving Hoffman in *The Hollywood Reporter*

For years the family had been saving to take their grandmother to Niagara Falls. When they finally succeeded, she stared at the water for a long while with a blank expression.

"Don't you like it, Grandmother?" the family asked. "Isn't it wonderful?"

The old lady shrugged her shoulders. "Well," she said deprecatingly, "what's to hinder?"   — Struthers Burt in *The Saturday Review of Literature*

Once Milton Berle played Pittsburgh for a one-week stand. On Monday he picked out a restaurant that looked attractive. "I always eat whole-wheat bread," he told the waitress, but she brought white. On Tuesday, he reminded her about the whole-wheat, but was served white again. Wednesday she made the same mistake, not to mention Thursday and Friday. Finally on Saturday when she took his order, Berle said, "Just for the heck of it, I think I'll take white bread today." "That's funny," said the waitress. "Aren't you the party who always orders whole-wheat?" — Bennett Cerf, *Anything for a Laugh* (Grosset & Dunlap)

A Bostonian was showing a visiting Englishman around. "This is Bunker Hill Monument, where Warren fell, you know."

The visitor surveyed the lofty shaft thoughtfully. "Nasty fall! Killed him, of course?"   — *The Pennsylvania Guardsman*

One raw winter night at Atlanta's Candler Airport, an old lady confessed that this was her first plane trip when I introduced myself as the flight steward. It was hardly a night for a first flight; rain mixed with sleet hammered on the ship as we taxied to the end of the runway. The old lady looked very tense. Breaking a strict rule, I unfastened my seat belt and sat on the arm of her seat, taking her cold hand in mine. She squeezed my hand tight and held on.

After we were safely aloft, as I started back to my seat, she said: "Now, son, if you are afraid when we go to land, you come right back here and I'll hold your hand again."   — Belvin B. Horres, Sr.

At the Stork Club, a bore was describing what happened to him on a trip to Grand Canyon. "There I stood," he orated, "drinking in the scene, with the giant abyss yawning before me."

At this point, Sherman Billingsley interrupted, "Was the abyss yawning before you got there?"   — Irving Hoffman, King Features

An American tourist in Paris was endeavoring to use some of his high school French to order his luncheon.

"Garsong," he said after a lengthy study of the menu, "je desire consumme royal, et un piece of pang et burr — no, hang it — une piece of burr —"

"I'm sorry, sir," said the tactful waiter, "I don't speak French."

"Very well," snapped the tourist. "For heaven's sake, send me someone who can."
— *Gags*

A young English officer put up at a famous Park Avenue hotel, neglecting to ask the room rate first. On his departure, he was given his bill. He gazed at it a moment, then asked the cashier, "Am I correct in assuming that suggestions from your patrons are welcome?"

"Certainly," he said. "Hasn't everything been satisfactory?"

"Everything has been fine," said the officer, "but I have noticed that you have a sign posted in your rooms which reads, 'Have you left anything?' Change the sign to read, 'Have you anything left?'"
— Bennett Cerf, *The Pocket Book of War Humor* (Pocket Books)

The Women

One of the girls in the senior class had received an engagement ring the night before but to her chagrin no one at high school noticed it. Finally in the afternoon, when her friends were sitting around talking, she stood up suddenly. "My, it's hot in here," she announced. "I think I'll take off my ring."
— Steve Benson

We were boarding at an old farmhouse in Milford, Conn., whose owner gloried in still having her family's original colonial grants to the land. On the morning of July Fourth we heard the sounds of martial music from the village. I asked our landlady if she weren't going down to the parade.

"Oh, no!" she replied. "I'd love to, but I've never felt *privileged* to go to the Fourth of July celebrations. You see, my family were Tories!"
— Mildred Wells

My sister and I were talking on the phone when the operator cut in: "You have a long-distance call." We immediately terminated our talk. Then the operator cut back in: "I didn't know whether to interrupt or not but — *this is a man!*" — Eileen O'Connor

Volunteering as a blood donor at a Texas hospital, a young woman was asked by the nurse, "Do you know your type?"

"Oh, yes," came the reply. "I'm the *sultry* type." — W. H. Shipley

An office manager was asking a girl applicant if she had any unusual talents. She said she had won several prizes in crossword-puzzle and slogan-writing contests. "Sounds good," the manager told her, "but we want somebody who will be smart during office hours." "Oh," said the girl, "this *was* during office hours." — Louisville *Courier-Journal*

My wife and I were enjoying a picture show in Redondo Beach, Calif., when suddenly an earthquake struck. For an instant we felt as if the theater were being carried on the back of a charging elephant. The majority of the audience started from their seats.

In the center of the theater, a woman stood up. "Don't get excited!" she cried shrilly. "Keep your seats, everyone!" Almost to a person the audience sat down. Then the lady calmly walked out. — Lee Arms

"She told me," a woman complained to a friend, "that you told her the secret I told you not to tell her."

"Well," replied her friend in a hurt tone, "I told her not to tell you I told her."

"Oh, dear," sighed the first woman. "Well, don't tell her I told you that she told me." — H. L. Gee, *Another Cheerful Day* (Methuen)

She's a good photograph of her father and a perfect phonograph of her mother (Bob De Haven) . . . She was born in the year of our Lord only knows (Leon Hale) . . . One of those large-chested women who always seem closer to you than you are to them (L. A. B. Hutton) . . . She's far from her old sylph (Jimmy Fidler) . . . A feminine question which gives a man his choice between two wrong answers (William E. Barrett)

The Woman's Way

Dick Ashbaugh in This Week Magazine

When I build my better world, I know one thing that is going to be outlawed. That's woman's intuition.

Take the little matter of starting the car on a cold morning. I am standing in the garage, already 20 minutes late for work, glaring at this large hunk of inanimate metal. I have primed the carburetor, checked the plugs and filed the points. At this point my wife walks in. "The license plate looks loose to me," she says. "That's probably why it won't start." In icy silence I tighten the license plate and step on the starter. The car not only starts but the dashboard clock starts ticking, and the dome light, which hasn't worked for four years, suddenly shines like a little star in the sky.

That's woman's intuition.

If the radio goes on the blink it is foolish to worry about the tubes or transformer. You slam the desk drawer three times and in comes H. V. Kaltenborn just like he was standing there in the room. My wife informs me of this in the tone one uses with a child. If my electric shaver doesn't work, do I worry? No. I go down in the basement and kick a certain water pipe. Sometimes I fail to kick the right pipe and have to be led down again and shown, but it always works. If the furnace goes off, I just reach up and put a drop of cologne on the thermostat. "I discovered that last winter," my wife informs me calmly.

Occasionally I get a little confused. Yesterday, for instance, I was tinkering in my workshop, and the electric drill wouldn't work. "Dear," I sang out, "would you know why the electric drill isn't working?"

"Certainly," she called from some place overhead. "You'll have to change your shoes."

Reluctant to tramp all the way upstairs, I searched around until I found an old pair of tennis sneakers. I put them on but still the drill didn't work. Just then my wife came downstairs. "What," she said, "are you doing in those old tennis sneakers?"

"I changed them so the drill would work," I said, and then added triumphantly, "but it doesn't!"

"Of all the egg-heads," she moaned. "I said change the fuse. It blew out yesterday morning. Who ever heard of making a drill work by changing your shoes!"

Of course nobody ever had.

Definitions

Oratory: The art of making deep noises from the chest sound like important messages from the brain.
— H. I. Phillips

Flirt: A woman who believes that it's every man for herself.
— *Country Gentlewoman*

Punctuality: The art of guessing correctly how late the other party is going to be.
— P.C.F. in *The Saturday Evening Post*

An historical novel: Like a bustle, a fictitious tale covering up a stern reality.
— Augusta Tucker, *The Man Miss Susie Loved* (Harper)

Budget: A method of worrying before you spend, as well as afterward.
— *Papyrus*

Bore: A person who has flat feats.
— Joe Harrington in Boston *Post*

Champagne: The drink that makes you see double and think single.
— Leonard L. Levinson

Football season: The only time of the year when a man can walk down the street with a blonde on one arm and a blanket on the other without encountering raised eyebrows.
— Bennett Cerf in *The Saturday Review of Literature*

Gambling: A way of getting nothing for something.
— Wilson Mizner, quoted by Walter Winchell

Modern bathing suit: Two bandannas and a worried look.
— Judy Canova Show, NBC

Child's definition: An adult is one who has stopped growing except in the middle.

Artichoke: Strip tease with mayonnaise.
— *The Kaserne Post*

Alimony: The high cost of leaving.

Rumba: A dance where the front of you goes along nice and smooth like a Cadillac and the back of you makes like a jeep.
— Bob Hope

Umbrella: A shelter for one and a shower bath for two.
— W. Hitchcock in London *Opinion*

The Dog That Bit People

Condensed from "My Life and Hard Times"

James Thurber

Probably no one man should have as many dogs in his life as I have had, but there was more pleasure than distress in them for me except in the case of an Airedale named Muggs. He gave me more trouble than all the other fifty-five put together. He really wasn't my dog, as a matter of fact; I came home from a vacation one summer to find that my brother Roy had bought him while I was away. A big burly, choleric dog, he always acted as if he thought I wasn't one of the family. There was a slight advantage in being one of the family, for he didn't bite the family as often as he bit strangers. We used to take turns feeding him to be on his good side, but that didn't always work. In the years that we had him he bit everybody but Mother, and he made a pass at her once but missed. Angered one day because Muggs refused to chase rats in the pantry, Mother slapped him and he slashed at her, but didn't make it. He was sorry immediately, Mother said. He was always sorry, she said, after he bit someone, but we could not understand how she figured this out. He didn't act sorry.

Mother used to send a box of candy every Christmas to the people the Airedale bit. The list finally contained forty or more names. Nobody could understand why we didn't get rid of the dog. I think that one or two people tried to poison Muggs — he acted poisoned once in a while — and old Major Moberly fired at him once with his service revolver near the Seneca Hotel in East Broad Street — but Muggs lived to be almost eleven years old and even when he could hardly get around he bit a congressman who had called to see my father on business. My mother had never liked the congressman — she said the signs of his horoscope showed he couldn't be trusted — but she sent

Thurber

him a box of candy that Christmas. He sent it right back, probably because he suspected it was trick candy. Mother persuaded herself it was all for the best even though Father lost an important business connection because of it. "I wouldn't be associated with such a man," Mother said. "Muggs could read him like a book."

Muggs never bit anyone more than once at a time. Mother always mentioned that as an argument in his favor; she said he had a quick temper but that he didn't hold a grudge. She was forever defending him. I think she liked him because he wasn't well. "He's not strong," she would say, pityingly, but that was inaccurate; he may not have been well but he was terribly strong.

One time Mother went to call on a woman mental healer who lectured on the subject of "Harmonious Vibrations." She wanted to find out if it was possible to get harmonious vibrations into a dog. "He's a large tan-colored Airedale," Mother explained. The woman said that she had never treated a dog but she advised my mother to hold the thought that he did not bite and would not bite. Mother was holding the thought the very next morning when Muggs got the iceman, but she blamed that on the iceman. "If you didn't think he would bite you, he wouldn't," Mother told him. He stomped out of the house in a terrible jangle of vibrations.

One morning when Muggs bit me slightly, more or less in passing, I reached down and grabbed his short stumpy tail and hoisted him into the air. It was a foolhardy thing to do. As long as I held the dog off the floor by his tail he couldn't get at me, but he twisted and jerked so, snarling all the time, that I realized I couldn't hold him that way very long. I carried him to the kitchen and flung him onto the floor and shut the door on him just as he crashed against it.

But I forgot about the back stairs. Muggs went up the back stairs and down the front stairs and had me cornered in the living room. I managed to get up onto the mantelpiece above the fireplace, but it gave way and came down with a tremendous crash, throwing a large marble clock, several vases and myself heavily to the floor.

Muggs was so alarmed by the racket that when I picked myself up he had disappeared. We couldn't find him anywhere, although we whistled and shouted, until old Mrs. Detweiler called after dinner that night. Muggs had bitten her once, in the leg, and she came into the living room only after we assured her that Muggs had run away. She had just seated herself when, with a great growling and scratching of claws, Muggs emerged from under a davenport where he had been quietly hiding all the time, and bit her again. Mother examined the bite and put arnica on it and told Mrs. Detweiler that it was only a bruise.

"He just bumped you," she said. But Mrs. Detweiler left the house in a nasty state of mind.

Lots of people reported our Airedale to the police but my father held a municipal office at the time and was on friendly terms with them. The cops suggested that it might be a good idea to tie the dog up, but Mother said that it mortified him to be tied up and that he wouldn't eat when he was tied up.

In his last year Muggs used to spend practically all of his time outdoors. He didn't like to stay in the house for some reason or other — perhaps it held too many unpleasant memories for him. Anyway, it was hard to get him to come in and as a result the garbageman, the iceman and the laundryman wouldn't come near the house. We had to haul the garbage to the corner, take the laundry out and bring it back, and meet the iceman a block from home.

After this had gone on for some time we hit on an ingenious arrangement for getting the dog in the house so that we could lock him up while the gas meter was read, and so on. Muggs was afraid of only one thing, an electrical storm. Thunder and lightning frightened him out of his senses (I think he thought a storm had broken the day the mantelpiece fell). He would rush into the house and hide under a bed or in a clothes closet. So we fixed up a thunder machine out of a long, narrow piece of sheet iron with a wooden handle on one end. Mother would shake this vigorously when she wanted to get Muggs into the house. It made an excellent imitation of thunder, but I suppose it was the most roundabout system for running a household ever devised. It took a lot out of Mother.

A few months before Muggs died, he got to "seeing things." He would rise slowly from the floor, growling low, and stalk stiff-legged and menacing toward nothing at all. Sometimes the Thing would be just a little to the right or left of a visitor. Once a Fuller Brush salesman got hysterics. Muggs came wandering into the room like Hamlet following his father's ghost. His eyes were fixed on a spot just to the left of the Fuller Brush salesman, who stood it until Muggs was about three slow, creeping paces from him. Then he shouted. Muggs wavered on past him into the hallway, grumbling to himself, but Mother had to throw a pan of cold water on the Fuller man before he stopped shouting.

Muggs died quite suddenly one night. Mother wanted to bury him in the family lot under a marble stone with some such inscription as "Flights of angels sing thee to thy rest," but we persuaded her it was against the law. In the end we just put up a smooth board above his grave along a lonely road. On the board I wrote with an indelible pencil, "*Cave Canem.*" Mother was quite pleased with the simple classic dignity of the old Latin epitaph.

Rejection Quips

The late R. K. Munkittrick, while editor of *Judge*, was pestered by daily effusions from an amateur poet. Growing impatient with this prolific lyrical output, Munkittrick finally wrote across one rejection slip: "Please curb your doggerel."

— F. P. Pitzer

"The best rejection slip I ever heard of," Russel Crouse told a group of authors, "was an editor's note attached to a heavy manuscript. It read, 'I'm returning this paper — someone wrote on it.'"

— Leonard Lyons

An aspiring author sent a manuscript to an editor with a letter in which he stated, "The characters in this story are purely fictional and bear no resemblance to any person, living or dead."

A few days later he received his manuscript with the penciled notation: "That's what's wrong with it."

— Blaine C. Bigler

A young English writer sent a number of his manuscripts to a celebrated newspaper columnist, asking his advice as to the best channel for marketing the writings. The manuscripts came back with this curt note: "The one channel I can conscientiously recommend as the greatest outlet for articles of this type is the English Channel."

— Guy H. Humphreys

Eugene Field disposed of a would-be poet who had submitted a verse entitled, "Why Do I Live?" by writing on the rejection slip: "Because you sent your poem by mail."

"For ten long, lean years," the author told the producer, "I've been writing this drama, working on it till my fingers were cramped and aching, my brain and body weary."

"Too bad," the producer murmured. "All work — and no play."

— *Counter points*

Men at Work

The Oppenheimer brothers were interviewing applicants for the job of private secretary. One Amazonian creature had excellent references, but the brothers did not enthuse after she waddled out. "I don't think she'll do," said one. "There's too much of her, in the first place." His brother added, "That goes for the second place, too!"

— Bennett Cerf, *Anything for a Laugh* (Grosset & Dunlap)

Last July I was helping a farmer with the season's haying. He was an old hand, and I felt self-conscious and amateurish around him. Also

I wanted to please him. So when we came to a patch that was heavy with weeds, I asked him, with my pitchfork poised for the next throw, if I ought to sort the hay from the weeds.

He thought it over a minute and said, "No, I think the cows have got more time than you've got."   — C. F.

Marc Connelly, a slow and meticulous worker, had promised a producer a new play, but when a full year went by without further word the producer waxed impatient and called Connelly on the telephone. "Where's that play?" he demanded. "I want to get my cast assembled." "It's coming along," Connelly assured him vaguely. "Just how much have you written?" demanded the producer. "Well," said Connelly, "you know it's to be in three acts and two intermissions. I've just finished the intermissions."   — Bennett Cerf

A young gal applying for a position answered the interviewer: "Certainly I can take shorthand — only that way usually takes me longer."
                                                       — H. R. Waddell

In Piccadilly Circus one afternoon, there were the usual number of panhandlers, but one seemed to be faring better than the rest. We watched as he approached various people, always with the same result: an uproar and then contributions. Finally, this beggar walked up to us. In his hand was a battered mandolin and holding it out he said in a pleading voice, "This is the only thing I have to make my living with" — then a pause — "and I can't play the damn thing!"   — J. T. Wakley

Boss replying to employe asking for a raise: "Of course you're worth more than you're getting, Morton. Why don't you let up a bit?"   — B. Tobey cartoon in The Saturday Evening Post

When Sam asked how he budgeted his income, he replied: "Oh, about 40 percent for food, 30 percent for shelter, 30 percent for clothing and 20 percent for amusement and incidentals."

"But, Sam, that makes 120 percent!"

"Lord, don't I know it!" Sam agreed.   — Liberty

Asked how she liked her new boss, a young secretary remarked, "Oh, he isn't so bad, only he's kind of bigoted."

"How do you mean?"

"Well," explained the girl, "he thinks words can only be spelled one way." — *Woodmen of the World Magazine*

Shaggy Dog Stories

A man went to a baker and asked him to bake a cake in the form of the letter S. The baker said he would need a week to prepare the necessary tins. The customer agreed, and returned a week later. Proudly the baker showed him the cake.

"Oh, but you misunderstood me," the customer said. "You have made it a block letter and I wanted script."

"Well," said the baker, "if you can wait another week I can make one in script."

A week later the customer came back, and was delighted with the cake. "Exactly what I wanted," he said.

"Will you take it with you," asked the baker, "or shall I send it to your house?"

"Don't bother," said the customer. "If you'll just give me a knife and fork I'll eat it right here."

— Quoted by Max Eastman, *Enjoyment of Laughter* (Simon & Schuster)

A man who had wanted a parrot for years was walking along a street and noticed a sign on a pet shop — BANKRUPTCY SALE. Here, he thought, is my chance to get a parrot cheap. He entered, and sure enough, there was a gorgeous parrot in a cage. When the auctioneer put it up for sale he began bidding; higher and higher went the bids, but finally the parrot was his.

Bursting with pride of ownership, he walked out of the shop carrying the parrot in its shiny cage, when suddenly it occurred to him that perhaps the parrot couldn't talk. Back he ran and, holding the cage up to the auctioneer, demanded: "Say, does this bird talk?"

"Whothehell do you think was bidding against you all that time?" said the parrot. — Clarence Budington Kelland

There's the story of the couple who furnished a 12-room house with premiums redeemed for soap coupons. They showed a friend around, proudly commenting on how many coupons each chair, table or carpet "cost." At the end of the tour the visitor said, "But you've shown me only five of the 12 rooms — what about the other seven?"

"Oh, those," shrugged the householder. "That's where we keep the soap."   — Julius Tannen, quoted by Hy Gardner in *Parade*

A man who made a fortune almost overnight was boasting to one of his cronies about his new estate with its three swimming pools. "But why *three* pools?" exclaimed the friend.

"One has cold water," the host explained, "one has hot water, and one has no water at all."

"One with cold water I can understand. I can even see a reason for one with hot water," conceded the friend. "But what's the idea of a swimming pool with no water at all?"

"You'd be surprised, Joe," the host confided sadly, "how many of my old friends don't know how to swim."

— Bennett Cerf in *The Saturday Review of Literature*

It was a cold November day and the football stadium was jammed. High up in the stands an alumnus, more than slightly inebriated, kept standing up and calling, "Hey, Gus," and each time a man down in the third row would ceremoniously stand up and doff his hat.

After many calls of "Hey, Gus," the gentleman in the third row shouted in a thick voice, "Now quit yelling at me! I'm tired of standing up, and besides my name ain't Gus."   — Mrs. W. H. Cunningham

At a tea the theory of prenatal influence was being discussed when a newcomer to the neighborhood arrived and was introduced. For several minutes she listened interestedly and then spoke up.

"I find myself in disagreement," she said, "for I am quite sure there is no such thing as prenatal influence. Take my case as an example. Shortly before I was born my mother tripped over some phonograph records and cracked every one. But it didn't affect me affect me affect me affect me affect me. . . ."   — Carl Brandt

Spontaneous and Unrehearsed

One night the announcer for the Pot o' Gold program telephoned a woman to report that she had won the $1900 prize. Since she was not at home, a boarder who answered the phone was asked the first thing the landlady would do with the money.

"Count it," was the prompt reply.
— David Skagerberg

At a warm-up of the Quiz Kids radio show, somebody asked, "Can you think of any proverb that helps you in your relations with your father?" One angel-faced moppet shot up her hand and piped, "There's no fool like an old fool."
— Maggy O'Flaherty, quoted by Bennett Cerf in *The Saturday Review of Literature*

During a sidewalk interview in Amarillo, Texas, an announcer asked a woman: "What did your husband say when he proposed?" She replied that he just said he loved her and wanted her to marry him. "Didn't he do anything to back up his statement?" the announcer said.

"Oh, yes," she replied brightly. "We have two sons!"
— Mrs. James A. McKnight

"If you dated a check on Sunday, it would be good. True or False?" asked a quizmaster. When the soldier contestant replied, "False," the emcee pointed out that the statement was true. "But you said if I wrote a check," said the soldier, "and I don't have any money in the bank."
— Earl Sparling in *This Week Magazine*

Bob Hawk, the quiz emcee, asked a contestant to "name a great time-saver."

"Love at first sight," she replied.
— Paul Denis in New York *Post*

Musical terms were to be used in answering a Dr. I. Q. quiz. When asked, "In what type of dwelling do so many people live?" the contestant should have said "flats." Instead he said "bars" and broke up the show.
— Jeanne Yount

When required by Bob Hawk to finish the proverb, "One man's loss —" the contestant immediately replied, "is another man's umbrella."
— C. J. Ingram

When "The Jersey Bounce" was played on Double or Nothing and the contestant was asked to identify a vacation spot from the title, she looked bewildered. The emcee hinted, "What kind of sweaters are very popular with young men?" Quickly she replied, "Sweaters with girls in them!"

A contestant on the Give and Take program, asked to name three ways of saying good-bye, replied, "Adieu, Adios and Arsenic."

They Asked for It

At the London Zoo a woman asked whether the hippopotamus was a male or female. "Madam," replied the keeper sternly, "that is a question that should interest only another hippopotamus." — Julian Huxley

"How can I ever show my appreciation?" gushed a woman to Clarence Darrow, after he had solved her legal troubles.

"My dear," replied Darrow, "ever since the Phoenicians invented money there's been only one answer to that question." — Walter Winchell

On a trip to Vermont, I did some research on agricultural statistics and noticed that the cow population of the state was larger than the human population. "How do you account for that?" I asked a native son. "We prefer 'em," he replied.   — Clarence H. Girard

At a golf club, a member was boasting about his strength when a puny fellow member bet him $25 that he could wheel a load in a wheelbarrow from the clubhouse to the street which the athlete couldn't wheel back. "You're on," said the boaster. A wheelbarrow was brought up to the clubhouse. "All right," said the little guy. "Get in."
— "A Philadelphia Lawyer" in
Philadelphia *Evening Bulletin*

At the close of a talk on King Hezekiah, a New York clergyman asked if there were any questions. A lady rose. "I've never been clear," she said, "how old Hezekiah was." The clergyman hesitated, then said, "Well, when? Hezekiah was different ages at different times, you know." "Oh," said the lady, "I never thought of that," and contentedly sat down.   — Ethel Tilley

The prairie tourist, marveling at New England's scenery, finally asked a New Hampshire farmer where all the rocks came from.

The native replied, "The great glacier brought them here."

"Well," demanded the stranger, "where's the glacier now?"

"It went back for more rocks," the farmer drawled.
— James R. Young, *Behind the
Rising Sun* (Doubleday)

Quotable Quotes

The way to fight a woman is with your hat. Grab it and run.
— John Barrymore

The thing that keeps men broke is not the wolf at the door but the silver fox in the window. — *Sunshine Magazine*

One of the greatest laborsaving inventions of today is tomorrow.
— Vincent T. Foss

Youth is a wonderful thing. What a crime to waste it on children.
— George Bernard Shaw

Keep your eyes open before marriage; half shut afterwards.
— Benjamin Franklin

A little girl's prayer: "O God, make the bad people good, and the good people nice." — Harry Emerson Fosdick

People who take cold baths all winter seldom have colds. But they have cold baths. — *Punch*

Some cause happiness wherever they go; others whenever they go.

Man is the only animal that can be skinned more than once.

One reassuring thing about modern art is that things can't be as bad as they are painted. — M. Walthall Jackson

There is no such thing as a dangerous woman; there are only susceptible men. — Joseph Wood Krutch

Most people have *some* sort of religion — at least they know which church they're staying away from. — John Erskine

Science is resourceful. It couldn't pry open the Pullman windows, so it air-conditioned the train. — Montreal *Star*

The real problem of your leisure is how to keep other people from using it.

There are three kinds of lies: lies, damned lies and statistics.
— Benjamin Disraeli

In America there are two classes of travel: first class and with children.
— Robert Benchley

A truthful woman is one who won't lie about anything except her age, weight and her husband's salary.
— Cal Tinney

Lines to a Daughter—Any Daughter

Condensed from Harper's Magazine — Agnes Rogers

One of the things that you really should know
Is when to say "yes," and when to say "no."
There aren't any textbooks, there aren't many rules,
The subject's neglected in orthodox schools.
You can't be consistent; there's often a reason
For changing your mind with a change in the season.
You may be quite right in accepting at seven
Suggestions you'd better refuse at eleven.
Perhaps you'll consider these tentative hints:
"No" to a dirndl of highly glazed chintz,
"Yes" to the bashful young man at the dance,
"No" to the man who's been living in France,
"Yes" to a walk in the park in the rain,
"Yes" if he asks for a chance to explain,
"No" to all slacks unless you're too thin,
"No" to that impulse to telephone him,
"Yes" to a baby, and "no" to a bore,
"No" if you're asked if you've heard it before,
"Yes" to a Saturday, "no" to a Monday,
"Yes" to a salad and "no" to a sundae,
"Yes" to a stranger (but use some discretion!),
"No" to three cocktails in rapid succession,
"No" if he's misunderstood by his wife,
"Yes" if you want it the rest of your life.
Remember, my darling, careers and caresses
Depend on our choices of "noes" and of "yesses."

Filling That Hiatus

Condensed from "Benchley — or Else!"

Robert Benchley

There is one detail of behavior at dinner parties which I have never seen touched upon in etiquette books, and which has given me some little embarrassment: What to do when you find that both your right-hand and your left-hand partner are busily engaged in conversation with somebody else.

You have perhaps turned from your right-hand partner to snap away a rose bug which was charging on your butter from the table decorations, and when you turn back to her to continue your monologue, you find that she is already vivaciously engaged on the other side —

a shift made with suspicious alacrity, when you come to think it over. So you wheel about to your left, only to find yourself confronted by an expanse of sun-browned back. This leaves you looking more or less straight in front of you, with a roll in your hand and not very much to do with your face. Should you sit and cry softly to yourself, or launch forth into a bawdy solo, beating time with your knife and fork?

Of course, the main thing is not to let your hostess notice that you are disengaged. If she spots you dawdling or looking into space, she will either think that you have insulted both your partners or she will feel responsible for you herself and start a long-distance conversation which has no real basis except that of emergency. You must spend the hiatus acting as if you really were doing something.

You can always make believe that you are talking to the person opposite, making little conversational faces and sounds into thin air, nodding your head "Yes" or "No," and laughing politely every now and again. This may fool your hostess in case her glance happens to fall your way, and it surely will confuse the person sitting opposite you if he happens to catch your act. He is naturally going to think that he had better not take any more to drink, or that he had better not go to any more parties until some good specialist has gone over him thoroughly. It is this danger of being misjudged which makes the imitation conversation inadvisable.

You can always get busily at work on the nuts in front of your plate, arranging them in fancy patterns with simulated intensity which will make it look as if you were performing for somebody's benefit, especially if you keep looking up at an imaginary audience and smiling "See?" Even if you are caught at this, there is no way of checking up, for any of the dinner guests might possibly be looking at you while talking to somebody else. It isn't much fun, however, after the first five minutes.

If you have thought to bring along a bit of charcoal, you can draw little pictures on the back on either side of you, or lacking charcoal and the ability to draw, you might start smothering the nicer-looking back with kisses. This would, at least, get one of your partners to turn around — unless she happened to like it. As time wears on, you can start juggling your cutlery, beginning with a knife, fork and spoon and working up to two of each, with a flower thrown in just to make it a little harder. This ought to attract some attention.

Of course, there is always one last resort, and that is to slide quietly under the table, where you can either crawl about collecting slippers which have been kicked off, growling like a dog and frightening the more timid guests, or crawl out from the other side and go home. Perhaps this last would be best.

Robert Benchley was drinking Martinis mixed with second-rate gin one day when a friend passed by.

"Don't you know," warned the friend anxiously, "that stuff's slow poison?"

"Oh, that's all right," said Benchley. "I'm in no hurry."
— Bonnie White Baker

Presenting the Lunts

Some years ago when Alfred Lunt and Lynn Fontanne were making a movie in Hollywood, they were asked to see the rushes (uncut scenes in the picture). Lynn saw them alone and was horrified. She hurried home to her husband.

"Well?" said Alfred.

"I was awful," said Lynn wildly, "terrible, unbelievable. I can't go on with it."

"How was I?" asked her husband.

"Oh, charming, dear, perfectly wonderful, as you always are. You'll have to do a little something about your make-up, because you look as though you didn't have any lips. But Alfred, I can't go on with this. My voice sounds impossible and I haven't any eyes, and my face is entirely expressionless and I don't seem to know what to do with my hands and feet."

There was a long pause.

"Alfred," said Lynn, "I tell you I can't go on. What'll I do?"

"No lips, eh?" said Alfred.

— Bayard Veiller, *The Fun I've Had* (Reynal & Hitchcock)

A little old lady, seeing the Lunts for the first time, relished the dash, the unblushing intimacy, the unabashed honesty with which they romped through a love scene on a sofa. When the scene was over, she sighed regretfully and turned to her companion, a dowager no less militantly respectable. Then she whispered, with more resonance than she had meant to muster, "It's nice, my dear, to know they are really married, isn't it?"

— John Mason Brown in *The Saturday Review of Literature*

At the opening of *The Taming of the Shrew* in Los Angeles, Alfred Lunt and Lynn Fontanne gave late-comers the works. As each laggard group came down the aisle, Lunt and Fontanne stopped dead in their lines, she to bow graciously, he to cry "Welcome!" Once he said: "For the benefit of those who have just come in, I'll play the scene again." And he did so.

— *Time*

About 20 years ago, Alfred Lunt, living in Genesee Depot, Wis., received a telegram from George Tyler asking how much he would take to play the lead in *Clarence*. Realizing the role's importance, Lunt decided to ask for $200 a week.

Tyler's response was immediate but puzzling. When Lunt received the wire at the railroad station, he read it over a second time: "One hundred fifty okay. The part is yours."

The chuckle of the stationmaster, who was also the telegraph operator, put an end to his perplexity. "Waal," drawled the old-timer, "I see you got your job. I thought you was plain daft to ask for so much, so I just changed it for you 'cause I was scairt you'd lose it."

— Russel Crouse in *Coronet*

When the Lunts, notoriously devoted to each other, started rehearsing *At Mrs. Beam's*, a play in which it was necessary for Miss Fontanne to strike Mr. Lunt in the face, she found she couldn't hit him. She pulled her hand back and let go — and then stopped dead before she struck. Her husband begged her to do it, but after 30 minutes she still couldn't. Finally Mr. Lunt shouted: "For God's sake, Lynn, you're the lousiest actress I've ever played opposite!"

The Fontanne hand made a direct hit. Mr. Lunt yelped in pain, then grinned. But when they put on the show he had to whisper, "Don't be lousy, dear," each time before she would hit him.

— Elliott Arnold in New York *World-Telegram*

The velvet rivalry between Lynn Fontanne and Tallulah Bankhead began with Miss Bankhead's greeting at a party: "How lucky you are to be married to Alfred Lunt, darling. His acting, his direction, his theater sense! Where would you be without him?"

"Probably," cooed Miss Fontanne, "playing your roles."

— Walter Winchell

Touché

A bumptious playwright who had a new show opening sent a couple of tickets for the first night to the mayor of the city with a note suggesting that the chief executive could bring a friend "if he had one."

The mayor returned the tickets with a courteous letter stating that previous engagements made it impossible for him to see the show the opening night, but he would purchase two tickets for the second performance — if there was one.

— Johnnie MacIntyre, quoted by Joe Harrington in Boston *Sunday Post*

Marlene Dietrich saw the first week's rushes of a new picture and complained that they didn't suit her. The cameraman had also photographed her in *The Garden of Allah*, one of the star's favorites; so they went to a projection room and had *The Garden of Allah* shown. When it was over Miss Dietrich said, "I looked gorgeous in that picture. Why can't we get the same result in this one?"

"Well, you see, Miss Dietrich," said the cameraman, "I'm eight years older now."

— Leonard Lyons

"Request five-day extension of leave. Just met an angel," a sailor on leave wired the personnel officer of a West Coast naval air station. The officer wired back, "Two-day extension granted for you to come down to earth."

— Virginia E. Beinecke

A salty Maine lobsterman, who made a tidy summer income hauling "trippers" in his small fishing boat, was known far and wide for the yarns he spun. One day a newcomer, an ample widow still sporting her city clothes and manners, raised her voice against the wind and shrilled, "Captain, they tell me you're the biggest liar on the Maine coast."

"Madam" — the battered straw hat came off in a sweep, the captain bowed in as courtly a gesture as the roll of the boat permitted — "Madam, you are the most beautiful woman I ever saw in my life!"

— Zulma Steele

In a crowded movie house, a young man was just about to sit down in one of a pair of empty seats when he was abruptly pushed off balance by a woman trailing behind him with her husband. Before he could recover, the couple had plumped into the seats. "Sorry, my friend," said the husband, "we beat you!"

"That's all right," said the young man. "I hope you and your mother enjoy the show."

— Leslie Paffrath

A contractor out in the Northwest had been trying for months to collect an overdue bill. As a last resort, he sent a tear-jerking letter, accompanied by a snapshot of his little daughter. Under the picture he wrote, "The reason I must have the money!"

The prompt reply was a photo of a voluptuous blonde in a bathing suit labeled: "The reason I can't pay!"

— Marveleen Holzback

Wolf Calls

A wolf lounging in a New York hotel lobby perked up when an attractive young lady passed by. When his standard come-on, "how-de-do," brought nothing more than a frigid glance, he sarcasmed, "Pardon me, I thought you were my mother."

"I couldn't be," she iced. "I'm married."

— Walter Winchell

As a Red Cross worker overseas, I found that an occasional officer was likely to try a little "wolfing." Nor did being a roving male always stop after marriage. One friend of ours, a colonel, married an Army nurse. Presently she had to go back home for the usual reason — their union had been blessed. Our colonel friend stayed close to his knitting for about a month, then one evening he got into his best tailor-made uniform to come to dinner with us. On the way he thrust his hand into his pocket and pulled out a piece of paper on which he found in his wife's handwriting, "So you're all dressed up — why?"

— Eleanor "Bumpy" Stevenson and Pete Martin,
I Knew Your Soldier (Infantry Journal-Penguin Books)

My English class was reading from the Journals of Louisa M. Alcott. We came to the section where Miss Alcott wrote, "I keep busy writing short stories which I hope to sell for $5 or $10 to keep the wolf from the door." I asked one boy, "What do you think Louisa Alcott meant by saying she was trying to keep the wolf from the door?"

"I suppose she just didn't want the guy bothering her," he replied promptly.

— Edith M. Penney

Wolves are like railroad trains — you like to hear the whistle even if you don't want to go any place!   — Ann Sothern

A pretty Army nurse, just returned from the South Pacific, was describing an air raid in New Guinea. "When the Jap bombers came over," she said, "I jumped right into the nearest wolfhole."

"You mean foxhole, don't you?" interrupted a listener.

"Maybe a fox dug it," said the nurse sweetly, "but there was a wolf in it when I got in."   — John O'Donnell in Washington *Times-Herald*

Fred Higgenstonough, accompanied by a beautiful blonde, entered a big fur store on Friday. "We want to look at a mink coat," he said. The $3000 model pleased her, but not him. Finally the saleswoman brought out the $25,000 model. "We'll take it," Fred said. "Here's my check. Put her initials in the lining, and we'll call for it next Tuesday. That will give you time to make sure my check's okay."

On Tuesday the couple came in for the coat. The saleswoman apologetically told Fred the credit manager wanted to see him. He left the blonde and went up to the office. Before the credit man could say anything, Fred asked, "Did you call up my bank? Did they say my family had millions but that I was the black sheep and my limit was $500 a month?"

"Why — y-e-e-s. But . . ."

"Good!" said Fred. "And thanks for a very pleasant week-end."
                                                          — Alex F. Osborn

One night the stewardess on my run had her hands full. No sooner did she break away from one heart case — a character who gave her the number of his hotel room and promised to have the place strewn with American Beauty roses — than another wolf waylaid her. "Little girl," he purred, "you might as well tell me where you live, because I'll find out anyway." She whispered an address, and added something about American Beauty roses. "Baby, I'll be there with both arms full of 'em," he promised. I'd have given a lot to see what happened when Wolf No. 2 turned up at the hotel room of Wolf No. 1.
                                     — Captain Hy Sheridan in *The Saturday Evening Post*

Prince of Wails

Marcia Winn in Chicago Tribune

Why is it that everyone refers to a baby as a helpless little thing? Give a baby a home of his own, and he is the least helpless object in it. All he needs to do to have his every want filled is to let out one small peep. If help does not come at once, he need only extend this peep into a wail. And by forcing a bellow, he can throw the entire household into a bewildered tailspin from which it may not emerge for days.

He can't walk, he can't talk, he can't feed or bathe himself, and in that he has an unmixed blessing. Unable to walk, he can lie in bed all day and kick his legs — the envy of every adult who sees him. Unable to talk, he need never answer unnecessary questions, become involved in a political argument, or politely tolerate a bore. When oppressed by the last, he can turn his head the other way, yawn, or blandly go to sleep, and have his actions approved by polite society.

He need never worry over what he is going to wear today or what he will eat for lunch. If he doesn't wear a stitch, he is perfectly content, and no one will raise an eyebrow. If he doesn't like his food, he can spit, blow, or bubble it out, no matter who is watching, or he can disdain to eat at all. He can emit, at the end of a meal, a resounding belch, and be applauded for what two years later will be considered most unseemly.

Soon the world at large will criticize the way his hair grows, although now his admirers are enchanted because it grows at all. It will criticize the way he eats, although now all are ecstatic if he gets it down any way. If he turns out to be beautiful, good, rich or successful, part of the world will envy him, and if he turns out to be ugly, mean, poor or a failure, the other part of the world will berate him, but now, for the last time in his life, he is eulogized by poets, chucked under the chin by old ladies, cooed at by Scrooges, and adored by all.

Far from being helpless in this world, he is the only human being who can chin on it. It wasn't idle conversation that prompted a pediatrician to muse, "In the next life I'm going to be a perpetual baby."

Present, But Absently

One season in Rome, George Ade gave a dinner for a number of friends including Booth Tarkington. About ten o'clock a woman guest wished to return to her hotel nearby and George accompanied her to the lobby. Then he stopped to speak to some friends standing at the hotel bar. Time was forgotten as stories and spirits flowed freely. About midnight Ade mentioned having dined that night with Booth Tarkington, who had told some wonderful yarns. "Who gave the dinner?" someone asked.

George thought for a moment, then, horror-stricken, bolted for the door with, "My God, *I* did!"

— Fred C. Kelly, *George Ade, Warmhearted Satirist* (Bobbs-Merrill)

Hiram Stevens Maxim, the well-known inventor, was plagued by absent-mindedness. After losing umbrellas, packages, books and drawings until he was desperate, he finally had stickers printed which he attached to practically everything he owned. Bordered in red, they announced boldly:

THIS WAS LOST BY A DAMNED FOOL

HIRAM STEVENS MAXIM

WHO LIVES AT 325 UNION STREET, BROOKLYN

A SUITABLE REWARD WILL BE PAID FOR

ITS RETURN

— Hiram Percy Maxim, *A Genius in the Family* (Harper)

The editors of the *Encyclopædia Britannica* sent an historical article, which had been in the book for a good many years, to the head of a western university history department for possible revision. It came back with the caustic comment that it was "badly disorganized and full of errors."

Curious to see who had written such an "inaccurate" article for them originally, the editors checked through their files. They were flabbergasted to find that the article had been written by the professor himself — so many years before that he had forgotten it.

— Warner Olivier in *The Saturday Evening Post*

Driving into a Laguna Beach, Calif., service station, a motorist asked for ten gallons of gas. Three servicemen hopped to work smartly — cleaning windshield, checking tires and water, etc. The driver paid his bill and drove off.

A few minutes later he returned and asked: "Did any of you put gas in my car?" The three attendants went into a huddle — then confessed nobody had.
— *Newsweek*

Dr. Frank H. Sparks, president of Wabash College, tells this story: My memory for names is notably bad, and at public gatherings I always rely on Mrs. Sparks to help me. But on one occasion we became separated, and I beheld a matron bearing down upon me whom I felt that I should recognize. I was greeting her with a warm handclasp when a man I knew rather well came along. Still clasping the lady's hand, I waved my other hand in greeting. "Hello, Fred," I called. "How is your lovely wife these days?"

"You ought to know," replied Fred. "You're holding hands with her!"
— *Quote*

My Financial Career

From "Literary Lapses"

Stephen Leacock

I have never been able to get over my fear of banks. The moment I cross the threshold of one and attempt to transact business there, I become an irresponsible idiot.

This is because as a young man I was badly frightened by a bank; the memory lingers painfully in my mind to this day.

My salary had been raised by $50 a month, and I felt, rightly enough, that a bank was the only place for it. I picked out the largest, most impressive one in town, and, after a few minutes of hesitation, shambled in and looked timidly round at the clerks. I had had no previous experience with banks but there was an idea in my head that a person about to open an account must needs consult the manager.

Feeling that this was a moment of grave importance in my life, and already affected by the hushed and somber atmosphere, I went up to a wicket marked "Accountant." The accountant was a tall, cool devil. The very sight of him rattled me. My voice was sepulchral.

"Can I see the manager?" I said, and added solemnly, "alone." I don't know why I said "alone."

"Certainly," said the accountant, and fetched him.

The manager was a grave, calm man. He looked at me with polite inquiry.

"Are you the manager?" I said. God knows I didn't doubt it.

"Yes," I said.

"Can I see you," I asked, "alone?" I had no desire to tack on that "alone" again, but I was trapped now. I had said it before and I had to be consistent.

The manager looked at me in some alarm. He could hardly be blamed for feeling that I had an awful secret to impart.

"Come in here," he said, and led the way to a private room. He turned the key in the lock.

"We are safe from interruption here," he said. "Sit down."

We both sat down and looked at each other. I found no voice to speak.

"You are a Pinkerton man, I presume," he said.

He had gathered from my mysterious manner that I was a detective from the most famous agency of the time. I knew what he was thinking, and it made me worse.

"No, not from Pinkerton's," I said, seeming to imply that I came from a rival agency.

"To tell the truth," I went on, as if I had been prompted to lie about it, "I am not a detective at all. I

"Literary Lapses" is published by Dodd, Mead & Co., Inc., 432 Fourth Ave., New York 16, N. Y.

have come to open an account. I intend to keep all my money in this bank."

The manager looked relieved but still serious; he concluded now that I was a son of Mr. Morgan, or a young Rockefeller.

"A large account, I suppose," he said.

"Fairly large," I whispered. I had it all in my pocket, clutched in a crumpled ball. "I propose to deposit $56 now and $50 a month regularly."

The manager got up and opened the door. He called to the accountant.

"Mr. Montgomery," he said in a peculiar voice, "this gentleman is opening an account with us. He will deposit $56. Good morning."

I rose.

A big iron door stood open at the side of the room.

"Good morning," I said, and stepped into the safe.

When they got me out of there I went up to the accountant's wicket and poked the ball of money at him with a quick convulsive movement as if I were doing a conjuring trick.

My face was ghastly pale from the harrowing experience I had just been through.

"Here," I said, "deposit it." The tone of the words seemed to mean, "Let us do this painful thing as quickly as possible."

He took the money and gave it to another clerk.

He made me write the sum on a slip and sign my name in a book. I no longer knew what I was doing. The bank swam before my eyes.

"Is it deposited?" I asked in a hollow, vibrating voice.

"It is," said the accountant.

"Then I want to draw a check."

My idea was to draw out six dollars of it for present use. Someone gave me a checkbook through a wicket and someone else began telling me how to write it out. The people in the bank, aside from the one I was dealing with, had the impression that I was an invalid millionaire.

I wrote something on the check and thrust it in at the clerk. He looked at it.

"What!" he asked in surprise. "Are you drawing it all out again?"

I realized that I had written 56 instead of six. I was too far gone to reason now. I had a feeling that it was impossible to explain the thing. All the other clerks had stopped writing to look at me.

Reckless with misery, I made the plunge. "Yes, the whole thing."

"You withdraw your money from the bank?"

"Every cent of it."

"Are you not going to deposit any more?" said the clerk, astounded.

"Never."

An idiot hope struck me that they might think something had insulted me while I was writing the check and that I had changed my mind. I made a wretched attempt to look like a man with a fearfully quick temper. But it was no use.

The clerk prepared to pay the money.

"How will you have it?" he asked.

"What?"

"How will you have it?"

"Oh." I caught his meaning and answered without even trying to think. "In 50's."

He gave me a 50-dollar bill.

"And the six?" he asked dryly.

"In sixes," I said.

He gave it to me and I rushed out.

As the big door swung behind me I caught the echo of a roar of laughter that went up to the ceiling of the bank. I could not blame them, but for a long time I squirmed under the memory of it and my devastating interview with the manager.

I am on excellent terms with banks now but it is still impossible for me to enter one without first getting a firm grip on my sanity, with both hands.

Clerical Errors

Many doctors and ministers who find themselves at a loss for appropriate words when called upon to admire newborn infants — attractive and otherwise — have adopted a standard comment which seems to satisfy everybody: "Well, that *is* a baby!" One pastor, however, became a bit confused when the christening hour arrived. Peering intently at the baby as it lay in a proud parent's arms, he exclaimed heartily, "Well! Is *that* a baby?"   — Betsy Hook

A visiting bishop delivered a speech at a banquet on the night of his arrival in a large city. Because he wanted to repeat some of his stories at meetings the next day, he requested reporters to omit them from their accounts of his speech. A rookie reporter, commenting on the speech, finished with the line: "And he told a number of stories that cannot be published."   — *The Sign*

A clerical friend of mine once told me of the most disconcerting experience he ever had in the exercise of his functions. An elderly lady of determined aspect took a seat in a front pew of his church. When my friend began his sermon, she opened a little wooden box and extracted an elaborate hearing device, which she arranged, screwed together and adjusted to her ear. After two or three minutes, she removed the receiver, unscrewed the mechanism and packed its component parts snugly away again in the box. And the preacher had to preach on. — Charles Hall Grandgent, *Prunes and Prism* (Harvard University Press)

A minister, preaching on the danger of compromise, was condemning the attitude of so many Christians who believe certain things concerning their faith, but in actual practice will say, "Yes, but . . ." At the climax of the sermon, he said, "Yes, there are millions of Christians who are sliding straight to hell on their buts."

The congregation went into gales of laughter, and the minister promptly closed the service with a benediction. — Dr. Emory W. Luccock

Woman, shaking hands with the preacher after the service: "Wonderful sermon! Everything you said applies to somebody or other I know."   — Robert Hoyt cartoon in *Redbook*

The elderly president of the Ladies' Aid Society in a small Vermont town was asked, after several years' determined opposition to the ideas of a "radical" minister, why she didn't try to have him removed.

"Well," she explained, "we all know that the Reverend Blank has very dangerous ideas, but I would rather not have him leave. After all, if he isn't here he will be some place else, and just think, *there* people might listen to him."   — V. R. B.

The Rev. Oscar Johnson, jovial St. Louis pastor, tells this on himself: Once, after a change of churches, he met a woman of his former flock and asked, "How do you like your new pastor?"

"Just fine," she beamed. "But somehow or other, he just doesn't seem to *hold* me like you did!"   — John Newton Baker

English Episodes

Two American soldiers, standing at the bar in an English pub, noticed an elderly, benevolent-looking gentleman sipping a glass of beer at a table in a corner of the room. One of the soldiers said to his pal, "Do you know who that dignified old man is? He's the Archbishop of Canterbury."

"You're crazy. The Archbishop of Canterbury wouldn't be in a pub."

"I'm positive it is," said the first soldier. "I've seen his picture many times, and I know I'm right."

"I'll bet you a pound you're wrong."

The bet was accepted, and the soldiers timidly approached the table. "Excuse us, sir, for intruding, but would you mind telling us something. We were wondering if you might be —"

"Go to hell and mind your own damn business!" the old gentleman roared.

The two soldiers quickly retreated to the bar, stunned. After a moment, one said to the other: "Isn't that a shame! Now we'll *never* know."

— John Durant

An Australian, returning to his London club after many years, found only an elderly and grim-looking man in the lounge. Said the Australian, "Excuse me, sir, I know I'm a stranger but I'm feeling lonely and I wonder would you have a drink with me."

Old Boy: "Don't drink; tried it once, didn't like it."

The Australian mooned around a bit, and thought he'd try again. "Sorry to barge in, sir, but I wonder if you'd smoke a cigar with me."

Old Boy: "No, thanks, don't smoke; tried it once, didn't like it."

The Australian, wandering off once more, noticed the billiard room, and decided to make a final approach. "Pardon me, sir, but perhaps you'll have a game of billiards with me."

Old Boy: "Sorry, don't play. Tried it once, didn't like it. . . . But look here — my son will be along soon. He will enjoy a game with you, I know."

Australian: "Your *only* child, I'm sure, sir!"

— James Montgomery Flagg

I once asked a London plumber why water pipes in England are not contained in the buildings but seem to wander outside and on roofs. "That's so they're easier to get at when they freeze up, guvner," he explained easily.

— Sam Boal in New York *Post*

An Englishman was pacing the floor of the waiting room of a London maternity ward. Finally a nurse came in. "You're the father of triplets," she reported. "Three beautiful girls." A little later she brought the triplets out to him. "Pick the one you want to keep," she instructed.

"One!" exclaimed the proud father. "Why only one? Can't we keep all three?"

"Under the present government," the nurse explained, "one is for you, and two are for export."   — Larry Le Sueur, quoted by Leonard Lyons

A chipper young lieutenant with an eye to the future approached a notoriously grouchy brigadier general at his club in London one day.

"Good morning, General," he saluted ingratiatingly.

"Grumpff," responded the general.

"Lovely day, isn't it?"

"Garumph."

"General, I trust you will pardon me for speaking of such a personal matter, but I read in the papers that you buried your wife yesterday, and I want to extend my heartfelt sympathy."

The general adjusted his monocle and stared at the young man for a moment.

"Oh, yes — yes," he replied. "I buried my wife. . . . Had to — dead, y'know."

A young lady found herself for the long week-end with a notoriously strait-laced country family in England. Fearing that the pajamas she wore instead of a nightgown might be considered improper, she carefully hid them every morning when she got up. But one morning at breakfast, she suddenly realized that she had forgotten them, that they were lying brazenly on her bed. Excusing herself, she rushed to her room. The pajamas had disappeared.

While she was feverishly hunting for them, looking vainly through closets and drawers, a dour, elderly maid appeared at the door and surveyed the scene. "If it's the pajamas you're looking for, miss," she said, "I put them back in the young gentleman's room."

— Westbrook Pegler

A British general, newly arrived in Washington to serve in the Combined Chiefs of Staff setup, was touring the War College with an American colonel. They came upon some colorful prints depicting the War of 1812. "War of 1812? Whom were we fighting?" asked the Britisher.

"We were fighting you, sir," mumbled the embarrassed colonel. "Don't you remember, the British burned Washington?"

"Burned Washington!" The general was thunderstruck. "We burned Joan of Arc, I know — but never Washington!"

— Mary Van Rensselaer Thayer in Washington *Post*

A gangster rushed into a saloon, shooting right and left, yelling, "All you dirty skunks get outta here."

The customers fled in a hail of bullets — all except an Englishman, who stood at the bar calmly finishing his drink. "Well?" snapped the gangster, waving his smoking gun.

"Well," remarked the Englishman, "there certainly were a lot of them, weren't there!"   — *Tit-Bits*

The Cocktail Hour

Frank Morgan was at a cocktail party one afternoon, holding a Scotch and soda, when the hostess suddenly appeared with a tray of silly-frilly canapés. She insisted on serving him. "No, thanks," grunted Frank, taking a firmer grip on his glass. "I belong to Hors d'Oeuvres Anonymous."   — Sidney Skolsky,
United Feature Syndicate

A brigadier general came home for an unexpected leave and a reception in his honor was whipped up. There was no time to hire an extra servant, and the offer of his ten-year-old daughter to help serve cocktails was gratefully accepted. She was doing fine, too, until her horrified mother heard her go up to an admiral's wife and say sweetly, "Won't you let me get you your eighth Martini?"
— Bennett Cerf in
The Saturday Review of Literature

At a party in New York, Mrs. Joseph Schildkraut said good-bye to the British consul, then shook many other hands, and finally found herself shaking his hand again. "But you've already said good-bye to me once," he remonstrated.

"Oh, yes," she replied, "but it's always a pleasure to say good-bye to *you*."   — Tom Powers

Alan Young tells about the man who stared into the mirror and, noting his bloodshot eyes, resolved never to go to a bar again.

"This television," he muttered, "is wrecking my eyes!"

— Erskine Johnson, NEA

At a cocktail party before a dance, one of the guests was a young lady noted for her beautiful face and her lack of figure. But that night her red, low-cut evening gown was surprisingly well filled. Her "new" figure was a whispered topic of conversation until two Manhattans had been consumed by one of the braver males. He approached her and complimented her on her figure, gazing steadily at the low-cut front.

Without batting an eye, the lady smiled and asked demurely, "Like it? It's the real decoy!"

— J. Knight Goodman

A man was complaining about his new son-in-law: "He can't drink and he can't play cards."

"That's the kind of a son-in-law to have!" said a friend.

"Naw," said the man. "He can't play cards — and he plays. He can't drink — and he drinks."

— Earl Wilson,
Post-Hall Syndicate

Groucho Marx saw a friend standing in the rain in front of a swank Hollywood night club. "What are you going to do?" he asked. "Stay outside and get wet or go in and get soaked?" — Erskine Johnson, NEA

Seeing an unpopular character at a cocktail party given for Joan Crawford, Thyra Samter Winslow said, "Why, people used to get up parties just not to have him."

— Earl Wilson,
Post-Hall Syndicate

Overheard toward the end of a cocktail party: "I feel a hell of a lot more like I do now than when I came" (W. D. in *Collier's*) . . . Nothing makes a woman look better than three cocktails inside a man (Richard B. Neff) . . . Though a fifth will go into three with none left over, there may be one to carry . . . A soft drink turneth away company.

Deft definitions: Night clubs are places where the tables are reserved and the guests aren't (Fred Casper, NBC) . . . Will power — the ability to eat *one* salted peanut . . . Alcohol — an excellent liquid for preserving almost anything but secrets . . . A pink elephant is a beast of bourbon.

All in Pun

The late Senator Charles B. Farwell claimed this was the only perfect triple pun in the English language: A woman's three sons went to Texas to raise beef cattle, sheep and hogs. Stumped for a good name for their ranch, they wrote home to Mother for suggestions. NAME IT

FOCUS, she telegraphed. Puzzled, they wired for an explanation. The reply came immediately: FOCUS — WHERE THE SUN'S RAYS MEET.
— Otis Chatfield Taylor in Croton-on-Hudson, N. Y., *News*

W. S. Gilbert, of Gilbert and Sullivan fame, was noted for his devastating comments. Once, when a player urged his untalented mistress on Gilbert for a star part, Gilbert turned to a friend, said: "The fellow's obviously trying to blow his own strumpet."
— *Time*

Bud Abbott and Lou Costello were discussing an actor they knew. "Nice guy," said Abbott, "but have you noticed how he always lets his friends pick up the dinner check?"

"Yes," said Costello. "He has a terrible impediment in his reach!"
— Andrew B. Hecht

A Park Avenue doctor's overdue bills now bear a sticker reading, "Long time no fee." — Bennett Cerf, *Shake Well Before Using* (Simon & Schuster)

Before Oliver Wendell Holmes was a writer, he practiced medicine, and taught anatomy at Harvard and Dartmouth. As a practitioner he was not successful, for people were a bit doubtful about the flippant youth who posted the following sign above his office door: "Small fevers gratefully received."

Called upon to address the guests at a Thanksgiving dinner, William M. Evarts, Secretary of State under Hayes, began: "You have been giving your attention to turkey stuffed with sage; you are now about to consider a sage stuffed with turkey!"
— *Journal of Living*

Coming into the Terminal

A friend of mine was waiting for her train on the platform of a Maine railroad station. The station was reached by stairs from the street above, and beside the stairs was a chute used to slide baggage onto the platform below.

Suddenly, my friend was astounded to see, coming down the chute, a little stout old lady — her legs stretched out before her, her hat clutched in one hand, and her suitcase gripped in the other. After a more or less dumpy landing on the platform, she gathered herself together, turned to my friend and said, "Land sakes! Wouldn't you think a big railroad station like this would have a better way to get down here?"

— Leola Daker

A traveler on the Milwaukee Railroad was giving the dining-car waiter his order. "And for dessert," he said, "I'll have some plum pudding and coffee."

"I'm sorry, sir," said the waiter. "We don't have any plum pudding."

"What!" cried the passenger. "You don't have plum pudding? That's absurd. My man, I am one of your biggest customers. I ship hundreds of carloads of freight every month. And once, once! — when I travel on your line I can't get what I want to eat. I'll take this up with the management. I'll go to the top."

The steward, interceding, called the waiter aside. "When we stop in Milwaukee in a few minutes," he said, "we'll get a plum pudding. Tell the chef to make hard sauce and serve some of that good brandy with it." It was done. Just out of Milwaukee the waiter reappeared at the customer's side, smiling proudly.

"Well, sir," he said, "I'm happy to tell you that we have the plum pudding, and the chef has been working all the way on the sauce. He hopes you'll like it. And with it, with the compliments of the line, we would like to serve you this 50-year-old brandy."

The waiter paused for the expected result. The customer paused, too, to digest this new development. Then he threw his napkin on the table with a gesture of fiery defiance.

"The hell with it!" he said. "I'd rather be mad."

— Chicago *Daily News*

The late Dwight Morrow, who was very absent-minded, was once reading earnestly on a train when the conductor asked for his ticket. Frantically Mr. Morrow searched for it.

"Never mind, Mr. Morrow," the conductor said. "When you find it, mail it to the company. I'm certain you have it."

"I know I have it," exploded Mr. Morrow. "But what I want to know is, where in the world am I going?"

The luggage-laden husband stared miserably down the platform at the departing train. "If you hadn't taken so long getting ready," he admonished his wife, "we would have caught it."

"Yes," the little woman rejoined, "and if you hadn't hurried me so, we wouldn't have so long to wait for the next one!"

— *The Wall Street Journal*

The Pullman porter had just roused me and, still half-asleep, I was sitting on the edge of my lower berth, unshaven and tousled. A mother and daughter passed by on their way to the diner and I got up and followed toward the men's lounge.

"Don't worry, dear," I heard the older woman say encouragingly, "they *all* look like that in the morning."

— H. F. Stern

Mark Twain met a friend at the races one day. This friend came up to him and said, "I'm broke. I wish you would buy me a ticket back to the city."

"Well," Mark said, "I'm nearly broke myself, but I will tell you what I'll do. You can hide under my seat and I'll hide you with my legs."

The friend agreed to this.

Then Mark Twain went down to the ticket office and bought two tickets. When the train pulled out his friend was safely under the seat. The inspector came around for the tickets and Mark gave him two. The inspector said, "Where is the other one?"

Tapping his head the humorist said in a loud voice, "That is my friend's ticket! He is a little eccentric and likes to ride under the seat."   — *Mark Twain Wit and Wisdom*, edited by Cyril Clemens (Stokes)

Some time ago the entrancing Clare Boothe Luce was on a train to Washington. A gentleman seated across the aisle recognized her and came over. "I'm Burpee," he said.

"That's quite all right," replied Mrs. Luce. "I'm sometimes troubled that way myself."

It turned out that David Burpee, the big seed man, was merely introducing himself, and wanted to name a flower after the Congress-woman.   — George Dixon, King Features

A waiter in the diner of a Canadian Pacific train approached a regal-looking woman and bent over her solicitously. "Pardon me," he asked, "are you the cold salmon?"   — Rod Maclean in *Rob Wagner's Script*

Three deaf gentlemen were on a train bound for London. "What station is this?" inquired the first gentleman, at a stop.

"Wembley," answered the guard.

"Heavens!" said the second. "I thought it was Thursday!"

"So am I," exclaimed the third. "Let's all have a drink!"
          — Bennett Cerf in *The Saturday Review of Literature*

Among the crowd hurrying through Los Angeles' Union Station to board the midnight sleeper was a tall, striking blonde. She wore an expensive fur coat, her hair was hidden by a becoming turban, and her sun-tanned legs were bare. Upon boarding the train she went right to her berth, and it was then I witnessed the last word in streamlined preparedness. To my amazement, when she took off her fur coat and turban, I discovered that underneath she had on blue silk pajamas — legs rolled above the knee — and her hair already done up in dozens of tight pin curls.

With one final movement, she kicked off her pumps, hopped into the berth, and was no doubt fast asleep long before the rest of us had even started getting ready for bed.   — Frances Lackey

The young lovers, trying to find a secluded spot for a long embrace, found people, people, people everywhere. Suddenly the man had an idea and he led the girl to the railway station. Standing beside the door of a car as though seeing her off, he kissed her fondly. After the couple had repeated the experiment at four or five different platforms, a sympathetic porter strolled up and whispered to the young man: "Why don't you take her around to the bus terminal? They go every three minutes from there." — *Jinx*

INDEX

(A Guide to Groups by Titles)